War in Aquarius

Special thanks to
Ann and Susan, Mike Kealey,
Don Nattier, and Renee Watson

War in
Aquarius

*Memoir of an American Infantryman
in the Vietnam War*

DENNIS KITCHIN

McFarland & Company, Inc., Publishers
Jefferson, North Carolina, and London

Pseudonyms have been used for all persons named in this account, excepting the author himself.

The present work is a reprint of the library bound edition of War in Aquarius: Memoir of an American Infantryman in Action Along the Cambodian Border During the Vietnam War, *first published in 1994 by McFarland.*

LIBRARY OF CONGRESS CATALOGUING-IN-PUBLICATION DATA

Kitchin, Dennis, 1946–
     War in Aquarius : memoir of an American infantryman in the
Vietnam War / by Dennis Kitchin.
          p.   cm.
     Includes bibliographical references and index.

     ISBN 978-0-7864-6729-7
     softcover : 50# alkaline paper ∞

     1. Vietnamese Conflict, 1961–1975 — Personal narratives,
American.   2. Vietnamese Conflict, 1961–1975 — Regimental
histories — United States.   3. United States. Army. Infantry
Division, 25th.   4. Kitchin, Dennis, 1946–   .   I. Title.
DS559.5.K58   2011
959.704' 342'092 — dc20   93-43782

BRITISH LIBRARY CATALOGUING DATA ARE AVAILABLE

Front cover: chopper on Eagle Flight; patrol crossing rice paddy with storm coming (photographs courtesy of the author)

Manufactured in the United States of America

*McFarland & Company, Inc., Publishers
     Box 611, Jefferson, North Carolina 28640
         www.mcfarlandpub.com*

For my family

Contents

Preface

Mix together ego, a sense of history, and a desire to pay tribute to the dead. The result is a war memoir. War memoirs—primary sources—can explain where, when, and how soldiers die. The world should at least know that. Only the why remains elusive, especially in the case of the Vietnam War. Historians will be amply challenged explaining the why of Vietnam. As for ego, what war veterans don't like to tell their stories?

The Vietnam War was a long, diverse war with many angles, pieces, lines. This book is an attempt to portray one combat platoon, to present a fragment in the vast mosaic of the Vietnam experience. I hope this snapshot of the war will contribute to its readers' understanding of what happened in Vietnam.

What's the matter with war?
It's a national tradition.

> —Archie Bunker
> "All in the Family"

And I'll obey our chiefs when
they lead well.
Not when they counsel crimes.

> —Euripedes

I ain't got no quarrel with the Viet Cong.

> —Muhammad Ali

There never was a good war or a bad peace.

> —Benjamin Franklin

Prologue

It is a lethal, blistering afternoon in 1966. My partner and I are working summer jobs for our hometown. We're supposed to be chopping weeds with sickles. Instead we're having a contest to determine who can kill the most butterflies as they flit around us.

"Splat! That's nine!" cheers my co-worker as he shreds a colorful one with a potent swing. He gazes at the hazy sun. "Hey Den, do you know that guys our age are being killed in Vietnam? I mean, shit, just think, only twenty years old and getting shot and killed in a war!"

"I never thought about it."

"You know, I heard some guy from Norristown was killed last month. Man, that shit really gets me."

"Then don't think about it."

"Well, doesn't it get to you?"

"No. It doesn't involve me."

We cease killing butterflies and go back to work.

1

Sentinel

"Tonight, new man," bellows Sergeant Ross while pointing at me, "you're goin' out with me and the squad on an LP. You're also gonna carry the radio."

"Me? Carry the radio? How come? I don't know anything about it. I don't know how to use it, or what to say."

"Don't worry, Kitch, I'll show you what to do. All you gotta do is stay behind me."

Twilight. My twice-wounded black squad leader from New Jersey is alerting his men to prepare for a night patrol. The soldiers gather around him. "We'll be settin' up this listenin' post about a hundred meters out. This'll be a short walk, no sweat. There's beaucoup berms out 'round there, so we'll have beaucoup cover. A snap LP, no sweat, everybody gets their sleep."

The seven men shuffling about him are silent. It's a routine night patrol.

"Be ready to move out in one hour," Ross says. "Don't forget, everybody brings a claymore."

The squad tramps off without a murmur.

"Sarge," I say as Ross turns to leave. "What about me?"

"Oh yeah, Kitch, follow me."

We saunter to Bunker III, the one with the radios. Ross introduces me to Kilcurry, the platoon sergeant's radioman. Kilcurry and I exchange pleasantries. Ross asks Kilcurry to help me and leaves. Kilcurry is benign of face and well-built, cordial, unpretentious, tranquil. In his slight Irish brogue he explains how to operate the radio. Each of us sensing a potential friendship, we promise to chat again in the morning.

At ten Ross assembles his unit on Bunker I. Reluctantly I don the radio. It's festooned with an extra battery and three smoke grenades. A cumbersome, twenty-four-pound appliance, the four-foot antenna vibrating above my head might entice some attention. I feel like a flag bearer in the cavalry. Or a mounted Revolutionary War infantry officer. Someone who is conspicuous. Someone to shoot at first. In training we were instructed that the enemy always tries to knock out our radio so we can't summon help. *Jesus*, I think, *why me? Because you're the fuckin' new guy, that's why!* RTO. Radio Telephone Operator. I feel ill.

Ross checks that each man has a claymore. He carries flares and a starlight scope, a clever device which enables its user to see things in the darkness. A classified instrument, all we know is that somehow it employs stars or moonlight to illuminate the night.

Ross orders us to fall in behind him. He takes the radio microphone from my hand and notifies the Command Post that we're departing. He whispers to me to keep close to him. We leave the bunker in single file and negotiate through the rows of wire and maze of claymores.

The evening is mild, still. The Milky Way glitters above like a magic carpet. The damp, thick air of Vietnam permeates our nostrils as we silently zigzag across wide rice paddies. I stumble along behind Ross, hoping that he knows where he's going. The heavy radio digs into my shoulders. I quickly work up a sweat. Achieving our LP coordinates, Ross finds a place with adequate paddy berms for cover. We deploy into an L-shaped formation with the machine gun team in the center of the L.

We have unobstructed visibility in every direction. Our fundamental mission is to provide a forward outpost for the fire base, and if we should detect any Viet Cong, to call in artillery on them. If the enemy should trip into us at close quarters we're expected to engage them. We aren't an offensive patrol. But we have the hardware to protect ourselves should the need arise.

Ross nudges me to put out my claymore. I nervously low-crawl to a point fifteen meters from our position, all the way crunching dead paddy reeds with my body. The noise seems loud and I wonder if anyone unfriendly is listening. I quickly set up the mine. I sneak back to our location, stringing the wire and making more noise as I crawl along. I attach the wire to the pocketsize firing mechanism and rest it on top of the berm. I look at Ross. He nods and gestures to our front. His expression says, *Good job, Kitch, now look for somebody to kill.* He maneuvers to one of the other groups.

The night is mute, except for the movement and whispers of our patrol. The silence frightens me. No airplanes overhead, no teenagers burning rubber, no distant sirens wailing, no faraway train whistles, no street lights, no dogs barking. Nothing but eight resigned, fearful men preparing their tools of war. I glare into the silver starlight blackness of rural Vietnam, a dreamy emptiness of shadows and listless air. I think of a jingle we often chanted at Fort Polk: "Vietnam, Vietnam, every night while you're sleepin' Charlie Cong comes a-creepin'." *Out at night on the prowl*, I shudder, *just like a skunk.*

I'm alert, trembling. I think my veteran comrades are making too much clatter. I feel vulnerable, mortal, alone, yet somehow joined with the others, like a star in a galaxy. I'm sprawled in the midst of a vast complex of paddies with seven other soldiers, some of whom I have yet to meet. *Are they good soldiers?* I wonder. *Can I count on them?* We're in an Oriental isolation chamber enveloped by absolute black and weird odors. And the relative safety of sandbag bunkers is somewhere behind us, a hundred meters distant.

As night submerges, I feel a kinship with other exiled night sentries in the world, like a hermit, monk, or *vaquero*. Partially. There really are few if any situations comparable to being on a night patrol in a war zone.

Ross scrambles back to me and radios to the CP that we're active as an LP. Two men will pull guard while six sleep. Ross and I take the first shift. That is the advantage of commanding a patrol: you can select your sleeping hours.

As the others go to sleep rolled in their poncho liners—lightweight, camouflaged quilt blankets—I ask Ross if he thinks anything will happen tonight. A typical question from a new arrival.

"No sweat, man, no sweat. Just keep awake on guard and watch for movement."

"Roger. Sleepin' on guard is the last thing you have to worry about with me."

Ross taps my knee and flashes his even white teeth. "No sweat."

Sure. I rub my hands on my fatigues to dry the sweat. Already the mosquitoes are dive-bombing with fury. I smear bug juice—insect repellent—over my exposed flesh. I examine my rifle and make certain that my magazine is locked in place. My stomach leaps when I recall that I haven't test-fired my rifle yet. If I make it through this night without using it I vow that I'll test-fire it tomorrow.

Infuriated, I grab a hand grenade Ross had given to me before we left. *My God,* I think, *a real bomb. I'm supposed to use this to kill people who are attacking us!* I try to make the pineapple-shaped grenade feel comfortable in my hand. It's impossible. I can't hold it like a baseball and get a good grip. Sometimes blasting caps fail to detonate. *What if my grenade is a dud?* I worry. *Christ, what if I run out of ammo?*

I ponder all the things that might go awry. What if the perimeter is mortared and the shells fall short? There aren't any bunkers to dive into like last night. What about a ground attack? What if we need artillery and they fire on us due to a miscalculation? What if we are forced to ambush a superior number of VC? What if our machine gun jams? What if, what if. . . ?!

Then from the caverns of despair I recoil, remembering from training that the percentages are in our favor: the majority of patrols fail to engage the enemy.

I'm hungry. My stomach fluids are screeching. It seems incongruous to be surrounded by such indeterminate danger and still be hungry. But I had lost my appetite for our evening repast once I had heard that Ross's squad would effect an LP tonight. And now I'm ravenous. So far the anticipation of going had proved to be worse than the actual operation. I resolve not to miss any more meals because of tension. If things became abominable, I'd probably puke it all up. But if things were okay, at least I'd have a full belly.

I need to urinate. Bad. I know it's verboten to stand up on a night patrol once you're in position. Perplexed, I whisper my dilemma to Ross. He says he has to go himself. We creep a few meters to our rear. We urinate while lying on our sides and propping ourselves on our elbows.

After our shift expires Ross wakes the next two guards: Hooper, a gangling cowboy from Idaho; and Tex, a panhandle Texan who drawls with the best of them. Ross gives Hooper a wristwatch and the radio to call in the situation reports to the fire base every half hour. The sergeant waddles back to his place and covers himself with his poncho liner. He notices me watching him.

"Kitch, go to sleep. Our guard's over."

"I'm not sleepy."

"Suit yourself."

Blinking, hoping, and computing the odds, I linger well into the third shift before my fear succumbs to fatigue. As the first pink-gray tint of dawn peeks over the horizon, Ross touches my shoulder.

"Kitch, get up and get your claymore in."

In a matter of minutes we're in formation and striving for our base. Stumbling under the unfamiliar weight of the radio can't siphon my ecstasy during the swift march to a breakfast of eggs, bread, bacon and milk. I had triumphantly weathered my first night patrol. And not a scratch! Not even a bullet fired!

But skulking behind my relief and exultation a squadron of questions are jabbing my brain: What is happening to me? Why am I trudging in this strange foreign land carrying a rifle and a radio? I'm in a war! A war! What am I doing in a war? How did I get into this mess?

2

The Television War

The year I became a conscript was a wild one. Early in 1968 in Vietnam the North Vietnamese launched their Tet offensive. Later in the year the My Lai massacre occurred. In the United States there were two shocking assassinations, campus riots, a president refusing to run for reelection, ghetto disturbances, and tanks skirmished with students at the Democratic convention in Chicago. The presidential election had the national conscience wrangling over one dominant topic: Vietnam.

In April of that year, about two weeks before I graduated from college, my attention gravitated to the election and the war. My draft reclassification notice had arrived: go to the front of the line. I suddenly comprehended that when Walter Cronkite gave the weekly body counts, he wasn't giving sports scores. When I saw the media's combat films, I realized I wasn't watching Marines in the Pacific during World War II. This was a startling experience, for the controversial Asian war thousands of miles from my life never had affected me before.

The university I had attended was a sedate Ohio institution that, for whatever reasons, seldom became emotional about anything, except basketball. The war was remote. While a poll might have indicated the majority of the faculty and students were opposed to the war, it simply wasn't a militant school. There were debates but no violence or student demonstrations.

It was difficult to locate someone who was directly involved in the conflict. The draft's tentacles had snared only a tiny percentage of the populace. Men enlisted in the Navy, Air Force, or Reserves to escape the draft and an infantryman's life in Vietnam. Postponements left and right. It seemed that everyone, except the minorities and the poor, had a formula to avoid the war.

That spring I also sifted the possibilities. I initially reckoned on getting a job with an inherent deferment. But I wasn't qualified for anything like that. I didn't have the money to secure additional training. So I decided to vie for any respectable job until I received the inevitable "Greetings." But my job interviews would turn sour when the issue of my draft classification was addressed. The interrogators always prematurely exposed their verdict with an embarrassed grimace when I said, "Class I-A."

Next I considered enlistment—"A choice, not a chance" proclaimed the ad—but after somber deliberation I eliminated this alternative simply because it would mean three or four years in uniform rather than a draftee's two years. I had already made the towering assumption that I'd dislike military life.

I decided to confront the necessary evil, to get the whole nasty military experience behind me as quickly as possible. Since I'd rather suffer from the heat than from the cold, I theorized it would be better to attend basic training during the summer months. So in May I went to my local draft office. I told them to register me for the July call-up. The prosaic bureaucrats recounted that I was already scheduled for the September allotment. But they accommodated me.

For some absurd reason I felt I was getting the last laugh on the draft by volunteering for it. Although I was submitting to the Army holocaust, I smugly reasoned that I was still retaining some control over my destiny.

Once I had made the decision I resolved to enjoy myself during the weeks before reporting. I returned to my old college summer job in the local park's maintenance department. Evenings I frittered away pursuing girls, guzzling beer, and basking in summer. My conversations with friends and my private reflections weren't dominated by the milestones occurring in America and Vietnam. Events seemed to be happening too swiftly anyway to have time to fret over them. The morality of the Vietnam War didn't interest me; I simply shelved the issue.

The war was escalating. But would it really involve me? I had extreme doubts that it would. Maybe it would end before I ever reported for induction. I faced eight weeks of basic training, then another lengthy training cycle. In all that time perhaps the fighting would terminate.

In May I was certain that if Eugene McCarthy or Robert Kennedy were elected, America's involvement in the war would cease in a matter of months. Hubert Humphrey appeared to be shaky, assailable. Candidate Nixon was the enigma trailing the pack. The antiwar juggernaut seemed to have the chart-minded policymakers in Washington teetering. The light, we were extolled, was visible at the end of the tunnel. Anything could happen.

I wasn't remorseful over my decision. I concentrated on having fun and getting myself into physical condition for the grind of basic training. I was simply going into the Army. Many people did that. Not everyone who entered the Army went to Vietnam, and of those who did, only a relative few went into combat. And percentage-wise still fewer had the misfortune to get wounded, let alone killed.

Therefore, I concluded, the odds were that things would be okay. Even if I did go to Vietnam I'd depart as a driver or typist — anything but an infantryman. I was simply too smart to be shuffled to the infantry. What purpose would I serve as a foot soldier? The Army personnel wizards surely wouldn't squander my talents by programming me to carry a rifle. After all, I was a college graduate.

3

Sweet Carolina Pine

On induction day in Selective Service America you report to your local draft office at 7 A.M. As your name is called you board a bus for downtown Philadelphia. Some fellows are frightened, but for most it's an adventure. That the adventure might end in the rice paddies of Vietnam is the last thing on your mind. There is much frivolity and bravado during the hour-long ride to the city.

At the induction center you're corralled inside, processed from station to station, signing here and there, progressively surrendering your privacy and vital statistics to the Army. Maybe for the first time in your life you're treated like nothing more than a chunk of flesh and bone. Due to the unique circumstances, conversation with strangers erupts easily, even for reserved individuals. There is still hilarity.

The assembly-line physical is lengthy, humiliating. Sometime during it you might encounter a biopsy of the Army's inefficiency. Several men had difficulty voiding for the urine analysis, so they borrowed fluid from others who had a glut. One man dispensed portions of his sample to a half-dozen unfortunates. Little did the technicians know that they were repeatedly testing the identical specimen.

Forty recruits are assembled naked. The physicians stroll by and inspect your male organs. Scenes of the embarrassed nude Jewry in Nazi gas chambers waiting for the "showers" to be activated might flash in your mind. You aren't going to be murdered. But you prepare yourself for anything short of that. When at the concluding station of the inspection you're pronounced "disgustingly healthy," you know that you're going to don olive-green for the next two years.

You get dressed. You're shepherded into a chamber with photos on the walls of everyone in the chain of command from President Johnson to the induction center commander. A podium stands in the front of the room. Next to it is an American flag. A major enters, jokes a moment with the other officers, then calls you to attention. He orders you to elevate your right hand. He solemnly administers the oath. You're congratulated. You're a soldier.

The atmosphere changes. The fact that we are no longer civilians and the looming specter of basic training smother the levity. We're hurriedly fed at a nearby restaurant and hustled onto a train for Fort Bragg, North Carolina. The train departs hours late. Most of us become unnerved by the brusque commands and the hurry-up-and-wait routine. As I snuggle into my berth I suspect that I'm not alone when I resolve to emulate the poised infielder, ready to respond at the crack of the bat.

A few days later we're on a bus taking us from the Fort Bragg Reception Station to our basic training company located on another part of the post. The bus makes a turn and climbs a steep hill. At the top of the hill it makes another turn onto a driveway between a row of dour barracks. It bounces to a halt. I don't see anyone board the bus because duffel bags obscure my vision, but I hear a heinous voice emanating from the front of the vehicle.

"Everybody out! Everybody out! Everybody out! Get your goddamn sorry asses off this bus! Get the goddamn hell off! Now, goddamnit, now!"

We scramble from the bus. The trick is to sprint with your unwieldy duffel bag fifty yards down the driveway and to come to attention in a formation initiated by previous bus loads. Our path to the assemblage is flanked by impeccably attired drill sergeants with Smokey Bear hats dipped low on their foreheads. If anyone stumbles while struggling to the formation a drill sergeant bombards him with a barrage of slurs while the soldier does push-ups.

Most of us, however, safely negotiate our way to the gathering and assume the attention position. The man before me is trembling so much that I think he's going to collapse any moment. I glance at the fellow to my left. He's shivering. I'm also apprehensive; my underclothes are soaked with perspiration.

The drill sergeants strut to the front of the formation. Glinting lodestones of military training, they brood before us like human volcanoes ready to erase anything in their track. Surely the Army had mastered cloning. From where I stand quivering the sergeants appear exactly alike: black, monolithic, sinister, poised, omnipotent. Their boots and brass are glistening under the afternoon sun. Protruding jaws are rammed tight. Inflamed, cunning eyes are fanning the formation. I had heard about drill sergeants being tough and furious-looking. But this crew has to be an All Star team.

A towering sergeant steps onto a small platform. With arms akimbo, he glares for several moments from one side of the formation to the other. He shakes his head no for twenty seconds while he paces around the platform. Then he says in a pathetic tone, "What a sorry bunch. Drop. Just drop. Everybody just drop right where you are. Drop!" Clerks at the reception station had informed us that "drop" was the command to commence push-ups. We sink and do twenty, everyone chanting out the numbers.

"On your feet! On your feet! Everybody on your feet! Demonstrator, front and center!" snarls the sergeant. A soldier who had just completed basic training leaps onto the platform. "Now, looky here," the sergeant continues, "I want all eyes on the demonstrator." Pause. "Demonstrator, hold up your right hand!" Another hesitation. "Demonstrator, prepare to grab your balls!" Another dramatic wait. "Demonstrator, ready, grab!" The grim private clenches his balls. The sergeant sneers across the formation. Then he turns to the demonstrator and says, "Good, good. Demonstrator, at ease!"

I hear some giggling behind me, but I don't dare turn around. None of the sergeants seem to notice the chuckling.

"Okay, okay," snorts the sergeant while rubbing together his mammoth hands. "Now, looky here, since y'all seen how it's done, I want every one of you goddamn sorry asses to hold up your right hand real high." He menacingly surveys the formation, hoping, I think, to catch someone with his left hand elevated. Before I move I think twice which hand is my right one. "Good! Good! Every swingin' dick knows which is his right hand. Now I want everybody to prepare to grab his balls." He halts a moment. "Ready, grab!"

Following the lead of the demonstrator a hundred and fifty men reach for their testicles. I hear more snickering. On the far side of the formation the sergeants catch a few gigglers and they're ordered to keep laughing while doing push-ups.

"Good! Good!" the sergeant shrills. "Take a real good fistful of 'em two soft things that should be hangin' there! For you numbnuts out there who don't know, us mens call 'em a pair of balls! That's it, that's it! Hold 'em real good an' tight. Now, looky here, up until this here point in your young an' sorry lives you jokers have been pussies. That's right, pussies! Every big long swingin' dick is a pussy! You don't deserve to have 'em family jewels in your hands right now. So what we're gonna do for the next eight weeks is to make you worthy of havin' 'em balls hangin' there. We're gonna make mens out of you! Well, some of you. I can already see some hardcase pussies out there. We know how to deal with pussies. We just recycle 'em for another eight weeks until they become mens. But most of you will become mens in one cycle. That's the tough job of us staff here! But we're ready for it!"

In unison the other sergeants scowl and cross their arms. I think I see one sergeant trying to stifle a grin. He starts coughing and turns his back on us. It's becoming more and more like a ridiculous sideshow act. Only we can't leave.

"Now," the sergeant yells, "do everybody understand me?"

Silence.

"Do everybody understand me?" he growls louder.

"Yes, Sir!" a few recruits venture.

"The answer is 'Yes, Drill Sergeant!' Let's get one goddamn thing clear right now: for the next eight weeks my first name is 'Drill,' and my last name is 'Sergeant!' And that goes for the other drill sergeants here! Do you goddamn pussies understand me?"

"YES, DRILL SERGEANT!"

"Good! Good! And just so you goddamn sorry asses don't forget it, everybody drop! Drop! Just start pumpin'!"

One of my principal goals in basic was to remain as inconspicuous as possible. In a platoon of forty men I calculated I could accomplish this by doing what I was told to do without having to be told twice. A close friend who had completed basic had advised me to do what the drill sergeants said no matter how stupid or unpleasant it was. Things would improve after training and the harassment would dwindle. He counseled me to avoid confrontation with the sergeants at all costs and never volunteer for anything—never.

After the sergeants concluded their welcoming drama, we were alphabetically dispersed into four platoons. At the initial formation of my platoon our muscular, stocky drill sergeant asked if anyone had attended college. Several of us raised our hands. He asked for those who were college graduates. Four of us stood at attention before him. He quizzed each of us about our university and our course of study.

"Kitchin, front and center!" he yelled. I stepped forward. He curtly dismissed the others. "Kitchin, you are my platoon leader!"

I stood speechless. His dark eyes glared at me like a tensor lamp. "Well? *You* are my platoon leader!"

"Yes, drill sergeant!"

He nodded, discharged the platoon, and sauntered to the company headquarters.

I was dismayed. This episode didn't concur too well with my policy of inconspicuousness. Under no circumstances did I yearn to be a platoon leader. If I had aspired to be a military leader I would have enlisted in the Army and vied for Officer Candidate School.

I decided to risk a million push-ups and expose my feelings. Later that day I went to the sergeant and told him that I didn't care to be his platoon leader. I explained that I felt extremely uncomfortable about it. Perhaps another fellow might handle the task more to the drill sergeant's satisfaction?

He didn't erupt like I expected. He encouraged me to do my best, promising me that he'd relieve me later if I didn't work out.

That evening three other K's and myself were subtracted from the Third Platoon and attached to the Second in a manpower realignment. The Second already had a platoon leader. My dilemma evaporated as swiftly as it had burgeoned.

Ebullience engulfed me over this incident. I had resurrected my anonymity! Now I could concentrate on accomplishing the routines one does in basic without having to be burdened with leadership responsibilities in an organization I didn't itch to be in anyway. All I wished was to complete my two years as painlessly as possible.

I subscribed further buoyancy from the fact that the Army, even the notorious drill sergeants, recognized the value of an education. There was little doubt in my swelled cranium that I'd be spared from the Vietnam maelstrom. The sergeants had proved it.

A few nights later I was on guard duty. My monotonous circuit took me around the dimly illuminated company HQ, down the block into the darkness and back again. About midnight, just as I was circling the HQ, three drill sergeants intersected my path carrying a squirming trainee crying, "No! No! No!" One sergeant approached me while the others toted the struggling private into the HQ.

"Hey, troop," he sneered.

"Yes, drill sergeant," I spurted, bewildered by the spectacle I had just witnessed.

"I want you to change your guard route so you stay away from this here building." He gestured to the HQ. "We got some disciplinary matter to attend to in there, and I want you to forget what you just saw." He glared at me ominously. "Get it, trainee?"

"Yes, drill sergeant."

"Good. Now get your butt on down the road."

He whirled and dashed into the office. I meandered into the shadows. I halted next to a telephone pole within eavesdropping distance. In a few moments the oppressive summer air was pierced by screams and shouts gushing from the HQ. The sergeants were beating the young soldier. The victim kept wailing, "Please, no! No! No! Please, no!" as they pummeled him.

Distraught, I considered trying to locate other witnesses. But the rest of the company was asleep. The other guards were nowhere in sight. I wanted to summon our company commander, who I assumed wouldn't tolerate such brutality by his drill sergeants. But I didn't know where to search for him. I rejected the notion of bursting in on the sergeants. Before I reacted, the thrashing ceased. The sergeants transported the man from the HQ while he whimpered something about "Not doing it" and "Being set-up."

I endured a haunting night trying to decide what to do about my experience. I hankered to retaliate against the savagery of the sergeants. Yet, with only a few weeks in uniform and my solitary word against theirs, I didn't feel confident about tangling with them. I kept recollecting my friend's advice to avoid confrontation.

My indecision was relieved the following morning at our five o'clock formation. Our CO made an unexpected appearance at reveille. He announced that any trainee apprehended with drugs in his possession would be delivered to the military police for prosecution under military law. He exhorted us to dispose of any drugs before his sergeants discovered them first. He stated that the sergeants probably would make our wait for the MPs "unpleasant." The captain further expounded that he and his cohorts hated the use of drugs because they "corrupted the mind."

The decorated officer had solved my quandary. I left the formation wondering how the man could ever identify a corrupted mind.

Basic training is an unforgettable, incredible experience. The itinerary is tedious, harsh, demanding. You're taught to do things you never conceived of doing, or thought you could do. You learn to run, jump, crawl (and how you learn to crawl!), march, eat fast, sleep little, and more saliently, you learn how to kill.

Basic is a vocal event. You learn to yell. You learn to sing. Whenever you move in groups you march and sing. Sometimes you march to the beat of drums, the universal call to arms. All the noise is ordered to nurture morale, to keep you awake.

You learn Army talk. You don't fail to qualify with the M14, you "bolo." If you botch inspection, you get "gigged." When you stand or sit, it's "on your feet!" or "seats!" When you march, you "rock steady." You're constantly reminded that you're a soldier so you always "maintain a military bearing."

If you commit a fundamental blunder you're corrected through physical reminders, usually push-ups. If you call your rifle a gun, you stand off by yourself with one hand holding your weapon and the other hand grasping your penis while proclaiming, "This is my rifle and this is my gun!"

The instructional commentaries are rudimentary, blunt: "Gentlemens, at this time you will be learned how to kill with the bayonet! And the spirit of the bayonet is to kill!" The results are equally elementary: after the training you may not have the spirit of the bayonet. But you do know how to slice a rubber tire.

The task of the drill sergeants is to prepare men for battle. To do this they must educate trainees in the correct way to act and think, especially who to love and who to hate. The sergeants make it very clear that there is only one correct way: the Army way.

The training regimen is as timeless as the patented scowl on the drill sergeants' faces. The mornings are identical: Everybody up! Everybody up! Up, up, up! Sweep! Scrub! Brush! Mop! Give that Brasso a workout! Wax that floor! Make those windows glow! Wipe that dust from the tops of doors! Clean those latrines! Line up those foot lockers! Tighten those bunks! Polish those insignias! Spit-shine those boots! Shave and dress! Out, out, out!

The nights and days run together: inspections, weapons' firing and cleaning, push-ups, KP, training classes, forced marches, calisthenics, fire watches, close-order drills, police calls, lines, details and formations. Hurry, hurry, hurry! Move, move, move! Faster, faster, faster! Wait, wait, wait.

The people who run your life for two months are lewd and brutal. For eight grueling weeks they have absolute power over you. All you have are your mates, who are in the same predicament as you. So you're drawn together, which fosters the love that you are supposed to learn.

And in the end the drill sergeants succeed. You bond with your buddies and you learn to shoot and kill. You're taught to hate your country's enemies because—as the drill sergeants remind you—they're the reason why you are in uniform.

The ultimate objective of the intimidation and the exhausting agenda is to subdue the mind of an already-sequestered body. Once you're mentally incarcerated, the discipline required to train and deploy an army becomes feasible. Without obedience to the leaders, how could there be armies? The military knows it must initiate this quest for mind-captivity from day one.

I was vaguely cognizant of all this before induction. So once in training I became determined to mimic soldiering without mentally submitting to the folly and ignorance which imbue the Army. I'd purport to be a "strack trooper." But my brain would be replete with independence.

I believed they could capture my mind only if I gave it to them. However, the military is alert for mental opposition. The days are crammed with physical activity. You never walk anywhere, you're always marching or running. Sleep is a luxury. Solitude is non-existent. The military knows the less time you have to ponder what an appalling situation you're in, the less time you have to sulk or debate going AWOL. They know that as the training drudgery is intensified, the more likely you are to waver.

During the first month I felt like I was managing things. I devised mental deterrents to resist as best I could. In class and while waiting in line—something I always detested—I daydreamed. I mentally composed letters to my family and friends back home. I carefully planned how I'd spend my leave time once training ended. Sometimes I concentrated on how the Philly sports teams were doing. Things like that. Countless ideas kept my head occupied with diversionary tactics.

One of my favorite subterranean maneuvers occurred during the half-hour jaunt to and from the rifle ranges. We rode in converted cattle trucks. The open trailers made too much din for conversation. Usually most of the men slumbered. We huddled close to keep warm during the chilly dawn journey. The benches were so low that you couldn't see over the wooden railings. All you could do was to peer up at the brightening sky and the imperial pine trees. The morning air was succulent with pine scent.

On one of the first rides I whispered to the trees. I greeted them with a hello and a smile. I asked them what would happen to us today at the ranges? Would I bolo or qualify? Would anyone get shot in the head erecting targets like happened in the training cycle preceding us?

As we voyaged back to the barracks I told my majestic comrades goodbye. I hoped they had received abundant sunshine during the day. I told them to get sufficient rest so they'd stand lofty and resplendent in the morning when I returned.

The vista and smell of the pine woods provided a mysterious therapy for me. I was doing something that I had never done before. I was taking the time to confront nature. Somehow I felt a euphoric oneness with the trees. I lamented that it took the internment of Army life to arouse my senses to nature, to life. I had heard that the military was a superb place to make lifelong friends. Fort Bragg's luxuriant pine forests became ample proof for me.

My mental barricading seemed to be effective until one day I was outflanked faster than Hitler's legions circumvented the Maginot Line. One afternoon in our fifth or sixth week, we were given an unexpected respite in the normal grind. This anomaly is usually a tiny incident, but it has the impact of a sledgehammer. Maybe you're permitted a free hour at the PX, perhaps an extra hour of sleep or an extended lunch break. From this abnormality jettison sporadic privileges during your concluding weeks.

As the noose slackened, I commenced to think that maybe the military wasn't going to be so terrible after all. *Hey,* I thought, *even the drill sergeants give us a break now and then.* So I began a retreat, a resignation. The war was over. I wouldn't attempt a bodily escape from the military because I had yielded mentally. The ironic part was that the Great Mental Stonewaller didn't even know it.

The Army was rife with rumors. My unit was no exception. The war was still magnifying. But near the end of our cycle we heard a rumor that combat units would soon be rotated home from Vietnam. More hearsay was that most Bragg basic graduates were henceforth being sent to Germany rather than across the Pacific. I was skeptical about this. Nevertheless I still felt my personal odds were outstanding for avoiding Vietnam. Nothing had happened in basic to convince me otherwise.

One afternoon in our eighth week we were summoned to formation. The sergeants requested volunteers to do office work for the balance of the day. They wanted no dummies, only smart trainees need apply. The typically seedy Army jest evoked the accustomed laughter.

It seemed like a juicy overture. But others had been lured into tantalizing proposals only to regret it later. A few men volunteered. When the sergeants fell short of the required number, other trainees suggested names of men who had, at a moment of indiscretion, exhibited a trickle of intelligence. Someone offered me.

Another fellow and I were ushered into a cubicle in one building while the rest of the volunteers were put to task in the HQ. The sergeants weren't deceiving us this time. We spent the afternoon shuffling papers. The final batch of work we had to accomplish involved, to our utter amazement, sorting the pending orders for everyone in our training brigade. The orders were scheduled to be dispersed within a few days.

Naturally everyone was anxious about where their next duty station would be. I was exuberant that I'd get a premature peek at the orders. We already knew which post one was assigned to for each particular type of advanced individual training, the next training cycle. Your assignment following basic was generally the training school for the job you'd perform once you reached a permanent duty station. I knew that any fort but Fort Polk would be okay with me. Polk was the eastern post for advanced infantry training. For most men it was the last stop before infantry service in Vietnam. It had a reputation for being a tough training cycle.

I flipped through the papers for A company. Our names were muddled. I furiously slid my finger up and down the list searching for my name. The superficial screening was portentous; about one-third of the company was assigned to Polk. I located my name with Polk next to it. A violent rage engulfed me. I ached to destroy the documents. I craved to rip apart the room. I cursed the drill sergeants, the Army, the president, the war, the Communists, everything, everyone. I felt like crying. But I was too irate for tears. Suffocating in self-pity, I memorized the orders for some of my comrades. That evening I was one of the most popular men in the company when word circulated about our glimpse of the orders.

I was horribly despondent. Why Fort Polk? How could this happen to me? Didn't these army assholes realize I had an education? Polk meant infantry and probably Vietnam! Why me? Why? Why? But I had no answers—only a skull teeming with delusions.

One soldier I had befriended in basic was a musician. He was a rotund, freckle-struck Virginian. He had enlisted for three years, assuring himself a drummer's life for his tour. He took the choice, not the chance.

Shortly before we departed Bragg we said goodbye in the mess hall. He was disconsolate over my misfortune. We had shared a bunk bed for eight weeks. Words seemed superfluous in the final moments. So we shook hands and wished each other luck. An hour later he met a Greyhound bound for the army band school in Washington, D.C. I boarded a jet destined for Louisiana and the infamous Fort Polk.

4

Tigerland

The principal entrance to Fort Polk was adorned with a wooden arch. It spanned the busy four-lane road which yawned into the post. On the arch colorful, leviathan letters announced the reservation's nickname as "Tigerland." Below the tip of the arch swayed another sign which proclaimed that the men training there were known as "Tigers." Other advertisements surrounded the entryway with slogans as superficial as those used in a political campaign. But make no mistake, the emblems blazed: beyond this gate we transform Americans into ferocious tigers to hunt and kill Viet Cong.

At Tigerland you master how to load, fire and clean everything in the military's arsenal from a .50 caliber machine gun to a .45 caliber pistol. I had belonged to .22 caliber rifle clubs in high school and college, thus I wasn't unduly intimidated by weapons. But in advanced infantry training you learn how to exterminate pop-up targets sculptured like men, which did succeed in intimidating me.

Everyone was issued an M-16 rifle, the primary firearm of the infantryman. It was a light, fully automatic piece with an effective range of over three hundred meters. It had all the amenities that twentieth century technology could concoct. In your hands it seemed like a toy. Parts of the rifle were indeed manufactured by Mattel, a prominent toy producer.

There were no flunkees in AIT. If you boloed a certain weapon, then you were retested until you qualified. If someone still didn't qualify after the fourth or fifth retest, then the exasperated drill sergeants doctored the scores so that the deficient trainee qualified. Every warm body graduated. Replacements were needed abroad.

Advanced infantry training wasn't as arduous or restrictive as my basic training itinerary. After our initial two weeks, we had more sleep and privileges than we did at Bragg, including Sundays and even an occasional Saturday afternoon off. The harassment and the usual military indignities were still rampant. There just wasn't seven days a week of it.

The theme of our training was strictly jungle-fighting-in-Vietnam. Each instructor began his class with the phrase, "*When* you get to Nam," not "*If* you get to Nam." Indoctrination and morale were purportedly enhanced by signs like "Bong the Cong" plastered all over the base. It was impossible to pass a wall, fence, or building without some pathetic poster reminding us of our destination and our mission once we arrived.

Like corporations vying for one's business, each division quartered in Vietnam had their insignias splattered about Tigerland. Inside my barracks a sprawling logo of the 25th Infantry Division was painted on the floor in the center of the aisle. My bunk was adjacent to the dazzling inscription, which was an arrow-shaped, red taro leaf with a gold border and a gold bolt of lightning centered in the leaf.

Nightly as I snuggled into bed, I'd glance at the mark on the floor. "I wonder if that's where I'll be goin'?" I often remarked to my bunkmate. "Don't fuckin' worry about it, chump!" my apathetic partner would always reply.

My drill sergeant was a whiplean, brooding, rough-tongued career man who had served with the 25th in Vietnam. A double Purple Heart recipient, his respect for the division was so overwhelming that he prohibited his trainees from walking on the insignia. He informed us that we weren't worthy of treading upon the symbol of such a grandiose unit. He commented that he had lost many friends in Vietnam; he wouldn't tolerate their sacrifices being defaced by our trainee boots which had never touched Vietnam's soil.

I'd often speculate on what had happened to this fellow in Vietnam. Was this what combat did to you or was the guy unstable before experiencing Vietnam?

Midway through our training cycle, our drill sergeant disappeared. Although we were curious as to his whereabouts, his exit was applauded by us because we were terrified of him. The other sergeants always became taciturn whenever his name arose. In our eighth week finally one of the sergeants yielded that our erstwhile leader was suffering from "traumatic war neurosis," a military euphemism for someone who had gone crazy from combat.

After his exodus we were permitted to trample wherever we preferred in our barracks. But I continued to refrain from pacing on the impression. Just in case I was assigned to that division, I rationalized. Already an idiosyncrasy of an infantry soldier was fomenting in me. I was becoming superstitious.

But after a week of avoiding the logo, I wondered if that didn't make me just as nuts as he was. I was compelled to admit that it did. So I bravely tromped on the red taro leaf, all the while praying that I wouldn't be allotted to that division.

During AIT other phobias crept into my mind. If I did get into combat the fear of my weapon jamming or running out of ammo haunted me. One solution to both of these quandaries might be to tote a small derringer, I theorized. Just when those lousy Commies thought they had me, I'd whip out my snub-nose and ruin their day! I felt so brilliant over this inspiration that one day I questioned a drill sergeant about carrying an auxiliary weapon. After he redeemed his breath from laughing so hysterically, he explained that if the firefight wasn't bad, then I wouldn't need another weapon. And if it was bad, he continued with a roguish grin, then there would be ample weapons being unused.

I pondered how I'd react to getting wounded or perhaps losing a limb. Well, I figured, if I lost an arm, leg, or eye, then that would make me different. I'd be unique. My disability would be an inconvenience. But no big deal for such a resourceful chap like me. Hell, so what? I'd be a Purple Heart medalist! Maybe I'd even be a war hero! And if I did lose an appendage, that in itself wouldn't stop me from living. I had a solution for every crisis: if I lost a member then I'd be a Black Patch, a Peg Leg, or perhaps an adept, lethal Captain Hook. I'd be a Mr. Cool, handicap and all.

This romantic nonsense was merely mental camouflage for my fear. Even then my gnarled rationale would topple under analysis because I really didn't think there was anything cool about walking around without a penis or testicles.

Among our concluding training exercises at Polk was a nighttime ordeal entitled "The Escape and Evasion Course." It was contrived to educate us on techniques to elude capture by the VC. A gigantic game of Cops and Robbers, the program consisted of releasing the entire company from one point with the object being for us to achieve the finish line without getting captured by a platoon of regular Polk troops who were masquerading as VC. Our adversaries were armed with sixteens loaded with blanks.

We had defined boundaries. The area that we had to journey through to reach safety contained an Interrogation and Torture compound. Another hazardous barrier was Texas Avenue, a two-lane paved road which we'd have to traverse to achieve the safety line.

While we waited for the Louisiana darkness to descend, we were tendered a class on how to sustain ourselves in the Vietnam countryside once we had escaped from the enemy. The riddle was posed how to kill a chicken one had snared in the wilderness. The drill sergeant had made the supposition that even us city slickers knew how to stalk and collar a wild bird.

The instructor called for the chicken. A drill sergeant coaxed a bewildered chicken onto a platform before the class. "Sergeant, we like our chicken fried!" a trainee next to me hollered loud enough for everyone to hear. All the sergeants exploded in laughter, signaling that it was permissible for the rest of us to release our mirth. The comedian was a favorite of the sergeants. If you were so ordained, then you could jest with them if they were in a gay mood.

If the sergeants had their pets, they also had certain trainees who they chided and abused. One trainee in particular was a *persona non grata* because of his admirable but indiscreet vocal opposition to the war. Early in AIT he had made it known that, while he'd go to Vietnam, he wouldn't engage in combat or kill anyone. The drill sergeants, who loathed pacifists, selected this trooper to function as a demonstrator. His task would be to exterminate the hen.

Smirking and strutting in vengeance, the instructor called the man from his seat. The soldier darted from the bleachers. He accepted the squawking fowl from the sergeant. But he refused to kill it. The incensed sergeants converged on the soldier. They assailed him with every expletive in the formidable military vocabulary. The reluctant executioner stood his ground until two drill sergeants took him arm-in-arm and ushered him off to an Article 15 and two horrid-looking black eyes.

After the "coward" was dispatched, the sergeant summoned a farmer's son front and center. Grinning and bloated with pride in his ability to snap a chicken's neck, the country boy disposed of the biddy and flipped it onto the platform.

As the man hustled back to his place in the bleachers, the impressed drill sergeant remarked, "You're a real man, troop!" The sergeant turned to the class. "And now, does any of you gentlemens got any questions on the material we have just learned?"

Nightfall. Formation was in a meadow fronting a dense, murky forest. Some hasty final instructions were given. Then the signal to begin the course sounded. Like one hundred and fifty inmates on a prison break, we scuttled for the woods.

Yapping, joking, and stumbling through the underbrush, a dozen of us merged into a group. The farther we plodded into the woodland, the darker it became. Our levity ebbing, we advised each other to keep closer together. When we halted to rest, only eight heads were present; we had lost four men in the void. Alarmed, we bunched together and held hands as we knifed onward. We made good progress.

We finally approached the dimly illuminated compound. We coiled around its fenced perimeter and advanced to within twenty meters of the treacherous Texas Avenue. We elected to try to cross the road simultaneously; we felt that if the surrogates were waiting for us, at least some of us would survive the ambush. I was trembling over the possibility of getting apprehended. Even though it was only a seasoning exercise, I knew that some of the thugs in the compound would relish getting their hands on trainees.

Just before the command was given for our group to scamper across the highway, another team bolted from the brush. There was much commotion, shooting. We seized this opportunity for our break. Whooping, we leaped from our shrubs and ran onto the artery. Halfway across, the "VC," who had been waiting for us, charged from their positions. I evaded one captor when he veered away from me and chased after the man running beside me. It was mass confusion. I was forced to dive back into some brush near the edge of the road.

Alone and quivering, I watched the captured prisoners being led away to the compound. Solitude returned to Texas Avenue. From my restricted vantage point, I surveyed the area as best I could. I couldn't see or hear anyone. I hesitated for a while hoping to effect my dash when another party tried their luck.

Less than forty meters from me a flock of men plunged onto the boulevard. Elated over being provided the diversion, I bounded from my concealment. My eyes burst from their sockets when an opponent sprung from the opposite side of the road. He fired several times. Then he tried to tackle me. Demonstrating my finest open field running since grade school, I side-stepped his lunge and scurried into the forest across Texas Avenue. He pursued me while hooting at me to halt. Ignoring his cries and bouncing off tree trunks, I galloped as best I could in the thick timberland. Suddenly I tripped and plunged cheek first into a tree. The collision flattened me. A scorching pain ripped through my head. I staggered to my feet and kept running until my enemy relented. Once I judged that he wasn't tracking me, I decelerated to a dizzying toddle.

I hiked for a half hour without sighting anyone or anything. As my head unclouded I realized that I was lost. I had been meandering about, dazed after I had struck the tree! I wasn't certain but I could have stumbled out of bounds.

I was desperate. I decided to risk capture by yelling for help. Hoping only trainees would hear me, I yelped for twenty minutes without results. Depressed, I sat on a fallen tree to assess things. I heard nothing. Only pine scent filled the air. I was lost, hungry, sapped, thirsty, covered with sweat and surrounded by total darkness. My head felt like it had an axe in it. My cheek was swollen, bleeding. I started moving again, not really knowing which trajectory to follow. I was as lost as a blind man in a labyrinth.

Suddenly I heard the cracking of twigs and brush before me. I froze. My heart cascaded in joy as three friendlies emerged from the blackness. Acting nonchalant, I asked if I could join them. Certainly, they said, since I was heading for Texas Avenue. And what was I doing with my cheek streaked with blood? Wilting under their interrogation, I admitted my dilemma and related my adventures to them.

We trekked close to the finish line. Since it also was a perilous locale, we circled through an off-limits area and climbed a lofty chain-link fence. Then we switched back in bounds behind the finish line. Safe at last, we boarded trucks that returned us to our lodgings.

Despite my throbbing head I was jubilant about not getting captured. Over one-third of the company had been netted. For me it had been a harrowing experience. I had a premonition that perhaps Vietnam would be a comparable escapade for me: injury, but not death or capture. *And, oh my God,* I shuddered, as I sank into my mattress that disquieting night, *what would Cops and Robbers be like when the enemy weren't proxies using blanks?* I prayed I wouldn't leave all my luck behind in the States.

Throughout AIT I kept embracing the ludicrous notion that somehow I'd escape orders for infantry duty in Vietnam. I persisted in believing that someone who made big personnel decisions would abort any attempt to send me to infantry. "Let's see here, what's this?" I fantasized some Very Important Person snorting. "We can't send this educated guy into infantry. Sergeant! Bring me the asshole who assigned Private Kitchin to infantry!"

But graduation day arrived and our orders were dispensed. And why should I be shocked at their contents? Why did the Army spend nine weeks training me how to Bong the Cong if I wasn't going to Vietnam?

With only two exceptions — and these two men had had brothers killed in Vietnam — our entire company was issued tickets for what we had christened "The Magical Mystery Tour."

5

Into the Abyss

The sadness surrounding a soldier leaving home, especially when he's destined for a battle zone, is monumental, overpowering. My departure wasn't unique. Since I desired to avoid any emotional airport scenes, I made arrangements for a friend to transport me to the airport. I said good-bye to my family at home.

Taking the latest possible flight out of Philadelphia, I arrived in Seattle about the time the bars closed. I passed the night at the terminal too depressed and fatigued even to think. Early the following morning I took a bus to Fort Lewis. The next forty-eight hours at Lewis were excruciating. Among "B" grade movies, equipment issue lines, and petty work details, I tumbled with the realization that this was my last opportunity to escape the war. Canada was but a few miles distant. Fort Lewis was replete with stories of those who had scaled the wall.

But in the end, the anchor of my background and experience out-weighed the temptation to flee. It really wasn't much of a contest either. My Catholic upbringing with its discipline at school and home, as well as the fear of censure by family and friends were the reigning factors in my reluctance to desert. I couldn't discard the years of indoctrination that in-spired me to do what I was told to do, to do the right thing, to do what was expected of me. I didn't want to go to war. But I had been *ordered* to go. There were *laws* against saying no to Uncle Sam.

Of course there was also the fact that I had already capitulated to military life. Maybe it would be a great foreign adventure. I had read my London and Hemingway. I loved to travel. I had heard that the harassment wasn't as extensive for field troops in Vietnam as it was for those in stateside posts. Maybe I wouldn't be in the infantry too long; surely a non-combat job would eventually come my way. Didn't I sometimes have fan-tastic luck since I'd been in uniform?

I was adrift about the legality and issues of the war. Who was telling the truth? The Communists? The Pentagon? The protestors? I had ex-perienced the Army with its brutality, stupidity. I knew that it was corrupt. But was the war wrong? Maybe this time America was right. Regretfully

I hadn't made the effort to evaluate the question. Doubt and fear plagued my last hours in the States.

As my jet taxied onto the McChord Air Base runway, I peered out the window at a magnificent Pacific Northwest winter sunset. Snow-mantled Mt. Rainier glowed in sun-drenched majesty. Golden shafts of sunlight pierced the oval windows of the plane. I longed to be anywhere but on that coasting cylinder of metal which was thrusting me into a dubious future in a land shredded by war.

But as titanic as that desire to escape was, it was eclipsed by another emotion surfacing from the dungeons of my mind. I felt a nebulous exhilaration. The anticipation of Vietnam was now over. Whether I approved or not, I was embarked on an Oriental odyssey. I'd determine for myself if this ambiguous Asian war was right or wrong. Another facet of this bizarre jubilance enabled me to settle back in my seat as my silver bird soared into the darkening sky and turned west: I also was going to discover much about myself.

It was dark eighteen hours later when our pilot announced that we'd land in seven minutes. Those who were asleep stirred. The shapely, exhausted stewardesses scrambled for their seats. A hush descended over the travelers. Necks strained to glimpse into the blackness. I encountered a numbing terror. My body began to perspire, tremble. My throat dried up. I couldn't talk even if I wanted to.

We were on our runway approach when the pilot was ordered to abort landing and assume a holding pattern over the sea east of Cam Ranh Bay. Once over the water, he divulged to us that the power station at Cam Ranh Bay had been sabotaged by the VC. There were no runway lights.

Fear. Foaming, boiling fear. *Damn,* I thought, *I wasn't even on the ground yet and already things were going wrong!* I revived myself with the hypothesis that for some this scare might be the worst they'd have to endure for their tour. For infantrymen like myself, maybe we'd look back on this incident as a mere inconvenience.

The emergency generators were finally activated. We landed. As we deplaned everyone wore an ashen, fleshy mask. We were bused to barracks and assigned berths. At dawn we were aroused and called to formation. My initial assignment on Vietnam's dust was to perform police call. I had assumed that police call in Vietnam meant gathering bloody arms and legs. Fortunately it was the usual cigarette butts and trash.

After breakfast I fled the barracks to escape the stalking sergeants who were searching for bodies to discharge meaningless details. They hated to see new troops, who were waiting for their individual unit assignments, lounging around unoccupied. My hike enabled me to inspect a portion of

Cam Ranh Bay. It was a sprawling compound with feverish activity. Pallid-gray mountains rimmed the base like reclining behemoths. Minute fleece clusters eked across an azure sky. It was hellishly hot. Everyone avoided the sun as much as possible. To my North American nose the morning atmosphere reeked with the odor of burning feces. I discovered later that my senses weren't deceiving me. Each morning in American complexes all over Vietnam, human excretions accumulated in make-shift toilet receptacles, fashioned from cut-off fifty-five gallon drums, were set ablaze.

The military's outdoor latrines did afford a little privacy: "shitters" were walled; "piss tubes"—metal pipes diagonally inserted into the ground—were ringed by a waist high wooden fence. The Vietnamese bobbing about the base generally avoided the American facilities. Both men and women utilized a strategic bush or tree. These extraordinary toilet procedures aided to slam home the reality that I was indeed half way around the world.

My second night at Cam Ranh Bay I was selected for guard duty. It was a beguiling tropical evening with a half-moon eerily illuminating our fortress. I was guarding an ammunition dump. My reflections rambled. I gazed at the dark silhouetting mountains, thinking about what would happen to me once I journeyed beyond the hills into Vietnam's hinterlands. Thus far the worst element about Vietnam had been the waiting. I hoped that I'd be spared any grievous troubles.

I was dumbfounded about life at Cam Ranh Bay. For sentinel duty I was intentionally issued an oily M-14 without ammo, albeit I had a razor-honed bayonet. I was angry. I kept reaching into my ammo pouches for bullets, but there weren't any to fondle. Wasn't this a war zone? What was the sense of being on guard without ammo? What kind of war was this where guards don't carry primed weapons? It seemed incredible.

I visualized VC sappers assailing the post while I walked the picket line. I pondered how I'd react. What could I do? Did the enemy know that sentinels at Cam Ranh Bay were unarmed? That probably didn't matter to our leaders. I assumed that as a fearless Tigerland graduate I was expected to engage the intruders with my glistening blade by parrying left and thrusting right while terrifying them by screaming, "Kill! Kill!" I hoped the VC would select another night to aggress the ammo dump.

The next morning I discovered why I had been denied ammo. Interior base sentries at Cam Ranh Bay weren't permitted to carry loaded weapons for fear of accidently shooting a friendly party.

My third day at the coastal perimeter I was issued orders to report to Cu Chi, the principal base camp of the 25th Infantry Division. *Oh shit,* I thought, *the insignia on the barracks' floor at Polk! And I'm going to an infantry unit!* I felt like I had a rope around my throat.

I was bused to the airport. My flight to Cu Chi was delayed. I collapsed onto a seat next to a thin sergeant in the waiting area. I unintentionally kicked over a metal ammo box which contained the man's scant personal assets. Several medals and ribbons scattered across the filthy concrete floor. I reached to help the sergeant collect his decorations.

"Sorry, Sarge."

"No sweat," he replied, unperturbed.

"What's this one?" I asked before tossing a medal into the receptacle.

"Purple Heart."

"Oh, that's nice."

"No, it isn't man," he snapped with an icy gaze. "Don't worry, if you spend a year in the field like I did you'll get one too. Everybody does. Only difference is some guys don't know they got one."

I was startled. Here was a soldier who had endured a year in the field! *My God,* I thought, *he looked terrible.* The sergeant's cinnamon-colored eyes were immobile, distant. A muscle in his cheek vibrated. He was drained, dirty, lethargic. He had the look of a sick, homeless old person. I wondered if his body would ever regain the buoyancy of youth. I wondered about his mental state. I wondered what I'd look like after a year at war.

"I don't want one," I said.

"That doesn't matter, man. Nobody wants one of those fuckin' things. But you'll get one anyway."

"Yeah, well, I hope not."

"Hope all you want." He rose as his flight number was broadcasted. He gathered his gear. I asked him where he was going. "Long Binh, to get ready for my Freedom Bird takin' me back across the pond. How about you?"

"Cu Chi. I just got in-country."

He shook his head. "I guess that gives you plenty of time for medals. Good luck anyway."

"Yeah, thanks. And good luck to you."

He gave me the peace sign and disappeared into a throng that funneled through an exit.

Later that day I was deposited in Cu Chi. A bus took me to the reception station. I had the misfortune to monitor a conversation between the bus driver and a new arrival like myself. The driver proclaimed with sincerity that units of the 25th would begin recycling home right after Christmas. His source was a trustworthy clerk at brigade HQ.

If that's the situation, I happily projected, I might make it home long before my tour expired. As a new arrival in-country you're susceptible to believing any optimistic tidings. You don't doubt the rumormonger because you want to believe him. So for the rest of the week I believed I'd be home by Memorial Day or at least by the Fourth of July.

At the reception station I met a fellow I knew from basic and AIT. Serene and articulate, Baxter was a black man from a North Carolina family of eight. We spent five days at the reception station waiting for our unit assignments. We labored on work details. We attended the reception station's Vietnam orientation classes: "Gentlemen, when in the field take a shower whenever you get the chance, because gentlemen, believe me, you will rot!"

We hoped to be shipped to the same unit. Our aspirations were thwarted when we were assigned to different battalions. We didn't have a chance to say farewell because I was on a work detail when Baxter had to report to his outfit. I privately wished him my best.

I was sent to Bravo Company, 2nd Battalion, 27th Infantry. The "Wolfhounds" had a celebrated history as a combat battalion: twenty-four battle streamers from the Philippine Insurrection, both World Wars, and Korea. They were a highly decorated unit. The battalion HQ was only a half-mile from the reception station. When I received my orders I trekked to my new home.

It was dusk when I reported to the HQ. A small wooden sign identified the building as battalion HQ. The unit's motto—*Nec Aspera Terrent* (No Fear on Earth)—was lettered under an engraving of a fierce-looking wolfhound. A nervous, flinching Spec Four directed me to the supply sergeant who would issue me a weapon and guide me to Bravo's barracks.

I found Sergeant McGinley and he greeted me with a smirk. He gave me an M-16 and three magazines. He remarked that I could get additional clips in the field. I wondered how many magazines a rifleman carried. *Five? Ten? Twenty? Shit*, I thought, *twenty of those things could be heavy.* McGinley accompanied me down a road to Bravo's building.

We went in the doorless side entrance of the shabby structure. McGinley explained that the front and rear ends of the barracks were partitioned into rooms. The front alcove was the private quarters of Bravo's non-commissioned officer-in-charge of the rear detachment. The chamber frequently alternated owners. It was complete with a fan, refrigerator, stereo, and *Playboy* centerfolds functioning as wallpaper. The rear cubicle housed McGinley and his two assistants. I assumed all the luxuries of the rear were also there; supply sergeants usually made themselves comfortable. McGinley gestured to the front of the barracks.

"Put your weapon in that footlocker up front there. Chow is at six. Formation at seven. I'll call you only once. Best get up then, okay?"

"Okay, Sarge."

McGinley left. Dejected and tired, I unbuttoned my shirt and sat on a cot. A voice from the back of the hall frightened me.

"New guy, huh?"

I whirled. Through the dim lighting I saw a gaunt black man sitting on a cot. He was dressed in olive-green Army underwear.

"Yeah, I'm a new guy. I didn't notice you when we came in."

He chuckled. "Yeah man, that's cool. I was hidin' from McGinley under this here cot. Don't want no motherfuckin' details you know, man, ha, ha. I'm Matthews. Been back here about three weeks now, man. Shammin' like hell!"

"O-O-Oh, w-w-well, err, why are you back here? Did you get wounded or what?"

"Fuck no, man. They sent me back in to see the shrink, ha, ha. They say I'm crazy. So I been goin' to the motherfuckin' doc once a day. Then I hide out from McGinley the rest of the day."

"How long were you in the field?"

"I was in the field with the First Platoon four motherfuckin' months. Man, that motherfucker can really get to you, ha, ha." In repulsion he threw his hands in the air. He began picking his nose.

Another fellow stumbled in. He was a gargantuan, brawny individual with curly brown hair. Wheezing and inebriated, he crashed onto the cot next to me. He had a blue-colored heart tattooed on his right forearm. One of his front teeth was missing. He surveyed me with his rolling bloodshot eyes.

"Hey, Matthews, whatcha got here—a new guy for Bravo?"

"Yeah, man. McGinley just brought him over."

"Well good. We can use him." The drunk burped loudly. He tried to focus his eyes on me. "I'm Angel. They call me that 'cause I rode with Hell's Angels in California."

We shook hands. His powerful grip squashed my hand.

"I'm Kitchin. Glad to meet you. Where's the company at now, Angel? What's it like out there now, anyway?" Like all new men, I was equipped with a catalog of inquiries.

"They're at Reed. It's pretty easy now compared to a few weeks ago. We lost beaucoup guys then, mostly on fuckin' traps."

"What's this Reed place? How big is it?"

"It's our November Lima. Night location. It's pretty big. There's no way in hell they can take us there." He burped again, spit on the floor, coughed, and wiped his mouth with his forearm, smearing phlegm over his heart. "They did get me in the ass one day though!"

My head perked up like a periscope. "Oh, who got you in the ass?"

"The goddamn gooks, that's who! Who the fuck do ya think I'm talkin' about? Ya fuckin' new guys are all alike! Ya don't believe there's gooks out there! Well, I'll tell ya one fuckin' thing: don't run when ya make your first contact! Don't run! 'Cause we'll shoot ya. Right in the fuckin' back. I'll do it anyway, without thinkin' twice. If ya go to the First Platoon, don't let me catch ya runnin'!"

Angel was spraying slime all over me. I tried to remain calm. "Well, where can you run to anyway?" I said while shrugging and looking at Matthews. Matthews was gaping at a light bulb overhead.

Angel laughed. "There's plenty of fuckin' places to run to. Just don't do it! And don't sleep on guard either!"

"Guard? How often do you have guard?"

"Every night!"

Angel's swarthy face was simmering with disgust. His eyes were afire, his face beet-red. His neck cords bulged grotesquely. He obviously had seen a lot of action. Maybe too much, I guessed, like Matthews.

"Angel, how much time you got left?" I asked.

"I'm a double digit midget, man. I got fifty-five days and a wake-up, and I'm gettin' short. You'll see. Just keep your shit together, and if ya go to the First, do what your sergeant tells ya. But don't listen to the fuckin' lieutenant 'cause he's an asshole. In fact, they all are. All officers are fuckin' assholes! I'm goin' to sleep. Night!"

He stretched out on the cot and pulled a poncho liner over himself.

"Good night, Angel," I said.

The dialogue with Matthews and Angel left me trembling. I couldn't believe that these were the type of men I might have to spend a year with in Bravo Company. One is a headcase. The other is prepared to shoot me in the back without even flinching. *Christ*, I shuddered, *he really meant it!* It was hours before sleep rescued me.

6

The Wolfhounds

Before reporting to their units in the field, new infantrymen were required to attend the 25th Division's Replacement School. The school was a five day refresher course for everything you learned — or didn't learn — in the States. There were no class sleepers in this cram curriculum. Everyone realized that it was your final training. You either paid attention and mastered how to fire the Army's arsenal, or you went to the field ignorant. There were no threats or jokes in this course. The groups were kept manageable in size. The instructors took their teaching soberly. They knew that within a week most of their class would be in combat.

I absorbed more in those five days than I did in nine weeks at Polk. I couldn't believe what was happening to me. I was extending rapt attention to an Army lecturer because shortly I might have to fire a grenade launcher or pop a flare. It was all so numbing, incredible. Only days ago, it seemed, I was a civilian in the States where no one carried weapons and discussed booby traps. And now it was zero hour. I was receiving my final instructions. I was expected to demonstrate in the field what I had learned in five months of classes. I was a fully-trained, fully-equipped infantry trooper.

One day we were dismissed early from class so we could attend Bob Hope's Christmas show. I recalled experiencing a performance of his while in college the year before. At the conclusion of the college show Hope expounded a stirring commentary about the grandeur of America and the brave fighting men in Vietnam. He didn't question the war. He lobbied that we should support the troops in Vietnam, regardless of the morality of the conflict. He was treated politely by the campus audience. Everyone joined him in an electrifying "God Bless America" finale. I shared in the celebration. Like most folks at my university, I didn't dispute his statements. Actually I didn't care about him or the war.

But Bob Hope's Cu Chi show was much different. There were no patriotic monologues in Cu Chi; it wasn't the time or place for it. Besides, we were more interested in the women he had brought along than anything he had to say.

The probing question for me was: did the attitude that Hope displayed a year earlier have any relation to the escalation of the war? To me Bob Hope *was* America. The statesmen and electorate in the United States who supported the conflict averred that all they wanted was peace. If they desired peace why was the war intensifying? Or more personally, why was I in Cu Chi? If they yearned for peace—at least for America—why didn't they simply disengage from the fighting and let the Vietnamese slug it out? I didn't have any answers. And I'd have bet that neither did Bob Hope—at least none that would've satisfied me. One thing I did know was that in my mind Hope was no longer an infallible deity in his exhortations about America. I knew Hope hadn't changed during that year. But I had. It was all very confusing.

The day after I finished the training I was ordered to the field via a truck convoy. One truck was filled with mess equipment, huge chunks of ice covered with canvas, red plastic mail bags, and ammo cases. Angel leaped onto the deuce-and-a-half ahead of me. He sat on C-ration boxes.

"C'mon, c'mon, get on up here! The convoy's formin' up!"

I was taking a final look around the battalion area. *When would I see this place again?* I wondered. I hoped it wouldn't be long.

"Okay, Angel, I'm comin'!"

There were seven vehicles in the convoy. A jeep with the convoy commander took point. This jeep had a radio and a machine gun mounted on it. A water truck and four deuces-and-a-half packed with men and equipment filed behind the command jeep. Another jeep pulled up the rear.

We took a sinuous route through Cu Chi in order to exit through the south gate. Cu Chi was a gigantic installation, as extravagant and comfortable as any stateside post. Like Cam Ranh Bay, everyone toddled around unarmed, except for the nighttime bunkerline watchmen. The base was the principal staging area for all operations of the 25th. Cu Chi had an airstrip, hospital, library, chapel, clubs, PX's, and even a 25th Division museum—open daily eight to five.

At the checkpoint the MPs signaled us through without delay. One MP had a grin for us. I wondered why he found amusement over us. Then it struck me that we infantrymen manning outposts corseting Cu Chi were providing security for the post, enabling our MPs to have sweet dreams in their air conditioned quarters.

For the troops stationed in Cu Chi the hostilities were remote. To me Cu Chi suddenly looked like a good place to spend a Vietnam tour.

The journey to Fire Base Reed was a thirty minute, serpentine fifteen miles. The road was unpaved, craggy. I debated if the potholes were natural or caused by shell fire. Our voyage took us through yellow-brown villages inhabited by diminutive, bustling people. The absence of young males not in uniform was conspicuous. Glossy-skinned children waved and jogged alongside the trucks as we lumbered through each town. Wrinkled elderly men and toothless women munching betel nut peered from doorways. Pungent cooking and burning smells lay heavy in the air. Palm trees shaded the hamlets; their drooping branches kept us ducking. Above the din of motor scooters some of the people exhorted us with singsong words. Startling young women with lengthy black hair scurried about on Hondas while their colorful silk dresses flowed behind them. Tiny Lambretta trucks zigzagged like butterflies between bicyclers and pedestrians. The colors and activity rivaled any carnival.

When we left Cu Chi, Angel instructed me "to put on your steel pot, load your weapon, and look for gooks 'cause they're watchin' us right now!" He did likewise except that the only people he observed were females. As we squirmed through the villages, he'd whistle and gesture at the women while shouting, "Hey, Mama-san, you boom-boom?" Some of them smiled and waved. Others replied with the finger.

The worst element of the jaunt was the dust. It clung to you like pelting wet snow. It left a thin red mantle on everything. One place I didn't care to see caking dust was on my sixteen. I inserted my thumb over the muzzle to prevent dust from entering there. I wrapped a rag around the magazine. I hoped I wouldn't have to discover if my weapon would fire encrusted with grime.

We left the villages and motored into the countryside. We came to a dusty intersection: a few ramshackle huts and an abandoned gas station with a teetering Esso sign. A skinny dog was relieving himself in the door of one place. Some old folks were gazing from the shade. There was a small outdoor cafe with three farmers sitting on stools and sipping 33 beer from bottles. A forlorn Asian crossroads on the road to where? We traveled down a road flanked by spacious rice paddies and lush hedgerows. Green, green, everywhere. Angel nudged me and pointed ahead. "Look! Reed! Big place, ain't it?"

I squinted through the heat waves rising from the dry paddies. In the middle of a vast expanse of paddies I saw a tiny base surrounding a sparse hedgerow. It was a brown American oasis in a green Asian desert. Reed looked pitiful to my Cu Chi–oriented eyes. It was much smaller than our battalion area in Cu Chi. The spectacle of it made me want to vomit. *Holy Jesus,* I thought, *this is where I must live and fight? This is the place where America must make a stand?* I couldn't believe that fate had brought me to this sweltering, isolated site.

The portal to the perimeter was just off the road. As we approached the gate a throng of baby-sans pursued us while jabbering, "Chop, chop! Chop, chop!" I thought these children were a segment of the deprived masses which we were rescuing from stampeding Communism. But no, the kids were beggars. Some generous soldiers threw novelties overboard. The urchins squabbled over a melting chocolate bar or a pack of crushed Marlboros.

Our truck halted adjacent to the CP tent in the middle of Reed. Angel vaulted off, gathered his gear, and departed without a word. With no one barking orders at me I lounged on the truck and scrutinized Reed. It was cordoned by a system of twenty-odd bunkers, each fabricated with sandbags and PSP, a perforated steel plate used as an overhead cover. The bunkers were ten to fifteen meters apart. Most of them were spanned by sandbag walls. To the front of each bunker claymore mines were dispersed in a staggered arc. Each bunker had a metal fence or screen standing before it whose purpose was to prevent enemy rocket-propelled grenades from striking the bunker. The bunker complex was looped by three rows of concertina wire approximately twenty meters apart. Enclosed wooden latrines and lister bags (punching bag–shaped water receptacles) dotted the fortress.

In the core of the perimeter was the CP tent and bunker, a tent mess, the mortar platoon's gun positions, and six 105 howitzers. Artillery pieces were a welcomed site to an infantryman. I was elated when I saw those sparkling tubes of destruction.

Intimidated and desolate, I jumped off the truck. I was gaping about, wondering what would happen next, when two fellows I knew from the Replacement School approached me. They also had arrived with the convoy. Before we could exchange greetings an officer emerged from the CP tent. He extended his hand to me.

"I'm Captain Hoy, the CO of Bravo Company. Who are you, private?"

"Kitchin, Sir."

He turned to the others. "Hi."

"Sheridan, Sir."

"I'm Litmis."

"Sir," the captain chirped, smiling.

"Sir," parroted Litmis.

Captain Hoy was a powerfully-built Texan with handsome features. His fixed, unblinking eyes complemented his well-modeled head. About thirty-five, his bearing commanded immediate respect rather than the disdain enlisted men sometimes reserved for officers.

"Welcome to Reed," he said, looking us over. "Where you men from?"

"Philadelphia, Sir."

"Columbus, Ohio, Sir," replied Litmis.

"New York, Sir," said Sheridan.

"We're glad to have you men with us. You'll find that the Wolfhounds are the best unit in the entire 25th. I've been the CO of Bravo Company for about three months. We're basically a reactionary battalion. It's our job to move quickly and to respond to VC impulses anywhere in our area of operations. Alpha Company is also here, and we have a battery of 105s here. So Reed is a secure base. We'll try to make your time with the Wolfhounds as pleasant as possible, and if y'all do what we tell you, then y'all go home safe and sound a year from now. Correction, less than a year," he snapped with a grin, remembering that we had already been in Vietnam about two weeks. "C'mon in now, and the first sergeant will take care of you."

Inside the tent the overweight first sergeant took our names. He called two of the rifle platoons on the radio. He ordered their platoon sergeants to the CP.

While we were waiting for the sergeants, a tall, lean black man burst into the tent. He shuffled to Captain Hoy. He swayed side to side with his hands in his pockets and said, "Splash!" The CO turned around.

"Well, Davis, what was the problem out there today?" quizzed the captain.

Davis shrugged and mumbled a few incoherent words. Abruptly he flashed an expansive smile and giggled, "Hee, hee, hee."

As a draftee barely out of training, I felt Davis was definitely mortgaging his future by snickering at the CO, to say nothing about reporting without saluting and saying "Splash!"

"C'mon, Splash, what was the problem, anyway? Sergeant Norton said that when you were about five hundred meters from Reed on a break you just got up and walked back in yourself. You know you're not supposed to do that. Well?"

Davis scratched his stomach.

"Well?"

"I . . . I . . . I just got hungry, that's all. Just wanted to eat, and get somethin' to drink."

"Splash, you know that Pineapple cooks big meals for you guys, and everybody is supposed to eat together. You stick with your buddies and your platoon leader out there. Lieutenant Jack knows what he's doin'. You listen to him, okay? I don't want to hear anymore of this bullshit from you, okay? Now get back to your platoon."

Davis chuckled and ducked through the exit. *What a crazy guy!* I thought. *Leave your platoon and hike across rice paddies alone in a war zone that has no boundaries?* I was stunned that Captain Hoy didn't get flustered by Davis's method of reporting. If we had pulled something like that in basic training we would've had our heads chopped off. Maybe Hoy was indeed unique from the other officers I had encountered in my abbreviated Army career. The first sergeant interrupted my reflections by summoning the three of us to him.

"Okay, okay, let's see now. Let's see now . . . Litmis and Sheridan, you're both goin' to the Third Platoon. And Kitchin, Kitchin, you're goin' to the First Platoon."

It struck me like a thunderclap. Crestfallen, I recalled what Angel had said about the First, especially his resolve to shoot me if I ran under fire. Not only was I anxious to elude Angel's platoon, but I was hoping to go with one of the other rookies just to have company. But no such luck.

A sergeant with E-6 insignias on his collars and jungle hat entered. He was six-foot-two with blond hair, cerulean blue eyes, and a reddish mustache.

"Kitchin," the first sergeant said, "meet Sergeant Norton, your platoon sergeant. He's all yours, Norton."

"Thanks," said Norton.

Norton and I shook hands while exchanging hellos. He was an imposing figure, ingratiating, clean, good-looking, confident. As we headed for the bunkerline, Norton explained that the First Platoon was responsible for Bunkers I, II, and III. He spoke in the mild but assertive tones of someone who expected to be heeded. We arrived at Bunker I where a half-dozen soldiers lolled. The air was alive with eyes.

"Fellows, a new guy," Norton announced with a smile. "This is Kitchin. Doc, take care of him, will you?"

"Okay," said Doc.

Norton ambled off. Everyone reciprocated mild greetings with me. My heart plunged when I noticed Davis, alias Splash, busy at something on the sandbag wall adjacent to the bunker. *First Matthews, then Angel, and now Davis,* I thought. *First platoon certainly seemed to have its allotment of nuts.*

After the brief amenities Doc Hernstein — all medics were called Doc — and I drifted to one side of the bunker. Whenever two soldiers met in Vietnam a predictable introduction usually ensued. Hello, I'm so and so. Where are you from? How long have you been here? What is your DEROS date? After those mandatory questions each man knew where he stood in relation to the other. In Vietnam all that mattered was time in-country. Time was like money in the bank. If you had six months completed then you were eons wealthier than someone with only two months in-country. Time. I never had confronted a status symbol like this before. The standards I was accustomed to were the usual ones: power, dollars, property.

"Two hundred and four days, Kitch," Doc said. "Two-oh-four and countin'. Next week I break the two hundred barrier. Gettin' short! How many for you? Have you started countin' yet?"

"No. I'm not countin' yet."

"You will soon. We all do. You'll count and know your days left better than anything you'll ever know in Vietnam. Your DEROS date is the most important date in the world."

"What's DEROS mean?"

"Your date eligible to return from overseas duty."

"Oh. Well, I believe you. It's just too depressing for me to count now."

"Uh-huh. Don't worry, you'll feel better once some guys come to the platoon after you."

Doc was slender, of average height with dark hair. He had a serious look about him, but he was very friendly. He was from Philadelphia. I was ecstatic that another person in the platoon was from my hometown. We noticed that everyone was leaving the bunker. Doc asked if I had eaten in Cu Chi.

"No."

"C'mon, let's go eat. Pineapple is supposed to have a real good one fixed up for us tonight."

I recollected the CO mentioning that funny name. "Who's Pineapple?"

"He's the mess sergeant. He's Hawaiian. He has about a dozen kids. He's a great guy. You know, not the lifer type. He's one hell of a cook. Man, he really puts out for us. Let's go eat."

Doc and I located a spot on the crowded bunker and ate Pineapple's mashed potatoes, gravy, carrots, ham, applesauce, bread and butter. Due to the excitement of coming to the field I wasn't too hungry. But for Army victuals it was a satisfying meal.

After we finished eating I asked Doc if he felt like cleaning his rifle with me. I explained that I didn't want Norton or Lieutenant Jack to see my sixteen in such a filthy state. Doc agreed; he was trying to make me feel at ease. While we worked on our weapons Doc asked about home. He told me about the fabulous holiday he had had with his wife in Hawaii on R & R. I was primarily interested in the Wolfhounds. I still had tons of questions bouncing like pinballs in my head.

I was grateful to Doc for his kindness. I sensed we'd become friends. Maybe we'd get together once we were home. But in the interval, there was a war to slither through.

7

Nec Aspera Terrent?

At twilight Captain Hoy mustered Bravo for a meeting. Doc explained to me that the CO believed in keeping his troops informed about all operations, especially what we could expect in terms of enemy contact. The company respected Hoy for this policy.

At the meeting our CO said that tomorrow's operation was a helicopter assault, also known as an Eagle Flight. We'd be deposited outside the village of An Phu before dawn. Intelligence had reported there were one hundred VC active in the vicinity. We could expect booby traps. It was a battalion-sized operation. Bravo's assignment was to sweep through the middle of the hamlet.

Hoy's briefing was succinct, becalming. He sparked my confidence with the statement that "the primary mission of Bravo tomorrow, men, is to walk back in through that gate tomorrow afternoon with every man that walks out tomorrow mornin'. I sure hope Charlie isn't at An Phu, but if he is, we'll kick his ass!" I departed the gathering with the feeling that Captain Hoy meant what he said and that he cared about his troops.

I pulled guard from eight to ten with Angel on Bunker I. At ten I wrapped myself in my poncho liner. Exhausted from the excitement of the day, I fell asleep rapidly.

It seemed I had been slumbering only moments when I was awakened by the cry, "INCOMING! INCOMING!" Confused and frightened, I grabbed my rifle. When I realized that a VC mortar barrage was in progress I threw down my sixteen and scrambled into the bunker with the others. We heard the distant plop of the mortars being fired. As the shells approached the perimeter their sound was unmistakable, haunting, terrifying. The rounds detonated well outside the bunkerline. After only four or five shells were fired at us, our artillery and mortar platoon returned fire.

The frenzy was over within minutes. Flares illuminated Reed. We crawled from the bunker. I was the last man out. I heard someone refer to the attack as "small shit." Another man mentioned how elated he was that the volley hadn't been a prelude to a ground raid. Hearing this comment ignited additional quivers across my spine. I realized that I had been so concerned over a mortar striking my bunker that I had completely forgotten about the possibility of an enemy ground foray accompanying the mortars.

My notions of personal ineptness were further intensified when I tripped over my rifle while I staggered around the bunker looking for it. I nonchalantly picked up my sixteen, hoping no one noticed that I had discarded it. I resolved to better acquaint myself with my weapon.

I found a rag. While I was wiping my firearm, Doc Hernstein approached the bunker. He was circling the bunkerline checking for injuries.

"Hey, Kitch," called Doc, "you okay?"

"Y-Y-Yeah, I-I think so," I sputtered, afraid to ask him what he carried for ravaged nerves. "How often does this happen, Doc?"

"Oh, maybe once or twice a week. But it happens every fuckin' night when a new guy comes to the platoon."

"What?"

"Yeah, it's true. Whenever a new guy reports to the First we always get mortared that night."

"No shit?"

"No shit."

I was skeptical.

Doc giggled. "Sure, we all knew it would happen tonight. Didn't you notice how funny everybody acted when you came to the bunker with Norton? They were all thinkin' about gettin' mortared tonight. Nothing personal, you understand. That's why I slept inside the bunker tonight. I knew we'd get hit sometime durin' the night."

"That sounds like a lot of superstitious bullshit to me, Doc," I said, conveniently forgetting my antics at Polk over a taro leaf.

"Superstition? Call it whatever you like. All I know is that it always happens. New men bring VC mortars. They go together, you know, like cake and ice cream. Don't worry, you'll get used to it."

"Sure I will."

I really believed I'd remain aloof from this foolishness. Three weeks later another rookie reported to the First. Of course, we were mortared that evening. Coincidence, I figured. When it happened again with the arrival of the next new man, I became a convert.

Less than an hour after the attack, we were aroused with a shoulder tap or boot kick by Norton. As the platoon shuffled around him on Bunker I, he called the names of the men scheduled to go on the An Phu operation. Twenty-four men would go. Norton permitted mostly short-timers to abstain. He assigned everyone to a chopper. He informed us that Bravo would be on the first airlift. Alpha Company drew the second wave.

Each lift had nine choppers, four ships to a platoon, six men to a craft.

The ninth aircraft was the CP chopper, which transported Hoy, his two RTOs, the CP medic, the artillery observer and his RTO. The Eagle Flight formation flew in two parallel rows, the extra ship making it a "heavy left" or "heavy right" alignment. In addition to a pilot and co-pilot, each chopper had two machine gunners, one to a flank.

When everyone was ready, Jack and Norton directed us through the wire. We assumed holding positions outside Reed. It was a ghoulish black night. Radiant dots glowed overhead. The pre-dawn air was chilly. In groups of six we reclined on berms waiting for the choppers. Some men had brought their poncho liners and they draped the blankets over their heads. No one spoke. Each man sat hunched over in controlled terror, alone, sullen, sleepy-eyed. Like secluded islands encircled by a sea of war we sat and wondered what the crashing waves of the day would bring. What's going to happen? Are the VC waiting for us or not? It was my first combat mission. *It's the real thing,* I thought. *No more training. No more games and bullshit.*

I prayed nothing would happen at least until it became light. *God,* I shuddered, *it would be terrible trying to fight in the Vietnam darkness. Maybe once it was light we'd be able to see the traps. Jesus, the traps.* I reached for my balls and felt them hanging there. I touched my knees and legs. Would I go to sleep tonight with everything still in place? *Oh God,* I thought, *a year of this? These people must be crazy! I can't stand a day of it! How many more days must I endure this?* I counted the days to DEROS. Doc was right.

I was trembling, awe-struck, drowning in anticipation and tension. My dominant fear was the possibility of making an acute mistake that either got myself or someone else hurt. I hoped I wouldn't make a fool of myself. I prayed that I'd duck when it was time to duck and shoot when it was time to shoot. I felt like I was going to puke when I heard the distant idle of the choppers. "Get ready!" someone in my group announced. I swallowed hard, took some deep breaths and suppressed the urge to be sick. I decided I couldn't get sick now. There wasn't time.

The choppers arrived, their loud engines making so much noise I was sure we were disturbing the sleep of Hawaiians. I wondered how we were going to surprise anyone with all this pre-dawn racket. Since I didn't desire to sit next to the open doors, in the loading scramble I grabbed a seat in the middle of the canvas bench behind the pilot. Four men could squeeze on the bench. Two men sat on the floor between the pilot and the bench.

It was my maiden flight in a helicopter. I didn't appreciate traveling in an airborne vehicle without doors. The cool air flowed through the craft and chilled my already-shivering body. Through the murkiness all I could discern were the glowing turquoise instrument dials of the chopper. It was eerie.

The flight took about twenty minutes. Back home it would have been a mere commuter flight, a little business trip. Except our business was killing.

As we approached our landing zone, I could see in the distance illumination flares and Cobra gunships swirling and diving. Once there we swooped down in formation about one hundred meters from a thick hedgerow. It was like daytime with all the flares. A chopper sprayed a dense smoke screen along the treeline. The doorgunners on the choppers nearest to the hedgerow fired ribbons of bullets into the foliage to provide us cover. Red tracers ricocheted into the night. The noise from the chopper's turbines and the firing was ear-splitting, nerve-wrenching. It was impossible to tell if the VC were firing at us or not.

Our choppers landed, nine venomous wasps zeroing in for the sting. We jumped out and sprinted as best we could with our heavy gear to the closest berm for cover. I hoped that the enemy wouldn't fire on us at that critical moment. As I hit the earth, I worried if the dike I had selected for cover was booby-trapped.

Escape from the choppers consumed only seconds. It was obvious why the choppers lacked doors: in a combat assault you want to get from the aircraft to the turf in the shortest possible time. There was no time for messing with doors. If anyone was sluggish disembarking, he found himself thrust out by the doorgunners. Once the last man was clear, the choppers flew off like a startled covey of quails, mission accomplished. Lying behind the berm and observing the choppers flutter off was to me a most disconcerting moment. I wanted to cry. I felt abandoned, helpless, much like a World War II Marine must have felt once the Navy had dumped him on a Pacific atoll and withdrew. While the flyboys scurried back to their bunks in Cu Chi, I wondered what was waiting for us in the treeline and in the village.

As yet there hadn't been any enemy contact. Jack and Norton established our formation. There was much confusion until everyone was located and matched with their squads.

We approached the hedgerow in a scrupulous on-line sweep. We still hadn't received any hostile fire, so Hoy had only our dupermen firing into the treeline. The Cobras orbited above the drifting flares, waiting for orders from our CO.

Slowly we progressed. The commanders were yelling, "Spread out! Spread out!" The dupermen continued firing. Their grenades flashed in the hedgerow, tiny explosions that didn't seem like they'd do much damage. I held my sixteen alert, safety off. I was quivering so much I could hardly walk. My heart was pounding directly into my teeth. I kept blinking wildly, my eyes straining into the hedgerow. Closer, closer we moved. I saw a thousand VC! I saw fifty machine gun bunkers! I saw the guys next to me being blasted away in a torrent of lead! Closer, closer. I saw rounds hitting all around me! Closer. Then, I saw nothing. Nothing! Nothing but a hedgerow of bamboo and shrubs. We were there. And everyone was unscathed. Empty! No VC! Nothing! *Oh God,* I prayed, *please make them all like this.*

Once in the hedgerow Hoy had us assume defensive positions five yards apart while we waited for daylight. The last flares died out. The village, silent and dark, lay before us: dozens of hootches surrounded by thick vegetation, fences, farm animals and what other lurking Asian phenomena?

Some men—the veterans—curled up and went to sleep. *It must be nice,* I thought. *I wonder if I'll ever become that accustomed to war?*

Trying to soothe myself, I inspected my equipment. When I checked my sixteen I nearly fainted. A round was somehow jammed between the bolt and the chamber! Beads of sweat popped on my forehead as I frantically tried to release the bullet. It wouldn't stir. Furious, I passed my rifle to Sergeant Ross. He didn't have success either. He returned it. I crawled to Norton. He patiently pried the round loose. As he reloaded my piece he whispered, "No sweat, Kitch. It should be okay now. Be more careful when you're loadin' up. We'll shoot it later in the day and try it out."

"Thanks."

I felt like a buffoon. I crept back to my position grateful that I hadn't needed my rifle on the assault. *Christ,* I shivered, *my first operation and my rifle jams! What next?*

With daybreak came the decree to advance. Much to my consternation the First was assigned point. Norton scooted around and warned us to be alert for traps and not to go looking for our own graves. Again we were on-line with weapons ready. We proceeded until some men pulled in front of others. Soon the entire formation became disorganized.

For an hour we aimlessly inspected the hootches and hedgerows, totally unconcerned about finding contraband. Most of us hoped we wouldn't find anything because that would only delay the operation. We just wanted to get out of there fast. Not caring about the damages, we yelled "Fire in the hole!" as we lobbed grenades in water wells and bomb shelters. There were only sad-eyed old people, women and children to be seen. I tried not to worry where the men were. Not ahead waiting to ambush us, I hoped. Suddenly I heard a muffled explosion followed by turbulent movement and shouts. In the dense milieu it was impossible to discern what had happened. The order was barked to hold up.

Norton circulated the news that Lieutenant Jack had hit a trap. His injury wasn't serious. Norton said the officer was joking about getting his million dollar wound. The disheartening thought in my brain was that on my initial operation my platoon leader gets wounded. *I hadn't even met the lieutenant!* I thought. *My God, yes, you're in a war, bachelor's degree and all!*

Norton suspended my depression by telling me to follow him. We slogged to a hootch where Taylor, a cordial, humorous, black machine gunner from Mississippi held his sixty on four women clad in black pajamas. Norton directed me to help Taylor until the CO arrived to question them with his Vietnamese interpreter.

Meanwhile Norton dragged a stoic, fiftyish man out of the hut. Screaming at the man to show us where weapons or equipment were stashed, Norton pummeled the puny Oriental with his fists. The helpless papa-san said nothing. When he tumbled from a blow Norton would pick him up and unload again. The scene disgusted me. Norton noticed it.

"You gotta rough 'em up a little first," Norton said while he sponged his forehead like a boxer taking a break from a light workout. "Don't worry, Kitch, you'll get used to it once you've seen some GI blood."

I shrugged and looked away. I wondered how Norton knew for certain the guy was a VC. I deduced Norton had been here long enough to know. I felt I might help myself by keeping my rookie mouth shut.

The CO came to the hootch with his entourage. Extending Norton a nasty look, Hoy led the disheveled, bleeding papa-san and the women away. We started back to the platoon when Norton told Taylor and me to investigate another hut.

We meandered to the hootch. While Taylor inspected the well I carefully entered the dwelling, rifle first. Squatting in one corner was a frightened mama-san holding two wide-eyed children. Just as I motioned for them to follow, a man leaped up from the floor behind a bed. With his hands elevated he bawled, "No VC! No VC!" I jerked my sixteen. I nearly fired out of pure shock. I summoned Taylor. He darted inside. He said that the man was very old and to let him go. We rejoined the platoon.

My nerves were in shambles. I felt sick. An instant of hesitation had prevented me from blasting into eternity an unarmed, nameless old man. Over a can-of-peaches lunch Taylor advised me to dismiss the incident. Even if I had shot the papa-san, Taylor asserted, nothing would've happened to me, considering the circumstances. He told me to count days; don't ponder past crises. His counsel didn't comfort me. How could it ever be okay to shoot an aged noncombatant who wasn't menacing you?

But I was rejuvenated when I realized that I had done the right thing.

It hadn't been a time to shoot and I hadn't shot. I had made the correct choice. I had passed the test and I was glad. The urge to eject my peaches waned. I wondered how many split decisions I'd have to make in Vietnam. Would I make the right option again? The next time someone surprised me a pause on my part might be fatal. It was going to be a long year.

The operation at An Phu lasted another hour. By mid-afternoon we were back at Reed gulping warm soft drinks on the bunkerline. We were informed that the women Taylor and I had guarded were VC seamstresses and the papa-san Norton had abused was their overseer. During the mission we contacted no regular VC. Nor did we capture any weapons, ammo or stores. In the process we lost Lieutenant Jack and a soldier in the Third Platoon to traps. Those results didn't seem to add up to me or to anyone I conversed with that afternoon. I found the whole episode to be befuddling, chaotic.

We learned that our burly first sergeant was going to be awarded the Bronze Star for heroism at An Phu. After Jack had struck the trap he was carried by two medics back to the vast paddy which we had swept across that morning. The first sergeant accompanied the corpsmen to the paddy. While the medics consoled Jack, the sergeant secured an LZ for the dust-off chopper and directed Jack's evacuation.

But the sergeant's heroism was a joke. He was no more needed on the scene than Superman. The real danger at An Phu was in the village and hedgerows lacing it. Furthermore, the weary medics didn't need a self-serving E-7 barking orders about a procedure they knew more about than he did. The medics later stated that all the sergeant did was to get in the way.

In the subsequent weeks the "heroism" of our daring Top was the fountainhead of sarcasm about the phoniness of many awards. During training I had had suspicions that military decorations were nothing more than ego inflators and career enhancers for military personnel who required such adulation. Our first sergeant's citation only confirmed for me that many medals were indeed worthless ornaments. No wonder that sergeant at the Cam Ranh Bay airport wasn't flustered when I booted his combat awards across the terminal floor!

After dinner Norton came to Bunker I and told us he'd be our platoon leader until a new lieutenant arrived from Cu Chi. He noticed me sitting alone on the sandbag wall cleaning my rifle. "Well, Kitch, whatta ya think of it so far?"

"I think it sucks."

My reply instantly won for me a half-dozen friendships. The guys knew I wasn't gung-ho.

Norton laughed. "Oh, you mean the work, don't you? Not the unit?"

Shit, I thought, *is this guy nuts? What the hell do I care about the Wolfhounds?*

"Yeah, the work, the work. I think the unit is fine."

"Right, Kitch, right. Ya did all right out there today."

"Thanks." I wondered if he realized how terrified and confused I had been.

Norton sauntered off. I rose and moved closer to my comrades. Together we resumed brushing our weapons in preparation for the next operation.

8

New Year's Eve

The last day of 1968 was like any other day for First Platoon. After breakfast we prepared for another operation—an Eagle Flight. Ross's squad was permitted to stay back because we had pulled the LP the night before. But Norton said I was going on the patrol as a replacement for a short-timer in another squad. When he assigned me to a ship he muttered something about new guys getting to go on almost all operations.

I wasn't unduly distressed about going when I should have had the day "off." As a newcomer in any situation you must pay your dues; in the military you learn to expect the worst.

At ten o'clock we boarded the choppers. My confidence was surging. This time I sat adjacent to the chopper opening. The view was marvelous. The Vam Co Dong river snaked through our AO like a glinting brown ribbon on an emerald carpet. Miles of sprawling rice paddies were punctuated by peaceful-looking villages edged by hedgerows. Like scars blemishing an ethereal face, bomb craters pitted the pristine countryside. In the distant north a majestic, solitary mountain named Nui Ba Den loomed serenely on the horizon. Its aberrance caused me to massage my eyes and look twice to be certain that I wasn't hallucinating.

It was difficult to comprehend that this bewitching land inhabited by Lilliputian-like people was engulfed in war. I wondered why humans mutilated the earth, their home. Why didn't they live in harmony with nature and each other? Why this unremitting struggle over territory?

In the euphoric limbo of flight such philosophical gymnastics erupted easily for me. Not surprisingly, the Eagle Flight became akin to the cattle truck jaunt to the rifle ranges in training. My mind perspired with thoughts and emotions heretofore alien to me.

But helicopters, like trucks, don't run forever. One instant you feel a sublime tranquility, then the choppers begin their descent. The trance is shattered. You make certain that your rifle is loaded and the safety is off. You adjust your helmet and take a grip on your ammo pack. While you watch the chopper gunners swing their machine guns into position, you try to rein your galloping fear. You show you're ready by flashing the peace sign or the thumbs up signal to your comrades flying parallel to you. You pray the landing will be a "cold LZ." But no one will know for certain until we're down.

We flew into an LZ with countless hedgerows – all potential ambush sites. The landing was cold. You could almost hear a collective sigh of relief. We were fashioned into formation by Norton. In the daytime the First maneuvered in two matching rows with the CP between the columns. Two flank men scouted on each side. The platoon leader and his RTO marched to the front of the arrangement while the platoon sergeant and his RTO trudged to the rear. Each file had a point rifleman succeeded by more riflemen or dupermen, then the machine gun section. Our velocity was governed by the pointmen who stalked cautiously. The platoon leader was usually in voice contact with his pointmen. In a terrain of open paddies the formation was dispersed so as to sometimes cover a tract larger than a football field. But in this compact locale the formation was tighter. Generally the short-timers lumbered at the tail of the patrol. The new troopers assumed the more hazardous slots.

The operation passed uneventfully. After lunch the choppers extracted us. While airborne back to Reed, Captain Hoy received new orders from battalion HQ. The Bravo Eagle Flight wouldn't return to Reed on New Year's Eve. We'd go to a dense area called the Hobo Woods, in order to pull two platoon-sized ambush patrols.

A doorgunner yelped this data to me. I distributed the depressing news to the others. As the choppers veered and began their descent, we all cursed and moaned.

Moments before landing, the gunner tapped me. He shouted that the Cobras softening up our LZ had detected some VC. Be primed for a "hot LZ." Before I had time to dispense these tidings we were landing with all the choppers' weapons blazing. I was upset about not being able to inform the others concerning the enemy sightings. But no one really needed to be alerted to the danger involved in Eagle Flight landings. My terror was short-lived because the VC had fled. The Cobras had chased them off.

Second Platoon was ordained to wait in a defensive perimeter while the First conducted a brief sweep of the area where the Cobras had engaged the VC. After a hasty, inconclusive exploration of only a click – a thousand meters – we rejoined the Second. Then we also effected defensive positions.

I had asked Norton earlier in the day if I could test-fire my rifle. He had refused, explaining that our operation was too precarious to unnecessarily herald our presence by test-firing a weapon. He unloaded and reloaded my sixteen several times and pronounced it fit. He said that if it jammed in a firefight I was to assist the machine gun crew. It looked like I'd have to endure another night without knowing for certain if my rifle would function properly.

A supply chopper brought us C-rations and water. After eating we settled down to await the dark—the most foreboding time of day in Vietnam. As the late afternoon sun glowed red on our faces, each man became mirthless, subdued, and edgy. The later it became the less movement and noise emanated from our laager.

With the explosive sunset one wonders only what the night will bring. Ambush? Mortars? Legions of VC? What the morning will bring is superfluous: you must first survive the night, the time when the enemy normally does his handiwork, before you think about dawn.

At twilight the Second left for their ambush site to the north. Captain Hoy accompanied them. I wondered if he felt safer with the Second than with us. Or perhaps he had more confidence in Norton as opposed to the young, brash Lieutenant Mills, who commanded the Second. Whatever the reason, Doc Hernstein and I forlornly watched the Second melt into the countryside.

Doc and I had just begun whispering about home when dozens of bombs detonated some miles away. It was a B-52 strike. Since we could neither hear nor see the aircraft, there was no forewarning. Frightened, we hid behind berms and observed the bombing of suspected VC positions. Great flashes of light, a distant thunderclap, then cauliflower clouds of gray smoke rose to a purple sky. We felt the earth tremble from the concussions. Palm trees quivered. It was all noise, smoke and massive destruction. It made you grateful that the VC didn't have B-52s or anything like them. Doc remarked that it would be some infantry company's misfortune to inspect the area in the morning.

By the time the bombardment ceased it was dark. Norton assembled our formation for the trek to the AP site. At night we marched in single file without flankers.

We proceeded to our night location. It was my first platoon-sized ambush patrol. I was appalled by the din raised by our platoon on a night march. We tried to be the stealthy night fighters we were trained to be but it was impossible. We were all noise and commotion, a long uncertain line plodding along like a maharajah's army. All we needed were the elephants. If VC were lurking about I was sure the pandemonium we made would discourage any attack upon us.

Norton led us through the spooky Hobo Woods. I wondered how he could see where he was going. I could barely see the man to my front. But

of course I could *hear* him. As we marched I worried about being ambushed, but mostly I worried about getting separated from the patrol.
Periodically Norton would stop and the order would be passed down to
hold up. As one man halted and turned to the trooper behind to relay the
message, the follower would often stumble into the guy in front like antics
from The Three Stooges.

After enduring this comedy-tragedy for twenty minutes, the First decelerated to a bumping halt. Norton and two squad leaders advanced to
the predetermined coordinates and scouted for a suitable site for an ambush. Within moments they returned and led us to the chosen location.
We deployed in a narrow hedgerow which ran parallel to and ten meters
from a dirt road. Our ambush was in a rectangular format with six men
in each corner of the paddy that adjoined the hedgerow. I was in a corner
nearest the road. Claymores were extended. Sentry duty for each position
was established. Norton radioed to Hoy that our ambush was active.

I was assigned last guard for our group. I could go to sleep. But there
was no drowsiness in my eyes as the others smeared bug juice on their
vulnerable surfaces and squirmed into their poncho liner cocoons.

I was alarmed, even more than on Ross's LP. An ambush patrol was
an offensive operation. If any VC came within range, it was our task to
spring the trap and to slay as many of them as we could. Battalion had
chosen the coordinates for the patrol. I knew they had selected a place
where VC were likely to be moving that night. After all, weren't we here
because of an unexpected change of orders? And weren't we the
Wolfhounds, the hotshot reactionary forces of the 25th?

I did wrench some comfort in having twenty-three other soldiers in the
paddy with me, rather than merely eight on the LP. The firepower of an
entire platoon was impressive. But what if the VC were migrating a division
down our highway this moonless, sultry evening? *Oh God,* I panicked, *I
still haven't tested my rifle!*

My imagination went berserk. What if we ambushed more than we
could handle? What if they didn't scatter when we attacked and they stood
and fought? What if they knocked out our radios and we couldn't summon
gunships or reinforcements? *What's going on here?* I wondered. *What am
I doing here? This is absurd!*

In all the ferment of the night I had forgotten that it was New Year's
Eve. But not the troops in the fire bases: at midnight the sky became a
panorama of Army-style fireworks. The men ignited green, red and white
star clusters and illumination rounds. It looked as if every flare in Vietnam
had been activated at once. It was spectacular and it made us homesick.

Munson, a Canadian citizen living in California who had the option of submitting to the draft or deportation to Canada, whispered to me how much he missed his wife and home. I told him that I would've settled to be at Reed rather than on my belly on an AP.

After the "show" we all shook hands and mutely wished each other a happy new year. Then everyone in our group but Munson and I went back to sleep. Again it became quiet. I rolled in my liner pondering what 1969 would portend for me. I'd spend all but seventeen days of it in Vietnam.

An hour later I was still absorbed in this macabre thought when Gibson, who was on guard in Norton's team, crawled to our section and tensely murmured, "Gooks! Gooks! Beaucoup gooks!" I bolted upright and gripped my sixteen. A tap and everyone, except Padbury, a rifleman from Missouri, was awake. Padbury was a deep sleeper. Neither Munson nor I could arouse him. We left him oblivious to our peril. I wished I had his confidence, or whatever it was.

Through a starlight scope Norton had seen VC to the north. Gibson, an urban, jazzy black man, was again dispatched to each position to advise us that roughly fifty VC had been counted moving away from us sixty meters distant. Minutes later our stress accelerated when Gibson sneaked around again and said that a force of twenty VC had been detected by Angel's unit to the south of us, albeit somewhat farther away than the fifty. We could hear clatter from the movement of both segments.

At night the VC usually strolled in single file and created as much, if not more, bedlam than we did. They'd utter aloud, cluster into groups, and often employ a flashlight to consult maps. These two units were too far from us to mobilize our ambush. I relaxed somewhat when word was circulated they had abandoned our area. In the interim Norton had relayed our observations to Hoy. Artillery from one of our installations fired on the VC columns.

The barrage woke Padbury. When we informed him about the VC he was piqued that we didn't wake him. He griped and snorted a few minutes, then he again lapsed into a profound slumber.

A half-hour after the artillery firing ceased Norton crept to our position. I was on my back studying the impartial stars, wishing they'd evaporate because that would mean dawn was imminent.

"Hey Kitch," he mumbled, "wanna see some gooks? I just spotted some right across the road."

My stomach rushed to my throat. A tremor ruptured up the back of my head like an earthquake. "Yeah, I guess so, sure," I said. I rolled over to him. *My God,* I thought, *the Hobo Woods are teeming with VC tonight! It will take a miracle to escape this night without a firefight!*

Norton passed the scope to me. My hands were fluttering so much I had difficulty focusing the instrument. Norton helped me. Forty meters across the trail I saw a squad of VC carrying a long tube. They were scurrying back and forth between three hootches: silent silhouettes in the starry blackness, presumably shuffling weapons of some variety. In the luminous green light of the starlight scope we watched them for an hour. At last they dissolved into the sootiness. They never did come close enough for us to ambush them, for which I was appreciative.

Finally I tumbled into an uneasy sleep one hour before my guard shift. Weaver, a rangy, educated duperman from Los Angeles, woke me at five. As I surveyed the burgeoning dawn I experienced a nebulous mixture of alleviation and gloom. We had observed at least seventy VC noisily prance like Santa's elves through our area. It paralyzed my mind to speculate on what might have happened. Already I was fathoming that I couldn't take breathing in Vietnam for granted. Angel was correct. There were VC out there!

At sunrise Norton called Hoy and requested authorization to search the hootches across the road. Hoy consented. We gathered our mines and formed up on-line. With the blazing morning sun on our backs, we stepped across the artery, weapons ready. Norton was certain he had seen the VC hide either a mortar or a 122mm rocket in one of the homes.

At the huts we were greeted by an ancient papa-san with a magnificent dove-gray beard, two mama-sans, and a half-dozen children. They were all unnerved. Norton ordered them to the front of one hootch where they were put under guard. Then he instructed us to tear apart the hootches looking for weapons.

This we accomplished with fervor. Everyone was still skittish over seeing so many VC during the night. We ransacked the abodes, absconded with souvenirs, pointed our weapons at the people, chucked grenades in the bunkers and wells, and, as I expected, Norton mauled the papa-san. Norton's patented mode of interrogation was to strike the individual, then bellow at him to confess to being a VC and tell where weapons were cached. Throughout the thrashing the powerless papa-san just shook his battered head and muttered, "No VC. No VC." Finally Norton let the old-timer crumble to his knees.

The melee upset the papa-san's five mammoth water buffaloes. They bucked and snorted in their corral. Suddenly the unpredictable animals burst through the bamboo fence and stampeded toward the open paddies. Norton commanded three of us standing by him to kill them. We fired. Displaying our customary Tigerland marksmanship, all the creatures escaped unscathed except one beast which galloped off bleeding from his nose, probably damaged while busting down the fence. Norton gazed at the sapphire sky and shook his head. Then he focused his attention on the latest addition to his souvenir collection: an exquisite cowbell.

To my amazement my rifle had barked a volley without jamming. I was jubilant about that. But it was the first occasion that I had discharged my weapon in Vietnam and I was perplexed as to why I was shooting at some farmer's livestock. We had been instructed in training that a water buffalo was a valuable commodity to the Vietnamese farmer, something analogous to a person's vehicle in the States. Why should we be decimating the man's livelihood, let alone slaughter mammals which weren't endangering us?

Our rummage of the hootches was fruitless. No rockets, no mortars, no AK-47s, not even a picture of Ho Chi Minh. Doc Hernstein bandaged the papa-san. As we departed for our pick-up zone, the grandfather nodded and smiled through a maze of dressings. Based on our ambush observations, he was probably a VC sympathizer. But we didn't uncover any contraband, so we let him go.

Our air taxis arrived to whisk us back to Reed. Once we took off I peered down at the trio of plundered huts and the motionless throng of Vietnamese who were watching us as we whirled over them. Their doleful expressions made me feel guilty, disgruntled. I looked away thinking, *What kind of a war is this? What is happening here?* I had participated on only a few operations. But already things were clouding up on me. Who are the VC? Who are we supposed to kill and who do we ignore? Why do civilians keep getting in our way? But were they really civilians? And if they were noncombatants, what are we doing destroying their property, to say nothing about their bodies? After all, the people we encountered this morning didn't try to harm us when we approached them.

The whole thing was too complicated for an uninitiated college man to comprehend at once. It was regrettable but true: I had a degree but it provided no wisdom about an Asian war which had raged for years. My indifference and laziness had come back to haunt me.

With his head and farm in shambles, I pondered how that aged papa-san felt that inaugural morning of 1969. Somehow I was certain that he'd recall it as the day the Americans came and raked his home, beat him up, shot at his buffaloes, and terrorized his family.

Thinking more about it at Reed that morning I wished that someday we'd return in peace to that farmer's remote home. I wanted to apologize.

9

Black Virgin Mountain

"Tomorrow, men," barked Captain Hoy, "we leave Reed for a stretch of easy livin'!" He grinned and wiped a droplet of spittle from his lips while he waited for the company's resounding cheer to subdue.

"Tomorrow," he continued, "we'll be picked up by chinooks and flown to Nui Ba Den, or for y'all who don't know Vietnamese yet, Mountain of the Black Virgin. Bravo's mission will be to man the bunkerline on the summit of Nui Ba Den. The mountain is considered to be the most important commo location in all Vietnam. Infantry companies have been rotatin' bunkerline duty on the mountain for years. Besides that, the mountain is sacred to the Buddhists and they have a shrine on it.

"Men, I lobbied long and hard to get this assignment. It should be a piece of cake. There'll be no sweeps, no APs, no LPs, no Eagle Flights. All we gotta do is work the bunkerline and keep alert at night. At night we'll be required to recon by fire the entire night so y'all get a chance to fire your weapons." Bravo burst into another applause.

"The VC are considered to own the mountain slopes and the surrounding countryside, but we hold the summit. Recently there has been little VC activity in the area, and so I expect a real vacation for us up there. Any questions?" There were none, only more cheers. "Okay, platoon leaders, have your men ready for the wire at zero seven hundred. Dismissed."

In the morning we assembled outside Reed. Our transports, the giant chinook helicopters, arrived in a cyclone of dust. These unsightly aircraft had two rotaries mounted front and rear. They were awkward-looking to the point of making you uncertain as to how they could ever get off the ground, much less fly. Inside its cylindrical recess each chopper could hold a platoon seated on two long canvas benches. In flight it was impossible to discern anything over the deafening thunder of the engines. Cumbersome and slow, when these forty-foot flying buses were landing they made excellent targets for the VC, a fact which mesmerized my mind during the entire flight.

By eight we landed on the peak of Nui Ba Den, a three-thousand foot green mountain in Tay Ninh province. The view was sensational. Ricefields, jungle, roads and miniature villages stretched from horizon to horizon. Billowing clouds scudded by literally within arm's reach. Communications apparatus housed in concrete buildings blanketed the rocky summit. A well-built mess hall and a chopper pad rested downslope from the commo site. Gigantic, well-fortified bunkers lassoed the isolated two-acre base. Telltale boulders strewn across the vertex were scarred from prior firefights on the mountain. All vegetation had been eliminated on the peak so that the timberline began roughly thirty meters down from the bunkerline.

The most dominant landmark in our AO, this peculiar mountain was steeped in Vietnamese legend. Centuries ago the mountain belonged to Cambodia, and a Cambodian ruler resided there with Nang Denh, his teenage daughter. A Buddhist who settled on the mountain converted Nang to Buddhism. Later her father wished to arrange Nang's marriage. The horrified daughter fled. Searchers later discovered a portion of Nang's body in a cave. Upholding a Buddhist life of celibacy, the devoted daughter ostensibly committed suicide rather than compromise her new religion.

Subsequently a pious Buddhist cleric thought he saw Nang Denh on the mountain, so he erected Nang a temple, the Shrine of the Black Virgin. Surviving years of war, the shrine still existed when we came to Nui Ba Den. It was located beyond our perimeter, so we couldn't visit it.

As promised it was a term of placid duty for Bravo. No operations. During the day we were occupied with countless chores. To improve our visibility, every day a squad was dispatched with bangalore torpedoes to clear the bunkerline farther down the slope. With a genuine mess hall in our midst we even had to submit to KP stints.

Often during the day we reclined on our roost and watched skirmishes far below us. We couldn't discern people or vehicles. But we could observe artillery barrages and bombing runs by jets. Smoke plumes from the maelstroms would sometimes rise as high as our towering pinnacle.

After dark we reposed on our catwalk and deliberated the dramas unfolding below us. Every night battles raged. Tracer rounds from gunships looked like red meteorites plunging into battlefields illuminated by flares. We felt like gods peering down at stupid human beings as they dueled with each other. It was bittersweet: we were glad not to be involved in the combat. But we felt glum because we knew people were being killed and wounded in those eerie cauldrons of light.

To dissuade enemy incursions, at night bunker lookouts were obligated to sporadically hurl grenades, fire weapons, and pop flares. We discovered that the principal hazard on Nui Ba Den wasn't from VC sorties. It was from being injured by your mates on adjoining bunkers.

Since the bunkers were staggered on the mountainside, an errant grenade or sloppy marksmanship would send guards ducking for cover. Sentinels were constantly railing at each other to observe their lines of fire. It wasn't uncommon to experience the ping of shrapnel on your helmet several times during your picket duty. It became so perilous that whenever the next fortress did their reconning, I always dived for shelter behind a sandbag wall until they finished.

It was prohibited for anyone to leave their bunker after nightfall. This edict was transgressed one night by a man in the Third. He wandered to the front of one bunker. The bunker sentry, a slim, hawk-nosed individual named Zimmermann, growled "Halt!" several times. He received no reply. When Briggs, the roamer, moved again Zimmermann emptied a sixteen magazine into him at a range of fifteen meters, killing him.

The accident left the company distraught, tense. The explanation was precise. Briggs was high on dope. He had become disoriented and strayed before Zimmermann's post. Briggs either didn't hear Zimmermann, or he simply ignored him. Zimmermann was a poor-sighted soldier who had endured numerous combat experiences. He wasn't taking any risks.

Since Briggs was black and Zimmermann was white, the incident temporarily ignited dormant racial sentiments. The blacks purported that Zimmermann was a trigger-happy fool who had no business being in the field in the first place. The whites countered that any black would've fired at Briggs given identical circumstances. The blacks, some of whom were as high as Briggs was that night, conceded that Briggs shouldn't have been where he was. Most admitted they shared some responsibility for not protecting him. More than anything the affair stimulated everyone's resolve to be more wary while on guard.

It was the first death in Bravo since my arrival. It happened not through enemy contact, but because of an accident. I knew that accidents occurred in war. But I never really understood it until I watched the medics lift Briggs onto a dust-off the next morning.

The episode demonstrated another troubling aspect of Vietnam. Besides looking out for the VC, you must also insulate yourself from your allies; friendly fire could exterminate you as surely as any VC trap or mortar.

As if this sobering deduction wasn't sufficient, one afternoon I was relaxing on the bunkerline reading *The Pacific Stars & Stripes*. While scanning a list of Bronze Star beneficiaries I stumbled onto the name of PFC Wilber Dexter Baxter, my friend from training and the Cu Chi reception station. Next to his name was an asterisk, which denoted a posthumous award.

This shattered me. It couldn't be true! We were together in Cu Chi less than a month ago! Baxter, dead? Dead? Dead! The verity left me numb with shock. We had gone to the field at the same time. Now he was deceased. I was depressed for the rest of the day. That sleepless night I scoured the star-laden heavens for the reasons why he was dead and I was alive. At daybreak the stars blinked off with my head still spinning in confusion and woe.

Days later another excruciating revelation reached our lofty outpost. Before Bravo's ascent to the mountain Doc Hernstein had been shifted to Charlie Company, which replaced us at Reed, because their medic corps had been decimated by traps. Doc was expected to rejoin us once we returned to Reed. It was believed by then new medics would have reported to Charlie.

One day Charlie was hustled to bulwark another unit in combat. During their trek to the fighting, Charlie was ambushed. Doc was killed.

I was stupefied. Doc's death left a chasm of emptiness inside me. I felt a morbid desire to engage the VC so I could requite Doc's demise.

When my fury subsided I initiated a search, as I had done with Baxter, for the reason for Doc's death. Who killed Doc? The VC, of course! But did they really kill him? Were the VC responsible for Doc being in Vietnam, or were the politicians and warmongers in America? Why were any of us in Vietnam? Was our cause moral and sensible, or were we merely intruders thrust by our government into an Asian conflict which wasn't our affair?

In my mind only one thing was certain: Doc, my friend from my hometown who had extended his benevolence to me when I most needed it, was in a coffin destined for a sad reunion with his family.

Like the mist that enshrouded our mountain each dawn, Doc's death cast a pall over the First. Our collective grief persisted until time began its protracted mending process.

On a dazzling, crystalline morning we departed Nui Ba Den to resume our functions at Reed. The prospect of again going on operations made everyone apprehensive. Except for the debacle with Briggs, the mountain had treated us well. But I was still confounded how the tally sheet was being computed for this war. We had had zero enemy contact for nearly three weeks, yet we lost Briggs and some others who were injured in disconcerting mishaps. *My God,* I reflected, *all the VC have to do is to sit back and wait for us to self-destruct!*

During the flight to Reed I thought of Baxter and Doc and the fact that Doc wouldn't be rejoining us. I wondered how their families were coping. I wished there was some way I could assist them. But there was nothing

I could do. I hoped they knew that Bravo shared their sorrow, even though the balance of America probably did not.

The deaths of my two friends recalled a poignant refrain I had heard at Polk from a crusty World War II sergeant: "Men, in war you make friends fast, and men, take it from me, you lose 'em fast."

10

Reed Revisited

While we were on Nui Ba Den I made two new friends. The first was a bespectacled midwesterner whom I immediately liked. Nash was an intelligent, affable, short, husky man. We became acquainted when we were assigned to the same bunker on the mountain. His brisk, incisive speech complemented his easy, broad smile and resounding cackle. Not one to suppress his opinions, Nash could make life uncomfortable for military superiors whom he considered incompetent. Like Doc Hernstein, his altruistic manner eased my adjustment into life with Bravo. Our friendship flourished.

The second man was an upstate New Yorker named Tremaine. One dusk I had been conversing with another fellow when I mentioned that I had read some novels authored by the late Robert Ruark. Tremaine overheard the conversation. A disciple of Ruark, he joined the discussion.

Perceptive, resourceful, slight of build, with angular cheekbones and sharp lips, Tremaine's thatch of sandy hair accented his piercing blue eyes. His teeth and some fingers on his left hand were tainted yellow by nicotine from his two-pack-a-day addiction. Volatile and headstrong, his ready wit and hearty laugh frequently swirled heads. Tremaine wasn't popular in the First. But his propensity for being in the midst of turbulence, whether enemy-related or not, made him known to everyone.

Whenever possible the three of us gravitated to each other and exchanged our philosophies, ideas, and aspirations. Together we explored the war and America's participation in it. Tremaine was opposed to the conflict. Nash, while not pro-war, was more unkind toward the military. I was still confused about America's role in Vietnam. We also discussed re-enlistment. Dangling over our heads was the realization that at any time we could get out of the field simply by re-enlisting.

To me it wasn't worth a Cu Chi job. I'd count the days and determine that I could make it. Hadn't I been lucky so far? Re-enlistment only seemed to be volunteering for more headaches and conflicts. Getting discharged as soon as possible was my primary objective when I entered the service and

I decided to stick by it, no matter the risks. Perhaps I'd get a Cu Chi assignment anyway without tacking on more time.

One evening after dark, as Tremaine and I contemplated the burning stars while on guard at Bunker III, our harmony was interrupted by the distant cough of mortars. We yelled "*Incoming!*" several times with all the gusto in our lungs. We grabbed our weapons and plunged into the bunker. With the others inside we assumed defensive positions at the bunker's portals. Grimly we watched the enemy explosions leapfrogging toward our perimeter. When shrapnel flew in and struck Munson in the cheek, we ceased peering out the windows. Two earsplitting detonations occurred near the bunker door. We scrunched down farther.

"The VC sure are hot tonight!" growled Doc Schmidt, our new platoon medic, as he bandaged Munson's minor wound.

Everyone agreed. Soon the attack ended. The "All Clear" notice was circulated by Norton. We were amazed at the unusual accuracy of the VC mortar team. One round had landed three meters from the bunker on the spot Sergeant Reynolds, a new squad leader from Chicago, had been sleeping. Another shell had burst even closer to the bunker, shredding Kilcurry's personal gear.

"The picture!" yelped Kilcurry as he sifted through his frazzled duffel sack. "I hope the picture's not ruined!" He found the portrait in question—a framed five by seven inch photo of him and his fiancée—and thrust it high for everyone to see. "Just a scratch!" Only a small piece of shrapnel had struck the likeness in the background space.

"That'll make a great souvenir," I said.

"Roger that," said Kilcurry as he kicked away the remnants of his gear.

The commotion from the attack subsided. Normal guard duty was restored. As I tried to sleep under the Centaur outside the bunker, my thoughts raced. Our good luck numbed me. I pondered how close we had come to death only minutes earlier. What if the initial round, not the last one, had landed where it did? Some of us surely would've been hit. Perhaps the survival of Kilcurry's portrait would be symbolic of the plight of the First as we groped our way through a war: close, but not fatal. Would my new friends and I emerge from this hurricane like Kilcurry's picture, with only a scratch? Or would we be swept away like Kilcurry's shrapnel-filled equipment? During the two months prior to my arrival, the First had sustained horrendous casualties from VC ambushes and traps. The platoon had a pattern of ill-fortune rivaling any unit in the Wolfhounds. But since my arrival it seemed that luck had been with us. Would I serve my time in the field before the pendulum drifted the other way?

I hoped I would. I knew that the odds were formidable. Only time would tell, I decided, as I tossed over for the fiftieth time trying to get some sleep. And I had more than ten months of time.

For the next few weeks the First was relegated to a routine of search and destroy missions, Eagle Flights, night ambush patrols, and LPs. The nights we didn't go on patrol we always pulled guard on the bunkerline. We were periodically mortared. But the VC bombs usually discharged outside the perimeter. The VC didn't damage anything except our nerves.

Day sweeps were always physical nightmares, strenuous contests against time, heat and danger. At the call "Saddle up!" you snap your canteen to a metal "D" ring that is attached to your belt loop. You pick up a few grenades, make sure that the pins are crimped, and hook the bombs to your ammo sack. You drop your lunch — two cans of C-ration fruit — into the baggy side pockets of your fatigues. You might remember to bring a plastic spoon and a P-38 (a tiny can opener). You place a folded olive-green towel on your left shoulder and balance your stuffed ammo sack on it. Then you lay low, hoping to avoid a last moment assignment to carry an extra sixty rounds, LAWs, smoke grenades or other equipment. Donning your helmet and grabbing your rifle, you respond to the command to move out. You wish you were going anywhere but on a patrol in a war. You load your weapon, and set it on safety. Your helmet, decorated with peace signs and names of places you've been in Vietnam, feels cumbersome when you first place it on your head.

The hike begins. After the first few hundred meters you commence to sweat, soaking your shirt and the back of your pants. The punishing sun drills into your shoulders. You beg for a cloud to shelter you, but there is nothing above except the vaulting blue sky. As your perspiration flows, you remind yourself to take some salt pills on break. Hyponatremia can be as deadly as the VC. Your equipment becomes weighty, uncomfortable. The towel cushion doesn't prevent your shoulder from aching from the twenty clips of ammo. You want to switch your ammo sack to the other shoulder, but you can't because it'll interfere with the mobility of your sixteen. Safety is paramount. If you're right-handed, your rifle stays on the right side and nothing is permitted to obstruct it. Your head throbs under the encumbrance of your steel pot. Remove it? Not until rest time.

Finally the objective: a hamlet, a road junction, a hedgerow, or anything. You haphazardly search for VC traces, hoping you won't find any. At lunchtime the patrol sets up in a defensive posture in the shade. You gulp your pineapple chunks or peaches, sucking the can dry of syrup. Solid food is out of the question. You're too hot and unsettled to taunt your stomach with slimy canned meat.

The mission-conscious patrol leader declares that it's time to go. You again file into the sunshine and start the wearisome trek home to the fire base.

It's midafternoon. Your water is gone. Your enervated body languishes in the pain of a forced march in soaring temperatures and one hundred percent humidity. Your mind floats away. You dream of an ice cold Bud, a swarm of snowflakes, aqua swimming pools, refrigerators, Popsicles, ice cubes, and water—clear frigid water. You smell the cool fragrance of moist earth, mountain forests, spring mornings. Your legs churn out the paces, your boots splinter and crack the dead paddy reeds. Like a pulsating automaton you propel onward, ever onward, knowing that each step takes you closer to shade, to rest, to water, to deliverance.

Wire and bunkers and RPG screens loom on the heat-rippled horizon. A mirage? You wipe sweat from around your eyes and squint. Yes! The perimeter! You lunge forward, accelerating. The formation expands across the monotonous paddies, everyone forgetting the VC and the traps.

The patrol rumbles into the base. Jokes, cheers, and barbs thunder across the bunkerline. "Hot coffee!" "Get your hot coffee at the mess tent!" "Let's go another twenty clicks!" "FTA!" "FTA!" "Fuck the Army!"

Another operation concludes. You have a few hours to relax, to cool down. You play cards. Drink sodas. Clean gear. Write letters. Smoke grass. Read books. Bullshit. Think. And as afternoon slides into evening, your thoughts mostly concern the pending night ambush.

Near the end of January the First was reorganized. I was assigned to Sergeant Reynolds's unit. Sergeant Ross, my former squad leader, had completed his year and was rotated home.

Reynolds, a friendly, engrossing individual was an "Instant Sergeant," or an NCO that came to Vietnam fresh from a two-month NCO course. Slender and astute, Reynolds approached his new assignment with caution, yet confidence. The arresting calmness in his voice and his open-minded attitude made him popular with his new squad.

Since I was one of the newer troopers, I was often designated to handle point on operations. On one occasion I was on point for a lengthy, rigorous sweep. During our trek back to Reed we had to traverse several canals. As I approached one expansive canal, I signaled for the platoon to halt. The waterway was lined with bushes and trees. It looked deep. With deer-like strides Norton hustled up to see what was amiss. I suggested that the place was an acceptable location for a VC ambush. Norton agreed. He summoned Tremaine and had him fire on the opposite bank with his duper. After Tremaine blasted some rounds Norton instructed me to cross the canal.

"What?" I bleated. "Sarge, hey man, I don't know. Let's look for another place to cross. It looks deep here!"

"Well, fuck, you can swim, can't you?"

"Yeah I can, but not with all this shit I'm carryin'!"

Norton stared at me. "Cross it, Kitch. These canals are usually no more than chest-deep. We all have to go across, and since you're the pointman, you go first. Don't worry, I'll cover you."

"Fuck!"

I waded in. I looked back at Norton and Tremaine. They were poised with their weapons. Tremaine nodded and grinned. Norton waved me onward. Pregnable and terrified, I negotiated deeper into the channel holding my rifle above my head. *If there are VC waiting for us,* I thought, *then certainly these are my final moments in this life.* In the center of the canal the water reached my shoulders. Here I momentarily stopped, realizing that I wasn't going to be in over my head. Norton yelled to get moving. I sloshed to the bank. *Stupid VC,* I thought, *you blew it! No way you're going to get me now!*

On the shore I took cover behind a small tree. I watched for movement while Norton and Tremaine forded the canal. As more of the platoon crossed I sauntered out on point again. I traveled only forty meters when I stumbled onto a gigantic mound adjacent to a berm. The abnormality had a tarpaulin over it. I peeked under the cover. It was a VC cache of 3700 pounds of rice.

Norton, bolting forward in response to my call, was ecstatic over the discovery. He called choppers to extract the prize. An hour later, after we had finished loading the last ship, Norton called me aside. Like I had really done something, he congratulated me on finding the food.

Norton knew that whoever had been on point would've found the rice because it was such an aberration. But he was probably just trying to spur my confidence. I thanked him for the compliments, informing him that I'd trade his praise for a safer place in the formation. He laughed and told me that my turn to ramble at the rear would come someday. Not soon enough for me, I advised him.

My first experience of being shot at occurred on a sweep. We were approaching a tiny village when sniper fire pierced the musty afternoon. I dropped behind the nearest cover, a small dike that afforded scant protection.

Taylor, Gibson, and Calhoun, one of the machine gun teams, had set up behind a substantial berm twenty meters from me. Their bulwark looked like the Great Wall of China compared to my dike. I decided to join them. Just before I moved, a volley of lead whined close overhead. Under Norton's command our pointmen returned fire. Then, except for the baying of dogs in the village, the paddy became silent.

Desperate for a more advantageous position, I committed a cardinal offense. I rose and scurried to the machine gun unit. Horrified, the three men yelped at me to get down. Ignoring their bleatings, I sprinted to their berm and belly-flopped next to them.

"You stupid ass, Kitch!" Gibson berated. "Don't you know bullets was just comin' through 'em bushes you just run past? What are you, some motherfuckin' Audie Murphy or somebody?"

"Hell no. I'm just tryin' to get to some decent cover! I didn't have a big enough berm over there!"

"Well," Taylor warned, "you better learn to stay down once the motherfuckin' shootin' starts! Medals don't do you no motherfuckin' good if you're zapped!"

"Medals don't mean a thing to me! I just wanted better cover is all."

"You right about that, Kitch," said Calhoun, a zany, congenial, big-city black man. "But from now on just keep cool. You a nice guy. We'd like to see you stay around awhile. So don't stand up in no firefight."

"Roger," I said, defeated.

The skirmish was over. Norton called a break. I rested behind the berm and reflected on what had just occurred. The entire thing had happened so fast that I really didn't know how long the clash had lasted. Time had been suspended. My senses collected. As my adrenalin slackened I felt an immense weariness. My stomach was in knots and my knees were shaking. Sweat covered me.

Despite my quivering I was elated over my performance. For some incredible reason it actually felt good to be shot at without results. I didn't run, freeze, cry, or get someone else hurt. I didn't even act scared—I didn't have time. But I was definitely terrified. My trembling body was proof of it.

I wondered if not running away made me courageous. No, I decided, because I had been simply reacting. Like everyone else, I was merely executing without cogitating about anything. Certainly that wasn't courage. Maybe bravery had more to do with just being in Vietnam in the first place.

The whole affair seemed like a little game. No one was hurt. We didn't see the enemy. I never fired my rifle. And after it was over we joked and clowned like a drunken crowd leaving a football game. I thought, *is this all there is to it? We tramp around the paddies, encounter our foe, exchange a few wild rounds, and the VC scamper off like jackrabbits. Then we get to relax, gloat, trade tales. No blood, no bodies.*

I recalled my boyhood times when I played at war. I remembered the

Great Cornfield War and the Great Snowball Battle when twenty of the neighborhood adolescents would divide into the Blue and the Gray or the Redcoats and the Rebels and try to inundate each other with snowballs or corn kernels propelled by slingshots. I had been scared then, plenty anxious about getting hit in the eye or being surrounded by bullies who'd bombard me unmercifully. The trepidation I experienced then was the same seething fear I felt now.

After a boyhood "war" you go home and prepare for another day of excitement. But in real war not everyone goes home after the battle. *And when,* I wondered, *would I see the real war, the blood, the death? Never! I had already come close enough. Enough! Let me go now! Oh God, to be a play soldier again! Childhood. Could it be forever lost?*

After the respite Norton took a squad into the hamlet. He returned with two women prisoners. They were middle-aged, slender. They wore black pajamas and sandals made from discarded rubber tires. Their black hair was folded into a bun in the back of the head. They were rumpled and filthy, probably because they had just crawled out of a bomb shelter.

Were they really VC? I imagined the enemy as being insolent when captured. But these women were reticent. They looked and acted like ordinary females seen anywhere in Southeast Asia. They whispered a few words.

"Mama-sans, you shut the fuck up and sit down!" Norton yelled, pointing a finger at them.

They seemed to understand. They sank to a berm. *Is this what we've been sent ten thousand miles to fight?* I wondered. *Forty-year-old women in sandals?*

"Kitch," said Norton, "these two gooks here are VC. I want you to guard 'em while I take the platoon back into the ville to look around some more." Like he was ready to ask me if I could handle it, he squinted at me dubiously.

"Sure, sure," I said confidently, although I was alarmed over my assignment. "Is that it?"

"Yep, just watch 'em. Don't let 'em talk or move."

"Okay."

He paused to blow his nose. "And Kitch, if they try to escape, shoot 'em."

"Err, you mean just shoot 'em? Do you mean that?"

"Yeah," Norton confirmed without a trace of a smile. "Blow 'em away." He took a mouthful of water from his canteen, swished it around, and spat it out. "But Kitch, hey, I mean, you know, make sure they're escapin'."

"Roger."

The platoon wobbled off. I brooded over the women with my sixteen. Pearls of sweat slid down my back, tickling me. The women commenced murmuring again and I screamed at them to clam up. I jerked my rifle menacingly. They quieted.

While I hovered over them I pondered how I'd react if they attempted to flee. Would I shoot them? *Christ,* I shuddered, *I had the power of a god!* It would be simple to slay them, even with my marginal marksmanship. It was frightening. *My God, shoot two unarmed women? Maybe they were innocent civilians. Maybe they had children. How did Norton know they were VC? No way, no way. No! Somebody's got to be trying to get me first.* So I continued to act mean and tough, hoping they wouldn't have the courage to simply get up and stroll away.

My charade worked. They didn't utter another syllable while I guarded them. When the patrol returned we blindfolded them, summoned a chopper, and shipped them to Cu Chi for interrogation and only God knew what else.

A week later Captain Hoy returned to Cu Chi to depart Vietnam. He had been granted emergency leave due to a family illness. The CO who relieved him, a likeable red-headed officer, promptly hit a trap on his third operation.

Later the same day we went on an Eagle Flight to establish a three day hardspot, a perimeter without artillery or permanent, sophisticated bunkers. While we were meticulously probing for traps in the hedgerow complex in which we'd construct our tiny base, our battalion commander, impatiently flying above, ordered us to accelerate our exploration. He directed us to get into the hedgerow and start building fortifications. If we couldn't quickly search a hedgerow, he screamed over the radio, then he'd land and show us how it was to be done.

Norton, who was still our platoon leader, laughed and radioed to Lieutenant Mills, our acting CO, to inform the battalion CO that we could use all the help we could get. Mills, the enthusiastic twenty-three-year-old fresh from the Second after the injury to Hoy's replacement, berated Norton for his gibe.

Meanwhile our impetuous colonel had decided to land and conduct a hedgerow-clearing class. Norton told us to freeze. We watched the chopper land. The portly colonel debarked the aircraft cursing the incompetence of today's soldiers compared to the troopers he had had the honor to lead in the good old days in Korea. Huffing, he assaulted the hedgerow with the élan worthy of a Kamikaze pilot. Boom! The colonel was critically injured. An RTO slogging behind him was killed.

While discussing the incident that night Norton commented that anytime an officer offered to demonstrate how things were to be done to let him do so. He said that it was an excellent method of discovering which officers had their shit together, and those who didn't.

With the inexperienced Mills as our acting CO until Hoy returned, company leadership teetered. This was a situation that alert, unsympathetic soldiers could exploit. We made the most of it. Whenever a squad from the First had to go on an LP, we simply consummated the operation right from the bunkerline. Once it became dark the patrol leader assembled us as usual and advised the CP that we were departing. Then instead of marching out the wire, we filed into one of our bunkers and spent the night there. We established guard shifts and called in the half-hour situation reports as if we were a thousand meters outside the perimeter. The regular bunker sentinels alerted us to be quiet whenever the bunkerline officer made his rounds. No one desired to participate on real LPs, so everyone conspired in the hoax. The personal survival of the men in the First superseded the welfare of Reed.

Since the war was assuming puzzling proportions in my mind, I was ebullient to be able to effect an LP from the relative safety of a bunker. Besides, if we were caught, what could they do to us? Send us to Vietnam?

The ruse became so widespread that eventually Mills became cognizant of the affair. When he threatened severe disciplinary action for everyone involved in future bunkerline LPs, the practice ceased. To make certain every patrol was leaving the wire, Mills would come to the departing bunker and witness us saddling up and leaving. It seemed ridiculous for the CO to have to do this, but the zealous Mills wasn't taking any chances. Our disenchantment with Vietnam and the military was surging. Mills sensed this. Perhaps our erstwhile colonel had a justifiable suspicion of the motivation of 1969 soldiers.

When we resumed the treacherous variety of LPs we often wished that we could have returned to the ersatz brand. One evening Tremaine took an LP eighty meters from Reed. About midnight Tremaine and I finished our guard shift. Tremaine reached for his poncho liner to cover himself.

"Kitch," he said. "Look! A snake!" The reptile was two feet long and resting comfortably on Tremaine's liner. "Hey, let's have some fun with the CP."

"What?"

"Let's call in and tell 'em we got a big thick snake in our position and ask 'em what to do."

"Yeah. Let's blow their minds. Maybe they'll even wake up Mills and piss him off!"

Tremaine giggled and called the CP. He reported that he had the biggest snake in the world, including the monsters seen at a zoo, curled on his poncho liner. He requested that the CP send immediate instructions regarding what to do.

"Roger, wait," was the reply from the RTO.

Moments later Lieutenant Mills's raspy voice grumbled sleepily over the radio. "Yankee ten, this is Foxtrot three-niner. Over."

"Foxtrot three-nine, this is Yankee ten," said Tremaine. "Over."

"This is Foxtrot three-niner. What's the fuckin' trouble out there? Over."

"Well, Foxtrot three-nine, we got a mean lookin' snake right in the middle of our position. Whatta we do? Over."

"Shit, chase it away! Over!"

"Roger, tried that, and it coiled up to strike. Over." Tremaine could hardly refrain from laughing while he was whispering into the microphone. Twice he cleared his throat to squelch his mirth. I was so hysterical that my head seemed like it would burst as I tried to muffle myself.

"Well goddamnit," said the Lieutenant, his voice cascading in anger, "try again you shit-head! It can't be that goddamn big! Over!"

"Negative on that, Foxtrot three-nine. This fellow is big and mean. Over!"

"This is Foxtrot three-niner. You listen here, Yankee ten: I don't give a fuck how big that fuckin' snake is, you just figure a way to get rid of it. Over!"

"Roger that, Foxtrot three-nine. But if we can't get it out of here can we call off the LP and come back in? Over."

"This is Foxtrot three-niner. Permission absolutely denied on that request, Yankee ten. Negative! Fuck no, you stay right the fuck where you are! I don't care if that snake brings his whole fuckin' family, you stay there! Over!"

"Roger that, Foxtrot three-nine. We'll do our best. Over and out."

"Out!"

Our escapade aroused everyone except Padbury. When we explained what had transpired, the squad had a good but subdued chuckle. Meanwhile our uninvited guest had slithered away, no doubt disturbed by all the human commotion.

In war it's fantastic how one's mood can change so swiftly. Still chortling, Tremaine and I had just squirmed into our liners when the grunt of mortars terrorized us. Instantly everyone, again excepting Padbury, awoke and grabbed their weapons and claymore firing devices. The mortar rounds crept toward our exposed position. My stomach did cartwheels and my head pounded.

Tremaine told Hooper to search for movement with the starlight scope. He emphasized that if we detected any VC, even one, we'd sprint for the wire regardless if we had permission to do so. I readily agreed.

Suddenly the mortars leaped over our site, exploding on the far side of the perimeter. We cringed as the projectiles whizzed over our heads. As usual our artillery and mortar section returned fire with intensity. The other LPs weren't reporting VC movement. It appeared to be merely another mortar shower.

It was over in ten minutes. The attack left us in a fearful state. For most of us scant sleep came our way the balance of the night. Padbury, despite Hooper's shaking, had slept through the entire episode.

With fifty days left in Vietnam Angel was promoted to sergeant. He called himself Sergeant Angel. His quackery was unmatched. His final mission, an LP one month before he left Vietnam, was memorable.

Two LPs from the First were dispersed with Reynolds and Angel commanding respectively. I was in Reynolds's group. About sixty meters outside the wire we found a suitable location and set up. Meanwhile Angel's unit, unable to find a satisfactory site, was floundering about the paddies. Angel had made it clear that he wouldn't spend his last night patrol in a spot without "mucho, beaucoup cover."

Finally Angel located a position, unbelievably, only twenty-five meters or so from our LP. We heard them approaching. Reynolds radioed to Angel that we were situated just to the north of him and to find another place farther away. No reply. Once he activated his LP, Angel, disregarding the radio, yelled over to Reynolds asking where he was. Reynolds, aghast over Angel's dangerous impropriety, radioed to Angel that we were only twenty-five meters to his north. Angel, unconvinced, informed the CP that he was popping a flare to "look around." No comment from the CP. Up goes the illumination. We all burrowed into the paddies. Under the spooky glow of the flare Angel stood up—a risky nighttime proposition for anyone, not to mention a man on his final mission—and crowed again to Reynolds to advise him where he was; Angel said he still couldn't see anyone. The Chicagoan, frustrated to the extent of no longer giving a damn, also rose, waved his arms, and hollered to Angel, "Here we are, you fuckhead!"

"Where?"

"Here, you fuckin' idiot!"

"Okay, great," Angel shrilled as he waved. "I see ya now. I just wanted to know where ya are so we don't get into a shootin' match! Go back to sleep!"

"Thanks a lot!" Reynolds shook his head and dropped.

Even the most stoic jungle fighters among us had a big giggle. We weren't far from the perimeter and the chances of a VC ground foray at Reed were remote. So we settled into our position and hoped that no VC had witnessed the antics of Sergeant Angel.

The following morning we congratulated Angel on completing his eleven months of operations. We marveled how such a crazy fellow could survive in the field for that long. Perhaps his flakiness tempered his nerves. After all, at Polk they had recommended that we not be ultra-careful in Vietnam.

Angel didn't help my nerves when he was around. I was glad to see him cease going on patrols. For one thing, it meant I could stop worrying about getting shot in the back by him.

On another sweep on which I had the misfortune to walk point, we explored an area that our artillery had fired into a day before. At the coordinates Nash and I were signaled onward by Norton to scout the terrain. To our shock we discovered a half-dozen dead VC littered in freakish shapes over a sun-scorched paddy.

They were the first regular VC I had observed up close. As the rest of the platoon sauntered up, we milled around the bodies and inspected the enemy. Like tourists in hell, we triumphantly hovered over the shrapnel-riddled corpses while snapping photos.

Of course, I was relieved that when we found the VC they were dead. But simultaneously I felt a sadness over their deaths. The deceased were no more than teenagers in black pajamas. It was difficult to imagine that these tattered souls were representative of an Oriental army which was checkmating a formidable American force. As I surveyed one lad whose left arm had been severed from his torso, I thought of the fragility of life. Here, only a day earlier, was some living and thinking young man, just like me. Did his mother know his fate yet? What were his hopes and dreams? Did he die believing in his cause? Or did he, like many of his foes, have doubts about the war? It no longer mattered what he thought. Now he was honeycombed with chunks of metal, lying unburied in a paddy with foreign men placing boots on his chest while comrades clicked Instamatics for girlfriends back home.

It was a sobering experience. I recollected how serene my relatives had looked in their coffins. They appeared as if they were merely sleeping, dressed in their finest garments, faces sedate, hands clasped, a rosary quilting their fingers. It was difficult to perceive them as dead. Indeed, they were referred to as "gone," or they had "passed away." But in war dead bodies aren't majestic. Unlike the dignity of my deceased relatives, war dead leer up at the living with ghastly expressions. Blood is splattered everywhere. They're simply unsightly, malodorous health hazards. They can't be alluded to as "passed away," only the term "dead" is apropos. As we gulped C-ration lunches not twenty meters from the cadavers, I pondered the timeless question of why men engage in war.

On February 23, First Platoon's winning streak expired. The night before my squad had gone on an LP, thus we were excused from the morning operation. As the platoon prepared for their dawn Eagle Flight, we all engaged in the usual joking and bitching, the eternal babble engulfing all camps of war since Cro-Magnon man. When the others departed Nash, Tremaine and I lolled on Bunker I and wished our friends a good day. A good day in the field in Vietnam meant that everyone returned healthy.

About noon the CP informed Reynolds to assemble his squad; we were to join Third Platoon for an airlift. The First had been ambushed. Casualties were substantial. But just as we readied ourselves, the order was canceled. The First was returning to Reed. The ambush had been brief, intense. Once the gunships had intervened, the VC had faded into the landscape.

When the platoon returned late that afternoon we learned of the lashing our unit had suffered. Six men were hit. Our new lieutenant, who had joined us only a week earlier, was shot in the mouth. One machine gun team suffered severe wounds. The saddest news was that Doc Schmidt was killed.

Our spirits plummeted. My personal thoughts were morose. How much longer before my luck ran out? It was only luck that my squad had fulfilled the LP the night before. *It could have been me!* It was unbelievable. Soldiers whom I had spent only a few months with, or in some cases, only a few days, I'd never see again. We had shared some conversation, meals, fears, and laughs. Now they were gone. I felt a gigantic emptiness, a cathedral of sorrow and depression.

The next morning the balance of the First was airlifted to the site of the ambush to ferret for dead VC. As we meandered around, Kilcurry described to me how the ambush had occurred. We lingered on the spot where our rookie lieutenant and Doc Schmidt had been hit. Doc's Army-issue glasses, gnarled and broken, lay on the blood-soaked earth. I longed to pick them up, but I couldn't. Paralyzed, I just stared at the forlorn spectacles.

Medics in the Wolfhounds usually served six months in the field, then were rotated to a rear medical company. Doc was short when he was killed; he had only one month left.

Days earlier at Reed, Doc and I had been conversing about our families. He had produced a photo of his two-year-old twin daughters. He had mentioned how proud he was of them and how much he missed rollicking with them. I had observed how glad I was that I wasn't married before I went to Vietnam, thus forgoing that complication. And now Kerry and Kimberly's father was coming home in a flag-draped coffin, his mangled glasses discarded in a rice paddy, his life's fluid soaked into Vietnam's already-red soil.

Why did this happen? I wondered. *Why must Doc's twins grow up without a daddy? Why had he been visited by the angel of death while I had been spared?* The questions gnawed on and on: the festering guilt of combat soldiers. My reflections were severed by the order to assemble for the flight back to Reed. Our dragnet was over. No VC bodies were found.

Back on the bunkerline Tremaine wondered how some politicians in Washington could keep boasting that we were winning the war. In our microscopic view this episode, at least, was a catastrophe. What had we won in the battle? Time? A parcel of ground? The heart and mind of the farmer whose paddy was damaged? Certainly none of these. Not even a body count. By our ledgers the ambush was a shutout for the VC. Of our half-dozen casualties only one—Calhoun—would ever return to the field.

"And furthermore," Tremaine stressed, "since I've been here I've seen more killed and wounded grunts than gooks. It makes you think."

"Yeah," I said. "And since I've been here I've seen our platoon go from more than three dozen guys to twenty-nine."

"Twenty-nine? How do you know?"

"I've been countin'."

"Oh. Well, there's only one thing I'm countin'."

"Days?"

Tremaine nodded. "Two-two-four."

11

Tropic Lightning

Without a replacement lieutenant in sight Norton again assumed leadership of the First. He savored the role. He was competent at it. His one befuddlement was that whenever the First had had any VC contact, he was staying back for something. The day when the devastating ambush had occurred he was in Cu Chi. His amazing luck astounded everyone but no one more than he.

Lieutenant Mills also relished his new job. On operations he was always snug with the pointmen, usually personally directing our movement. His alacrity frightened us. We often remarked how sooner or later his stateside gung-ho attitude would get someone hurt.

Two days after the First was ambushed, we went on a mission to investigate a suspected VC village. As we moved on-line toward the hamlet we received sniper fire. We took cover. Mills called for Norton and "Doofus," a Chieu Hoi or rehabilitated VC who was attached to the First as a Kit Carson scout. Doofus was Norton's little novelty. The guide had even been nicknamed by him.

The lieutenant instructed Doofus to use a loudspeaker and order the VC in the hamlet to surrender or be annihilated. Doofus, after hesitating for Norton's approval, followed the orders. The only reply was additional sniper fire. Mills, incensed that the enemy had spurned his offer, called an air strike on the village. Doofus advised the noncombatants in the town that they would be attacked by jets in fifteen minutes and to vacate the premises immediately. Acting on cue from the comedian Norton, Doofus asked Mills if he had any further instructions for the VC. Mills shouted at Doofus to tell them to surrender. The slender man giggled and dived behind a berm. Norton was laughing so hard he had difficulty crawling back to his position.

Old men, women and children, faces stiff with terror, clutching whatever few personal items they could carry, streamed from the hamlet. Soon two glistening F-100 Super Sabres roared out of the cobalt-blue sky and commenced their work. Cowering behind dikes, we watched the air strike on the VC enclave. The sky vomited fire and destruction: frightful detonations, squealing animals and birds, zooming debris and mushrooming thick gray smoke.

Meanwhile, the sizable throng of villagers cringed next to us, wailing and holding their ears. I wondered how the pilots in their Lysol-clean war machines would have felt about their labor if they could have seen the terror on mothers' faces as they tried to protect their bawling toddlers from a metal storm. It was a sterile war for the Air Force.

After the strike we lumbered on-line toward the village while Cobras hovered above. The jets had done their job; we met no resistance. We hurriedly swept through the ravaged hamlet. It smelled like a smoking city dump. No VC bodies were found. We did discover two dead chickens.

Lieutenant Mills, determined to teach the VC a lesson they wouldn't forget, resolved to burn the village. He said he wanted the enemy to sample fury from the Tropic Lightning Division. Norton and others in command positions tried to dissuade the CO from such action. They felt that if we did burn the place, certainly the VC would retaliate by planting numerous traps. Then if we or another unit ever returned to the village things might be much worse for us. As it was, they argued, the hamlet had been sufficiently damaged. But, the CO countered, if the village was "neutralized," then the VC could no longer use it as a sanctuary. Mills had been indoctrinated well. Norton threw his hands in the air and ambled off. The lieutenant ordered us to disperse and to burn any undamaged hootches. Cursing our CO, we followed orders.

No doubt recalling our bunkerline LPs at Reed, Mills darted about the village making certain the job was being done. When he was watching us we made ourselves look busy. Once he altered his attention we scuttled off, hoping to spare at least a few huts.

It was over in a half hour. As we trekked from the hamlet, the tears and anguish on the faces of the villagers made us sick. We had totally destroyed their homes, food, gardens, and possessions. We left them with nothing but their lives and a smoldering village. It was the contorted American mentality of guerrilla war in Vietnam: you must destroy a community in order to save it.

Back at Reed, Kilcurry, Nash, Tremaine and I discussed our foul venture. We were perturbed over the incident. I felt guilty for not refusing to burn the village. Our scorn for Mills was burgeoning. None of our men had been hit by the sniper fire. It seemed a monstrous reprisal to leave women and babies without food and shelter.

Two weeks hence our worst foreboding was realized when we were ordered to return to the hamlet. As we waited for the choppers outside Reed that ominous morning, an unusual feeling was pulsating in my brain.

Somehow I knew something was going to go wrong that day. It was like a sixth sense. Recalling "Ultra," the British code-breaking triumph of World War II, and the immeasurable service that its forewarning provided, I christened my novel emotion Ultra.

Ultra had been brewing for several weeks. As my duty in the field progressed, I was becoming more familiar with the environment and my rifleman's job. I became adept at knowing when peril was imminent. This combination of an early-warning mechanism and an infantryman's savvy was priceless. You knew when to be alert and when to relax. You were able to strike a certain balance. Or, in army lingo, to keep your shit together.

Certain omens spurred Ultra into action. It seemed that whenever an operation had a rush-rush atmosphere, or whenever we were working an unusual area, Ultra would be bobbing in my head.

Superstition was another catalyst. Whenever a rookie reported to the First, beware of mortars. Since the First had been ambushed twice on Sunday, it was a marked day. Look out for Sundays. Another precarious period was the twenties of any month. Misfortune, more often than not, struck sometime during the twenties. On the first day of a new month the First always released a huge sigh of relief. We had made it through the twenties!

Intuition and superstition had become brothers. Whenever Ultra slipped into high gear I believed something bad was going to happen. It didn't always materialize. But I was definitely ready for it.

On this stifling morning, Ultra was vibrating even before we left the ground. When the choppers flew in to pick us up only some of the ships were able to land; others had to fly off because some of our six-man groups weren't lined up properly. It took nearly twenty minutes for all the choppers to land, gather their reluctant passengers, and establish their flight formation. Lieutenant Mills was embarrassed over the foul-up; he was responsible for it.

The sloppy pickup, which was the first occasion I had seen such an escapade, left me trembling. As I exchanged anxious glances with Nash and Tremaine, I wondered how much more fright they'd feel if I shared with them that Ultra was popping flares and launching rockets in my sweltering mind.

The aircrafts deposited us outside the village. We established our alignment and approached the somber town. As expected our pointmen found traps. Mills sent Doofus and a squad from the Third into the village to enlist volunteers to show us where the other traps were located. With no takers, Mills instructed Sergeant Houston, who commanded the patrol, to abscond with two old men and make them walk before our pointmen. Of course. We wended our way into the hamlet uninjured.

The inhabitants had removed most of the rubble and had erected makeshift structures with scraps of tin, cardboard, and bamboo. They glared at us with hatred. Nervous and disconcerted, we searched the village. We discovered nothing in the way of contraband.

Mills, repulsed over our inconclusive rummage and the aversion of the villagers to cooperate with us in ferreting the traps, ordered a withdrawal. Since the First was the last platoon in, we had to pioneer the way out. With our Vietnamese helmsmen blazing the trail we were safely ushered through the booby-trapped area. Then we dismissed our gloomy trap monitors and accelerated from the locality.

The end of the operation. It appeared that Ultra had failed. The chopper snafu at Reed was just that—another common Army muddle. Nothing had happened. No VC contact. No casualties. Not even any accidents. And just as I had convinced myself that Ultra had erred—the First was over two hundred meters from the village—a thundering explosion lurched through the afternoon's tranquility. We all twirled around bleating in crescendo, "What was *that?*" The detonation occurred just outside the hamlet. A dark, macabre tower of smoke spiraled towards cirrus clouds.

Norton turned to Tremaine, who was carrying the radio. He grabbed the microphone from Tremaine's hand. "Tango one-seven, this is Lima four-zero! Over!" Norton toweled his forehead and tensely juggled the transmitter in his hand. We clustered around him and waited for the reply. "Tango one-seven, this is Lima four-zero. Over!"

"Lima four-zero, this is Tango one-seven. Over," a fluttering voice said.

Norton recognized the voice and told us that it was Sergeant Houston, the Third's platoon sergeant. "This is Lima four-zero. What the fuck happened back there? Over!"

"This is Tango one-seven. We got one man blown away from a trap. Looks like maybe a booby-trapped bomb from one of our jets. I don't know. We're goin' to be here awhile to, err, pick up all the pieces. So just relax awhile up there, okay? Nobody else hurt. Over."

We waited for Norton to ask the obvious question. He looked at us. "Go ahead," chirped Tremaine. "Ask!"

"Roger that, Tango one-seven. Who hit the trap? Over."

"This is Tango one-seven. Lieutenant Mills. Out."

12

A Lawyer, a Pirate, a Face

With the demise of Lieutenant Mills, a new CO, the fourth since I joined Bravo, was sent to the field as an interim CO until Captain Hoy rejoined us. He was a tense, bespectacled officer who was a military lawyer from Cu Chi. Inexperienced as an infantry commander, he wasn't bashful about verbalizing that he wasn't sure how to load a rifle, much less fire one.

The dearth of infantry officers in the Wolfhounds frightened us. Even though we generally had a vinegary view of officers, we still preferred one disciplined in infantry as opposed to one seasoned in courtroom tactics or some other irrelevant artistry. Lieutenant Duncan of the Third, who was the only other officer in the company, and the platoon sergeants—excepting Norton who was on R & R in Hawaii—were aware of the potential hazards. They tried to monitor our counselor-captain so that he didn't get anyone hurt.

Our premier operation with our beleaguered CO was an Eagle Flight. We were flown to an area where a VC unit had been traced by a Long Range Reconnaissance Patrol. It was rugged, uninhabited terrain with enough woods to excite John Muir. Once on terra firma in the LZ, we found ourselves floundering in a clearing ideal for a VC ambush. The CO, mystified over his bearings, relied on Duncan to align us and get the patrol moving.

With the sergeant's assistance, Duncan was able to get the sweep expedited. We assembled for the choppers. Then came orders to assume defensive positions; a unit of VC had been detected by a reconnaissance aircraft. The VC were approaching us. Abandoning our customary posture of standing in vulnerable groups like passengers at a bus stop, we snuggled behind berms, weapons primed. Tension mounted. The basic question: who would reach us first, the VC or the choppers?

A towering black man from another platoon suddenly bounded over to our detachment. He knelt behind our berm, glaring and sniffing at a distant treeline.

"Who's he?" I whispered to Calhoun.

"The Pirate."

"Who?"

"The Pirate. He's from the Second. A bad dude. Stay clear of him. Let him do his thing."

"His thing? What the hell's his thing?"

"Smellin' out the gooks."

"What?"

"He can smell 'em out before we can see 'em."

"Yeah, sure," I said with a smirk and an irritated wave.

The Pirate was six-foot-six with the arms and chest of a colossus. About his massive oblong head he wore a bush hat rather than a helmet. His lengthy hair was the closest mode to an Afro I'd seen since leaving the States. He was reputed to be a virtuoso with the duper. Like any worthy brigand, on his hip he sported a machete, which he supposedly liberated from a dead VC. During his tour he had served with various companies in the Wolfhounds. His prowess in discerning the enemy by smell was legendary. Although wounded thrice, he returned to the field each time after he recovered.

Glistening with sweat, he rotated his pock-marked face up and down the hedgerow. "I smell 'em! I smell 'em! I smell the li'l mothers! There's some of 'em motherfuckers movin' behind that hedgerow over there!"

"Where?" asked Calhoun, straining to see what the Pirate smelled.

The Pirate gave Calhoun an expansive grin, revealing a mouthful of chipped, rotting teeth. He sniffed at the treeline. Dissolving in laughter, he fired a round into the hedgerow. "There!"

Kilcurry radioed to Duncan that the Pirate had detected VC. The lieutenant advised the converging choppers to be vigilant for a hot LZ. Then the Pirate leaped up. "I'm goin' to get 'em li'l fuckers!"

Stunned, we watched him march towards the hedgerow while firing. The distant drone of the airlift infected our ears. We howled to the Pirate that the choppers were approaching. He waved at us, then fired again. Soon the choppers dropped into our LZ with their M-60s blazing. Kilcurry yelled that he just heard over the radio that some of the choppers were receiving ground fire. *Jesus,* I thought, *we're in for it!*

When our chopper landed we scrambled aboard, content to rescue ourselves while the Pirate played John Wayne for us. There was so much tumult from the shooting and the aircrafts' engines that it was impossible to tell if our ship was under fire. I took the outside seat and looked at the Pirate. He was standing with one hand on his hip gazing at us like an outfielder killing time between pitches.

I waved at him to come. With cool detachment he raised his index finger, indicating only he knew what. I glanced at the chopper pilot. He was flailing his arms at the Pirate. The Pirate, unperturbed, fired another round, then strode toward the chopper. With horror we watched him stumble as if he had been shot. But he quickly recovered and sprinted for the airship. The pilot anticipated his arrival and began to lift off. I reached for the Pirate's hand as he tried to hurtle himself onto the elevating chopper. We missed each other's grasp. He tumbled to the paddy. The doorgunner, who had been blasting into the bush like a gangster from "The Untouchables," told the pilot through his intercom to lower the craft. He did so. This time I grabbed the Pirate's shirt while Nash clenched his tattooed arm and we pulled him aboard.

As the chopper rose I yelled into the Pirate's ear and asked him if he was okay. He gave me a sugary smile. The pilot turned to me and by reading his lips I determined he was asking if the Pirate was hit. I shook my head no. The pilot nodded and within moments we joined the formation for the flight to Reed.

Back at Reed I asked the Pirate how he was able to smell the VC.

"I just learned myself to get deep on smellin' 'em li'l fuckers." He lit a joint. "But I won't be smellin' out 'em gook mothers no mo'!"

"Huh?"

"In a few days I go to Cu Chi for DEROS. That's why I volunteered to go out today with the Second. Just wanted to get a few last shots at 'em li'l motherfuckers!"

"Oh."

The Pirate wasn't your ordinary Wolfhound. There were some in Bravo — not to mention the VC — who applauded his departure.

Some days later Alpha and Bravo dismantled Reed. We were transferred four thousand meters south of Reed to establish another fortress dubbed Fire Base Aires.

Erecting a perimeter was always a tedious experience. For security purposes the bases were usually constructed in open terrain. We toiled all day without shade. We splintered into squads and each unit would manufacture its own bunker. The work pace was lethargic and not entirely because of the heat. We knew we had to have the bunkers completed by nightfall in order to have cover for that sinister time of day. We were cautious to temper our progress, however, so that we didn't complete our bunkers too soon because then we'd only be put to task fabricating the CO's or someone else's outpost. It was one thing to drudge under a relentless Asian sun building a structure which might in a few hours save your own ass, and quite another to slave over another's citadel — especially if it was for someone you didn't respect.

Our initial night at Aires was inauspicious. Enemy movement was detected all about us by radar. Our ordnance expounded fire the entire night. We were mortared. The VC's marksmanship was, as usual, errant. Remarkably, all the night patrols from the Third trudged back in without incident.

As the last strips of sunlight radiated into our eyes on the second evening, First Platoon assembled for three LP assignments. Reynolds was doling out the orders in Norton's absence.

As I wandered around Reynolds, Ultra commenced beaming. We were experiencing a disturbing hiatus in leadership. We had already been mortared once. Our resident attorney was floundering about the CP quizzing the sergeants on what he was supposed to do if we were bombed again. The perimeter site was deplorable and our breastworks were sloppily constructed. Unlike at Reed, our visibility was diminished. At some points hedgerows were within forty meters of the bunkers. The VC, through their network of civilian informants, undoubtedly were aware of these tactical deficiencies.

Additionally, some shuffling was required to substitute for furloughed men. Our squad was partially dismembered. Tremaine, one of the fellows I most desired to be with when in battle, was going out with another unit. Ultra's influence had attained absurd proportions: having the right people with me on a patrol had become the most notable feature of the operation. My desperation was such that before departing I asked Tremaine to switch LPs with Hooper so we could be together. They agreed to switch. But at the last moment Hooper altered his thinking, figuring that he'd be safer in the locality assigned to our LP.

With all these burdens prancing in my mind, the instant we departed Aires I began trembling. Scherbarth, a nineteen-year-old recently promoted sergeant, directed our patrol, which included Nash, Munson, Splash, and Hooper.

It was a brief jaunt to our coordinates and Scherbarth selected an LP site and got us set up. I tried to relax and sleep. Near one o'clock a report snapped over the radio that VC were moving east of Tremaine's LP. Our artillery fired at them. Soon we learned that VC activity was determined just west of us. "Stay low," Scherbarth warned. "Here comes the arty!"

Explosions detonated in a hedgerow close to us: a dreadful blast, the sky flickered, the ground shivered, buzzing jagged splinters shredded ferns and bamboo. We could hear the foliage being sliced, like sharp scissors cutting paper. We cowered flat as hot steel fragments shrieked over our heads. We yelled at Scherbarth to tell them to back off the artillery. "Goddamnit," he screamed into the microphone, "the arty's too close, push it back, push it back!" The CP replied, "Wait, out."

Hooper, improvising, snuggled parallel to our berm rather than the usual perpendicular position the balance of us had assumed. By having his entire body adjacent to the berm, he reckoned he could better protect himself. Then there was another close burst. Lethal debris thumped about us. Hooper screamed and rolled away from the dike, writhing in pain. He had been lying between Nash and me. We pounced on him until his twisting slowed.

"What the FUCK?" Hooper exclaimed. He winced in anguish and fright. "Who's throwin' ROCKS?"

"WHAT?" Nash crowed over the roar of another discharge in the treeline.

"Somebody just hit me in the back with a ROCK!"

"What?" I shrilled. "Are you hit, Hoop?"

"Jesus Christ, I'm hit!"

"Where you hit? Where? Where?" pumped Nash. He rolled Hooper over. "Where the fuck you hit?"

"In my fuckin' baaack!" Hooper wailed through clinched teeth.

Nash ripped open Hooper's shirt. He had a wound in the small of his back. Blood bubbled from the injury. Nash produced a bandage he always stored inside his helmet, tore open the package, and covered the rupture.

On it went. Earsplitting salvos. Blood and fire and smoke. Horrible tearing sounds. Iron hail kicking up dirt around us. Flares hanging overhead. The vile smell of gunpowder in the air. But still no VC. I looked behind me at the perimeter. Angry orange flames spit from the howitzer muzzles. Friendly fire. *My God*, I thought, *they're going to kill us! They're going to hit us all!* Scherbarth radioed to the CP that we had a man wounded. He requested permission to quit the LP and bring him in.

Our novel CO, overwhelmed by the proceedings unfolding about him, summoned Duncan and Houston to his bunker. They counseled him to immediately withdraw all the LPs. He procrastinated for ten minutes during which time Scherbarth pleaded over the radio that Hooper was looped over in unbearable torment. Nash and I did our utmost to soothe him and squelch his bleatings. His agony was excruciating, irrepressible. Finally the artillery barrage lifted, then came the order for us to retreat. We squandered not a second. Scherbarth seized the radio and took point. Nash and I took Hooper arm-in-arm, stood him up, and followed Scherbarth. Munson and Splash screened our retirement. As we approached the wire we shouted to our compatriots on the bunkerline not to fire at us. They ignited flares and yelled that they were covering us. We sped for the wire as best we could with our injured mate.

It seemed like hours, but within minutes we safely cleared the wire. We dragged Hooper to the CP bunker where the company medics attended to him. A dust-off was hailed from Cu Chi. Hooper was whisked to a hospital.

Infuriated and still shaking, Nash and I rested outside the CP bunker. We were vexed over the needless dalliance in letting us return to the perimeter. When the CO emerged from his bunker, Nash and I exchanged expletives about what we thought of insensitive, incompetent officers. We did this loud enough so that the CO could hear us. He ignored us. But Houston, racing about trying to get a handle on the situation developing beyond the wire, told us to shut up and to return to our bunker. We quieted and remained near the CP hoping to watch things progress.

In the interim, Tremaine's LP had perceived some VC close to them. The VC were erecting bamboo rocket launchers—crude devices which enabled the enemy to catapult warheads at our perimeters from close range. Reynolds, who commanded the LP, requested consent to withdraw to Aires. Again the lawyer, no doubt sifting the merits of his decision, vacillated for twenty minutes. He finally acquiesced. Reynolds radioed his thanks and advised the CP that it was too late for his unit to flee because two VC were groveling towards them on the opposite side of the berm. They were towing a rocket launcher.

Nash, raving over hearing these tidings, unleashed another verbal tempest. Houston, tired of our bitching, told us that if we desired to help Tremaine's LP, to go to the bunker nearest them. There we could caution the men on that barricade, if they weren't already aware of it, that one of our LPs was posted before them. Mustering our senses as well as our rifles, we scuttled for the bunker. There we discovered from a radioman in the Second, who was auditing the transmissions between the LPs and the CP, that the other LP from the First had been recalled and had safely reached Aires.

We stared into the night, hoping for the best for our buddies stranded in the paddies. Suddenly, in the vicinity of the LP, riflery and detonation rent the air. There were flashes of light, distant yells, and a spray of gunfire, then silence. Then came another withering volley of lead, followed again by silence. We gathered around the RTO. In a wispy voice Reynolds said that they had engaged the prowling enemy. They had killed the VC. None of our comrades had been injured. Under the dull milky light of the flares we saw them rise and scurry like frightened mice for the bunkerline. We alerted the adjoining bunkers to contain their fire.

Our comrades bolted into our sandbag haven. Tremaine was the last man in. Once he was close I called to him. He heard me and looked blankly in my direction. As he did so I nearly leaped from my skin. Tremaine's expression was one of sheer terror. His pale lips quivered. His eyes pierced me with the stare of a zombie. His face was ashen, ghostlike. It was the face of a man who had just witnessed the abyss, the Inferno. And for the first time, in Tremaine's grotesque countenance, I saw the horror we all were experiencing as we endured a desperate struggle for survival in an unholy, baffling war.

Tremaine staggered to us. He sank to the ground. His clothes, face and hands were covered with grime. Swallowing his fear, he told us what had happened. He was the outside man in the formation, closest to the Vietnamese. Through the starlight scope, he had detected the VC slinking down the paddy. He alerted the rest of the patrol. Once they were ready, Tex and he and some others lobbed grenades and fired their sixteens. They waited for the smoke to clear and peered over the dike. There was no movement. At that point Reynolds relayed that they were able to sprint for the wire.

Tremaine's throbbing account was lanced by the voice of Duncan requesting volunteers to go inspect the LP's work. His fright ebbing and his curiosity rallying, the resilient Tremaine offered to go and see exactly how many VC had been killed. "I gotta see what's out there!" he said. Tremaine asked if I'd go. Recalling my Fort Bragg commitment to refrain from volunteering for anything, I declined.

First artillery fire softened up the area. Then under cover from the bunkerline the patrol wobbled its way to the LP site. They verified a body count of two VC. Soon they were back inside our refuge.

Exhausted to the point of collapse, we retired to our respective bunkers. One by one we found our poncho liners and went to sleep. Tremaine, unable to locate his liner, foraged around for something to cover himself. He found a messy, tattered rag. He flung it over his shoulders, snuggled beside a bunker, and dozed off. We ignored establishing guard shifts.

Two hours later at daybreak we were aroused. Our first command of the day was to assemble at the CP for a company meeting. Tired and numb, we stood before our CO. Emanating buoyant zest, our barrister proclaimed that Alpha and Bravo would dissolve Aires forthwith. By noon we had to be prepared to embark for the north. Enemy infiltration had accelerated in the triple canopy jungle of Tay Ninh province and, in accordance with the reactionary mission of the Wolfhounds, we were being cast into the rift.

With obvious delight, the CO further divulged that he was being relieved of his duties because Captain Hoy would be rejoining us in Tay Ninh. He thanked us for our cooperation and bravery. He remarked that without these he might have been killed, which was probably true.

As we boarded chinooks destined for Tay Ninh, our reprieved CO stepped into a Loach. His time with Bravo concluded, he was destined for Cu Chi and imminent challenges in the world of the Uniform Code of Military Justice.

13

Rocket City

When we arrived at Fire Base Washington, a compact perimeter northwest of Nui Ba Den in Tay Ninh province, Captain Hoy was waiting for us. Once we were assigned bunkers he circled the bunkerline shaking hands with his company. He was ecstatic to be back. And considering our fortunes with previous COs, we were glad to have *him* back.

Also back in the saddle was Sergeant Norton. He was stupefied to learn of all the excitement he had missed. "We always get in the fuckin' shit when I don't go out! Nothin' ever happens when *I* go out!" he remarked with genuine disgruntlement.

Within a week we departed Washington. We were ferried to Fire Base Mills, so named by Hoy for Lieutenant Mills. Our duties at both bases involved the usual day and night patrols probing for infiltrating North Vietnamese. The jungles of Tay Ninh were impossible. The Garden of Eden gone to seed: a jumble of trees, ferns, vines, exotic flowers, thickets of bamboo, and clusters of plants of every size and description—all a different shade of green. The jade towers were tangled so thick you couldn't see the sky. As the stalks swayed in a breeze from above, the jungle canopy squeaked and moaned. It was truly a living thing, a murky, emerald twilight world. Odors of moist, decaying vegetation. A boundless compost heap. No sun, no air, no trails and, perhaps worst of all, no visibility. But there were plenty of spiders, screaming monkeys, fat snakes, weird insects and colorful birds. And heat. Incendiary heat. It was our job to hack through this awesome green monster with dull machetes. Certainly paradise for Charles Darwin or Alexander von Humboldt. But for beer-starved draftees, it was Hades.

In the jungle Charlie could have slaughtered us. We were as helpless as the Wehrmacht mired in winter on the steppes of Russia in World War II. Fortunately we never found Charlie there. So we returned from our two-canteen patrols joking and bragging about how the VC had fled once they heard the barbarous Wolfhounds were coming to Tay Ninh.

After two weeks of these exhausting operations Bravo was rotated to the 25th's principal northern base of Tay Ninh for a stand-down. Comparable to Cu Chi in facilities, the camp was smaller and more hazardous because there were more VC in the area. We were quartered in barracks at a place known as Tay Ninh West, a refitting-resort complex complete with showers, cots, and a massive rubber swimming pool. The retreat also presented daily stag movies, the Army's idea of wholesome entertainment. For three days we frolicked in the respite from operations and nightly guard duty.

One night Bravo was convened for a memorial service for its five recently deceased members: Lieutenant Mills, Doc Schmidt, Briggs, and two men from the Third Platoon killed at Reed. During the eulogy Captain Hoy disintegrated into tears when he endeavored to speak about Mills. The ceremony concluded with the "Sounding of Taps," played on a tape recorder. Shivering with depression and sorrow, we filed from the open-walled chapel, each of us praying that we'd never achieve the ranks of the Memorial Roll.

Vacation over, we were sent—to our absolute astonishment—to another part of the Tay Ninh base. We were assigned to barracks. Our only missions were daylight Eagle Flights. The basic imperfection with this arrangement was that nightly Tay Ninh experienced 122mm rocket attacks. At the first clamor of "Incoming!" we sprang from our berths, shouldered through doors, and plunged into bunkers next to the buildings.

The rockets seldom descended in our locale. But one evening after dark Tremaine and I slithered from the barracks. Like two alcoholic escapees from a detox facility, we proceeded directly to a bar about a quarter mile across the post. At the pub we drank tepid beer for an hour. We sauntered outside. It was another hot, star-shrouded Asian night. While conversing with some fellows from the Second, who also were AWOL from the Bravo area, a huge explosion nearby sent us scrambling. Someone yelled "Rockets!"

Tremaine and I ran towards our barracks, hoping to encounter a bunker along the way. Unable to locate one, and with rockets blasting too close for debate, we curled next to a building until the assault ceased.

We knew that one rocket had exploded back near the club. Our inquisitiveness lured us back to inspect the damage. We discovered that a rocket had hit where we had been chatting only minutes earlier. Two men who had fled the saloon after us were killed. That was the last time we went gadding about Tay Ninh in quest of spirits or anything else.

The inevitable order finally came for us to return to a fire base in the field. This meant more ambush patrols and LPs. On our last twilight in Tay Ninh we had a boisterous party that endured well into the dank night.

In Tay Ninh, like everywhere else in Vietnam, alcohol and marijuana were as plentiful as soda and hot dogs at a picnic. As long as your perimeter was coiled by the eager, capitalistic natives, you were never bereft of wartime sundries. About two-thirds of Bravo used marijuana, while nearly everyone drank. It was virtually impossible to find someone who used neither drug.

If you had to fight a war, especially one as mind-twisting as this war, then one way to do it was by being stoned half the day. It definitely wasn't Willie and Joe's army.

In the First there was no animosity between the heads and the juicers. At night on the bunkerlines, whoever was on guard would cover for the others inside from any prowling, not-with-it officers. Each of us were pursuing our individual formulas for mental deliverance from the war. We cultivated a brotherhood of respect in this regard.

On our closing night in Tay Ninh, however, there was no need to be anxious about getting hassled over possessing a joint or a fifth. For even Captain Hoy, whose liver was overdosed by midnight, joined in the merriment. He was indeed exultant to be reunited with his beloved Bravo. Norton, a guitar player, stroked the chords and led in the singing until he went hoarse.

Norton liked me. He occasionally did things to display it, such as leaving me back from an operation when fellows with more time in-country were participating. I was grateful for this. But his cruelty to prisoners remained disconcerting. I desired to question him about it, but I decided that it could wait. Maybe someday I'd look him up in the States and then ask him. There was no sense in risking becoming a permanent pointman.

14

Bloodswirl

Bravo was reassigned to Fire Base Mills. Within a week we destroyed the base and relocated back down south. A more startling development involved Captain Hoy. Again he left us to journey home for personal affairs. This time he was permanently relieved.

We became melancholy over this event because we knew we were losing a leader who truly cared for us. The consummate professional, Hoy's prudence and leadership somehow helped us to endure. He was stern but fair. His fundamental concern was always the safety of his men. Perhaps, like many of us, fomenting in the catacombs of his mind was a conviction that the war was absurd, thus not worth one additional life or dismemberment. We disengaged from our CO with respect and friendship, waning commodities between officers and enlisted men in Vietnam in 1969.

Another officer was assigned to Bravo. Volcanic and balding, Captain DeFreeze was an experienced infantry veteran. An earthy individual with a paunchy face and deep-set eyes, he had the annoying habit of barking rather than speaking his words. With a .45 pistol on his hip and two grenades clipped to his chest pockets, he made no pretense about who was now in command at Bravo. Aptitude-wise, he was a capable infantry officer. But from our view it would be difficult for anyone to replace Captain Hoy.

Fire Base Jackson, our next duty station, was the size of Reed. Waiting for us there were three new First Platoon recruits. Yerby, a hillbilly from Fort Bragg country; Mortensen, a runty, solemn Instant sergeant who seemed like he'd fit into the platoon; and Dougherty, a reserved yet amiable eighteen-year-old from Southern California who, like Kilcurry, was a fair-skinned Irish citizen.

When I first talked with Dougherty, he was bruised and frightened to be serving in Vietnam with a rifle company. Just tough luck, I told him. What I didn't tell him was that his haunting glances and trembling hands unnerved me. His bewildered, innocent expressions symbolized for me that war is a young man's enterprise; it's mostly the young who pay the supreme price of war. After that first encounter I pretty much avoided Dougherty. In Vietnam if someone made you nervous, you acted accordingly.

Of course the replacements weren't hailed with the warmest of greetings because of what new men usually meant. Sure enough, that evening we were mortared.

The following day Bravo was supposed to stay at Jackson to refurbish and expand the bunkerline. At ten o'clock came an order to prepare for an Eagle Flight. We were gathering our equipment when a man with lieutenant's bars on his collars paraded up and down our bunkers.

"Saddle up, First! Saddle up, First!" he exhorted in a squeaky voice while evading everyone's eyes.

"Who the fuck's that?" asked Rojas, a soft-spoken, smiling rifleman who had come to the First about a month before me. Around his neck Rojas wore a huge peace medallion, two rosaries, and three or four medals honoring various saints. We wondered how he could hold his head up.

"Our new lieutenant," said Norton, trailing behind the officer. "He was back in Cu Chi when I got back from Hawaii. His name's Wortman. I checked him out. He's okay."

"Sure he checked him out," Tremaine said to me out of earshot of Norton. "Just like he checked out that last louie of ours who walked into an ambush and got himself shot in the mouth!"

"Everybody saddle up! Everybody saddle up!" Wortman ordered. He was twenty-one, cherubic-faced, and had buck teeth.

"No, no, not everybody!" Norton boomed after the lieutenant. The officer froze. "Everybody gather around me!"

Before the platoon Norton explained to the officer that only twenty-four of the unit's twenty-eight soldiers would go on the Eagle Flight. Mabry, a fleshy-faced, six-foot black man who toted the duper, was exempt due to minor medical reasons. The same was true for Nash. Munson had only twenty-five days until DEROS and he was excused from operations. Gibson had left the field en route to R & R.

"What's goin' on out there?" Tremaine drilled Norton.

"Charlie Company's been ambushed. They've been in the shit all morning."

"What about casualties?" someone asked.

Norton gave an unworried shrug. "No report on casualties. We'll find out once we get out there."

It was another of those Condition Red situations which always sent Ultra reeling. While Tremaine and I loaded magazines on the bunker, Munson told us to take care of ourselves. I glanced at Tremaine. He grinned.

"Shit Munson," I boasted, concealing my terror, "don't worry about us. We'll be okay. I wasn't born into this world to get blown away on some damn rice paddy in Southeast Asia!"

"Hell no," said Tremaine. "Me neither. Besides, I've only got a hundred and ninety-two days to go!"

"Yeah? And I've got twenty-five! In twenty-five days I'll be lyin' on the beach in California!" gloated Munson.

"Okay, short-timer," I said, "don't rub it in."

Munson laughed and blinked his eye. "You guys take care out there. See ya tonight."

The chopper pickup outside Jackson was reminiscent of the ill-fated Eagle Flight on the day that Lieutenant Mills was killed. We blamed our new CO for the foul-up. Later we discovered that the airmen were erroneous in their landing pattern.

In twos and threes, all of the other choppers landed and took off with their troops while my group was left standing in the PZ. My ship consisted of Norton and his RTO Jackel, a likeable country boy from the Midwest; Dougherty, the rookie; Rickenbrode, a competent, dependable machine gunner; and Foos, another new rifleman who had joined us in Tay Ninh. While we waited for a helicopter to pick us up, I remarked to Norton that it would be fine with me if they forgot about us. Norton, exhibiting his fanatical streak, told me no chance. And why did I want to miss out on any good shit waiting for us at the LZ?

The last empty chopper landed. We scrambled aboard. I sat on the floor across from Dougherty. As we joined the formation and cruised towards our LZ, I drooped my legs out the open doorway. I noticed Dougherty staring at me. I thought perhaps that my fearless, Cong-zapping Green Beret posture probably hypnotized him. In training they never told us that we'd be riding in choppers with our legs hanging over the side. Then I realized that my flapping legs weren't the focus of his attention. It was something else—something grisly. His face was locked in terror. He clenched his rifle tightly between his legs. His Paul Newman eyes glared at me like blue searchlights. When he realized I was looking at him, he tried to kindle a smile, but he couldn't. He couldn't do anything except plead with me with his eyes. His expression asked, What am I doing here? Why am I flying off to battle in a controversial war? What's waiting for us ahead? You're the combat veteran, Kitch, what's going to happen when we land? Something? Nothing? It's my first operation. Will it be bad or will it just be an ordinary patrol, one of many I'll endure in my Tour 365? Help me, Kitch! Help me!

I yearned to growl at him not to look at me like that, but I merely gave him a quizzical glance. Then with a shiver, I turned away and prepared for the LZ.

As we approached the LZ, a spacious paddy that likely concealed no

VC, Norton warned us to be alert for a hot LZ. I peered at Dougherty and he almost fell out the door. I gazed at Jackel and he grinned like a circus clown. I turned to Rickenbrode and he rotated his head no. I nodded agreement.

The landing was routine. Once we assembled in our squads, DeFreeze ordered us to assume defensive positions in a line facing a hedgerow a hundred and fifty meters distant. Beyond the treeline was a village where Charlie Company was doing battle. They were trying to flush out the VC and push them into our waiting armory — a neat little plan.

It was a big firefight in the hamlet. Norton came around and said that the VC body count was into double figures. Fatalities for us were "light," a term which always instigated harpooning mockery in our ranks.

The battle raged. Finally an air strike, complete with jelly-like napalm, was rent upon the village. From our protected vantage point it was like watching a Hollywood war movie in horrible, vivid color. "Wow! Look at that! Wow, man, look at 'em trees and huts flyin'!" we exclaimed like youngsters at a Saturday matinee. It was easy for us to exchange sassy jokes about the happenings unraveling before our eyes. The shock of war was beginning to erode for us; we were becoming accustomed to it.

As swiftly as the jets appeared they dissolved into the cloudless heavens. The burning village was declared subjugated by Charlie Company. "Another village liberated by bombing it out of existence!" Tremaine groaned while igniting another Lucky Strike.

Norton, who had been monitoring the action on the CO's radio, meandered to us. In place of his helmet he wore a baseball-type Army cap with four general's stars adorning it. Thinking our chores were completed for the afternoon, we were hoping to learn when we'd embark for Jackson. Norton was intent on impersonating General Creighton Abrams, the American commander in Vietnam. "How's the war going for you, soldier? I'll speak to my staff about getting you grunts better chow. Go ahead and take a break in place, troop! As you were, soldier! I'll be in the area all day, troop!" On he went, clowning and exaggerating, not concerned about when the choppers were coming.

Norton succeeded in melting our tension until our new lieutenant ambled over. He ordered us to form up for a sweep into a hedgerow complex west of the vanquished village. Wortman told Norton to leave behind two men to guard our extra ammo and provisions which we had carted along. Norton selected Splash and me to abstain from the patrol.

With Ultra subdued and my confidence burgeoning, I thanked Norton for the opportunity to refrain. I requested that he pick someone else to stay back. I explained that I'd rather accompany the platoon and get to some shade. The heat we had tolerated in the sun-splashed paddy for over an hour was grueling, choking. "Besides," I spurted to Norton while gesturing toward the smoldering village, "the VC have been put out of business in this part of town." Norton shrugged and elected Tex to forgo the sweep with Splash.

I suddenly felt squeamish about rejecting Norton's overture. *Jesus,* I thought, *don't ever volunteer for anything! But Ultra couldn't always be right. No. Of course not. It's too late. It's also too hot out here. Fuck it.* I gathered my gear.

We established our normal two column formation with Dougherty as pointman for the left wing and Foos on the right. I was behind Foos. We inched towards the hedgerow. Since Wortman was inexperienced, Norton abandoned his usual post in the rear of the formation and moved up front. Within fifty meters of the timberline I noticed some four-foot cone-shaped dirt mounds ahead.

"Sergeant Norton," I said, "there's some hills up there the VC might be usin' as bunkers!"

"Where?"

I pointed at the pillars. "Right up there!"

"You mean those ant hills, Kitch?"

"Yeah."

"No, no, they're just ant hills, Kitch. The VC use underground bunkers, not dirt hills like that."

"Okay," I said, feeling stupid.

"But we'll go ahead and put a few recon rounds into 'em just to be sure. Tremaine and Weaver—you guys put some rounds into 'em ant hills up there!"

Tremaine and Weaver trooped forward. They fired several missiles. There were no direct hits. Tremaine giggled and eddied back to his place behind Dougherty. Weaver, who often articulated his dislike of military life, grumbled something about what a mammoth waste the war was.

Satisfied with the reconning, Norton waved the pointmen onward. We threaded our way past the sinister ant colonnades, through the hedgerow, and across a four-foot ditch, which was a dried-up irrigation canal. We entered a tiny clearing. Another hedgerow was just ahead. As our movement decelerated we dangerously bunched up. I stepped over a scrawny, foot-high berm making a mental note of its existence and thinking what a horrible dike to ever have to use for cover.

We lumbered a few meters more. We halted for more recon fire. Suddenly the whole world exploded in automatic rifle fire. "AMBUSH! AMBUSH!" screamed several voices. The shouts seemed to dangle in the muggy air as First Platoon instinctively dropped to the earth. If a second was ever an hour—or a lifetime—it was that moment.

I whirled to my right and dived behind the small berm I had just traversed. Some VC had us in a crossfire. They were in fortified bunkers with slit openings for their AK-47s. One VC was located in the hedgerow directly in front of me less than ten meters distant. He was firing into the center of our patrol, thus I wasn't in his field of fire. Like a jackhammer, he was kicking up a dust storm around his bunker as he peppered the nucleus of our formation.

Once behind the berm I started cursing. The ambush had frightened me beyond anything I had ever experienced. I vented my rage as I squeezed off three magazines at the bunker before me. I didn't really aim at anything; I just rested my rifle on top of the berm and fired in the direction of the bunker. I glanced to my left and saw Weaver firing his duper. He gawked at me, then crawled over.

"Kitch," he cried over the din of rifle fire, "who's that layin' in front of you?"

I peeped up and saw a green-uniformed body sprawled midway between myself and the VC. Foos! I had completely forgotten about him being on point.

"It's Foos!"

"Kitch, I think he's dead! He's not movin'!"

"There's nothin' we can do. Let's just keep firin' over him!"

"Okay." He reloaded and fired. "Fuck! Oh Christ, my rounds are goin' right on through the hedgerow! They're hittin' way back in 'em trees! Look!"

He fired two rounds. They whizzed through the brush and harmlessly exploded beyond the VC bunker.

"Fuck!" I rammed another magazine into my sixteen. "What can we do? Just keep firin' and hope you get one into the bunker hole!"

"Fuck! Fuck! Fuck this fuckin' war!" said Weaver. He launched several more grenades, all of which missed the bunker. "Kitch, how many gooks are there?"

"I don't fuckin' know."

Weaver nodded to our point blank foe. "I can see this one here. But where are the rest of 'em? There's got to be plenty of 'em considerin' all this fuckin' shootin'!"

"Christ, I don't know, Weaver." I signaled to additional hedgerows twenty meters to our right. "Maybe you should put a few rounds over there."

"Are there gooks in there *too*? Have you received any fire from over there?"

"No, no, but put some rounds in there just to be sure!"

"Okay, but if there are any VC in there, we've had it!"

Weaver told me to lie flat and to keep my head down. He rested his weapon on my back and fired three rounds into the area. Then we resumed firing at the verified VC in front of us until Weaver exclaimed, "Kitch, I'm out of ammo!"

I couldn't hear him over the drumfire of bullets. "What?"

"I'm out of ammo! What am I goin' to do now?"

I tossed a hand grenade to him. "Here!"

"What am I supposed to do with that?"

I shrugged. "I don't give a shit what you do with it! Keep it in case they rush us! It's somethin' to have anyway!"

After a pause Weaver cast the grenade back to me. "Here, I don't want that thing!"

"Why?"

"Because those fuckin' things are dangerous!"

We heard sudden shouts of "Start firin'! Start firin'! Keep firin'!" Our volume of fire had diminished considerably from when the ambush had begun. Norton, like a hockey coach discovering his players coasting through skating drills, was exhorting everyone to fire. Amid cries of approbation, our dormant weapons erupted in a spasm of firepower.

I rapidly expended three or four magazines. Realizing that I had nearly halfway emptied my ammo sack, I began to worry where our gunships were. "Where the fuck are the gunships, Weaver? They're always around right away when we don't really need 'em! Where are they now? Where are the gunships?" I was possessed with fury over their tardiness.

Weaver buried his flushed face in his dirty hands. I primed a magazine and ripped another eighteen rounds at the submerged VC before us who was intermittently spraying our comrades.

"Kitch."

"Yeah?"

"Kitch, somebody's layin' on top of a berm way over there!"

"Where?"

Weaver pointed towards the pivot of our patrol. "Over there! He isn't movin' at all! He has brown hair. I think it's Tremaine! It looks like Tremaine!"

I glanced up and noticed a body slumped on a berm with its limbs diffused. There was so much smoke and debris in the area that it was impossible to discern who the person was but it definitely wasn't a VC.

"No! No! No!" I said. "It's not Tremaine!"

"How the fuck do you know?"

"Because I know!"

"It looks like Tremaine! The guy has brown hair!"

"I don't give a fuck! It's not Tremaine!"

"Fuck you, Kitch!" Weaver scolded as he looked at the sky. "Kitch! Look! The gunships!"

I squinted upward. Two swirling Cobras. It seemed like an eternity, but finally they made their first attack run. Weaver and I laid on our backs. We watched the sleek, yard-wide gunships as they whizzed into our faces to engage the hedgerow. Their initial barrage of rockets landed well beyond the VC. On the second sweep one Cobra hit the target. Diagnosing their range, the choppers assailed the treeline.

Under the bombardment of the rockets, we cowered into the earth. One shell missed the hedgerow and detonated on the other side of our berm. The universe became a flash of dead white light, a gray instant of silent nothingness. I was closer to the explosion than Weaver and its impact hoisted me several inches off the ground. It sent me reeling, screaming.

"Kitch, Kitch, are you all right? Are you all right?"

Weaver's frantic yelps told me I was alive. "I-I-I think so."

Dazed but unharmed, I gathered my rifle and ammo and braced for another rocket. We had waited and pleaded for the gunships to assist us. Now we desired nothing more than for them to leave. Our aspirations were realized. After that nearly fatal assault, the Cobras evaporated into the smoke-engulfed sky.

In their wake three Huey choppers, the ones which always took us on Eagle Flights, loomed above. Unarmed with rockets, these ships made their runs with the doorgunners furnishing the fireworks. Again we shifted onto our backs and observed the gunships as they raked the hedgerow with machine guns.

One doorgunner was firing so intently that he was precariously hanging out of the chopper. With only his toes edging the chopper floor and his hands locked onto his sixty, he protruded himself into virtual thin air to help us. Certainly an All Pro in what the flyboys called "air follies," we were mesmerized by the doorgunner's ardor and marksmanship.

When their ammunition was consumed the Hueys scattered into the stench-filled atmosphere. After the smoke dissipated Weaver and I peered hopefully over our meager berm. In seconds we had our answer. Waiting for some bobbing heads, our wily opponents, including the VC barricaded before us, dispensed an avalanche of lead over the once peaceful paddy.

"Well, what the fuck do we do now?" Weaver said.

"One fuckin' thing for sure, Weaver, this sure ain't no Disneyland out here today!" I said, referring to Weaver's home state.

"How the fuck can you joke around at a time like this? Never mind fuckin' Disneyland!"

"I don't fuckin' know! I guess it's how I try to control my fuckin' nerves!"

"Fuck you! I'm gettin' out of here!"

"Where you headin', Weaver, Disneyland?"

I reloaded my piece. When I finished firing I looked around for Weaver. He was gone. I peeked over the berm to see Foos. There wasn't a trace of him. Either he was only wounded and he had crawled away, or during the gunship storm he was blown to pieces.

Realizing that I was alone, I wasn't in any mood for wisecracks. Panicky, I glanced in the direction of the man with brown hair to see if he was still on the berm. As I did so, three AK-47 bullets kissed the top of my dike only inches from my eyes. The impact of the slugs spewed dirt into my face.

Overcome with the terrible sensation of not knowing what was going to occur next, I covered my head with my hands. I hugged the ground and heard the earpiercing chatter of a machine gun. I heard bullets slice the air overhead, then crackle through the palms and bamboo. I could feel my heart thumping against the Vietnamese soil. Since the arc of fire of my foe before me couldn't reach me, that meant someone else had me in their gunsights, which meant there were still at least two VC alive. I understood that if I made an incorrect decision now it would be my last mistake. It would be my final anything, ever.

I was too afraid to try to scramble away like Weaver. I inserted another clip into my sixteen and fired again at the bunker in front of me. I glimpsed over the berm. The Kalashnikov muzzle was still ominously shifting from side to side like a Cyclopean eye.

Sick to my stomach, I burrowed into my helmet wishing I could shrink small enough to fit my entire torso into it. My adrenalin was pumping so furiously that I felt my body drifting in it. How long, I debated in an instant, could one swirl in that stuff before you collapsed?

I felt very hot. Heat currents danced around me. I felt myself literally boiling. I looked to my side. Some weeds were burning right next to me! I scouted about. The parched paddy was inflamed in several places! In the intense heat of the firefight some reeds had burst into flames. *Oh God,* I thought, *I've survived VC bullets and American rockets only to be burnt to death!* Terrified, I smothered the conflagration beside me with my leg, singeing my pants.

The idea of capture haunted me. I was alone, exposed. If any lurking VC got the drop on me I'd either be a KIA or a POW. In training they had advised us to try to escape as soon as possible after capture. The theory was that the longer the VC had you, the fewer chances you'd have to flee. So if the unthinkable happened, I resolved to escape at the first opportunity.

The morbid thoughts proliferated. Since the shooting had tapered off into only sporadic bursts, perhaps the platoon had withdrawn a considerable distance pending another Cobra sortie. Or worse yet, maybe an air strike was imminent, an eventuality which would definitely eliminate me. Perhaps I was already considered killed or lost by my allies. In the confusion maybe I was just plain forgotten. Hadn't I forgotten about Foos, a man right in front of me?

I realized probably the best formula to solve my problem would be to sneak backwards to the ditch we had crossed what seemed like eons ago. But I was too terrified to move. Thus far I had endured the battle where I was. What would it be like in another place on that godless paddy?

I knew time was on my side. Sooner or later the VC would either be killed or retire into the hinterlands. We had been enlightened at Polk that if you survived the initial thirty seconds of an ambush, your odds of outlasting the competition were outstanding. Of course, the instructor had neglected to edify us about what you're supposed to do if you're still alive after the opening thirty seconds and ensnared in a crossfire. If I abandoned the berm, perhaps the fellow who had me pinpointed would have an unobstructed line of fire. I resolved not to move unless the situation absolutely dictated it.

Somewhat rejuvenated, I jammed another magazine into my weapon. As I prepared to fire, a familiar voice called.

"Kitch, Kitch, you okay?"

It was Reynolds. I told him I was coping. He smiled. "Great! What are you doin' over here by yourself?"

His last few words were muffled by an earth-shattering explosion. More automatic rifle fire erupted.

"I don't know. But I'm sure glad to see somebody!"

I relayed to him what had transpired. I alerted him to the two villains entrenched before us. "Let's just keep firin'!" was his reply.

"There's one good thing we can say about all this," I said after firing. "At least we won't have to pull any LPs tonight!" Reynolds frowned. "I mean, after all this shit today they won't be sendin' us on LPs tonight!"

I was effecting the colossal assumption that we'd be airlifted out of the area once we quit the battle. And once back at Jackson they surely wouldn't inflict LP assignments on the First. After fighting on our bellies all afternoon, how could we be expected to pull LPs?

"Probably not, Kitch. But don't bet on nothin' in this damn Army!"

A voice hailed our names from somewhere behind us.

"It's Taylor!" barked Reynolds.

"Reynolds! Kitch!" Taylor yelled again with cupped hands. With three belts of sixty rounds slung over his shoulders, he had lugged his machine gun up to the canal fifteen meters behind us. "Y'all have to get the fuck out of there right now! Some tanks are comin' and they're gonna blow this spot of Nam! Start movin' back! I'll cover you!"

I gawked at Reynolds. He rubbed his eyes, thinking. "It's now or never time, Kitch! Let's go! I'll try it first!"

"R-R-Roger! I'll cover you!"

I shoved home another clip. Reynolds left and I fired at the elusive Communist before me. As Reynolds crept rearwards Taylor scoured the hedgerow with his sixty, firing right over our heads. I glanced over my shoulder and noticed Reynolds drop out of sight ten meters behind me. Taylor roared at me to get moving. Confused as to what had happened to Reynolds, I waved at Taylor, put in a fresh magazine, grasped my ammo sack, and slithered backwards. Under Taylor's cover I maneuvered back to the cavity into which Reynolds had vanished. It was a dried-up six-foot well. Reynolds was sitting on the bottom, reloading. I plunged in headfirst, nearly spearing myself on his rifle barrel.

"Welcome to the dungeon," he said. "Man, will you look at these fuckin' spiders! I wonder if these fuckers are poisonous?"

I flicked one of the vicious-looking creatures off my forearm. "Not as poisonous as the ones above us!"

The hollow was permeated with spiders of various sizes. It seemed as if every spider in that war-engulfed sector of Vietnam had retreated into the well, converting it into one gigantic spider-bunker. I'm normally intimidated by spiders with bodies as large as dimes but in this instance I felt a strange kinship with them. They were also being threatened by war.

Reynolds wiped a spider web away from his face. "I guess we should get our asses out of here before Taylor runs out of ammo but I sure hate to go back up there in the shit!"

"Yeah, I know. Let's spend the rest of the war in this hole."

Reynolds laughed. "Kitch, once Taylor opens up again I'm gonna ditty-mau!"

"Roger!"

Taylor began firing. "Here goes!" Reynolds said. He vaulted out of the pit and slinked to the canal. I clutched my equipment, said goodbye to a spider treading up the side of the well, and thrust myself out of the depression. Utilizing my Fort Bragg low-crawling technique, I squirmed back to the gully. I had always wondered why they made us do so much crawling in basic. Just as I rolled into the gorge, Taylor's sixty jammed.

"She's gone," he snorted. "Second barrel today. Kitch, let's get the fuck out of here!"

"Roger that!" I extended my hand. "And Taylor, thanks!"

"No sweat, man."

We wended our way down the ditch until we stumbled upon several members of the First. I yanked out my canteen. I sucked it dry. Warm water never tasted so good.

The spectacle in the canal was incredible; the battlefield had assumed an inanimate atmosphere. The Third, spearheaded by Duncan, Houston, and the CO, had inherited the bulk of the fighting. Meanwhile, the residue of First Platoon lounged between the walls of an empty aqueduct, each man dazed from a swipe with death.

Kilcurry, punctured in the thigh with shrapnel, lolled smoking and calmly holding a blood-drenched bandage to his wound. Trickles of blood streaked his leg. Next to him rested Foos. Sporting a bandage around his head, he was showing Rojas his helmet, which had a bullet hole through the top of it! I overheard Foos explain to a grim-faced Rojas that in the initial burst of VC fire he had been shot in the head. The slug had penetrated his helmet and grazed his scalp, rendering him unconscious. He recovered quickly, however, and crawled to the canal.

Weaver and Rickenbrode, both unscathed, squatted motionless, glowering at each other. Our new lieutenant, who had a head wound, sat benumbed. His huge teeth were chattering. Doc Addison, a personable youth of nineteen who had joined us in Tay Ninh, was next to Wortman. Doc was simultaneously crying and laughing as he searched his medical pouch for another bandage.

Realizing that my personal peril had diminished, my interest veered from my own welfare to that of my chums. A preliminary head count revealed there were many missing faces. I waddled to Kilcurry and asked him if he was okay. He peered at his injury with sad eyes. "Yeah, but it's startin' to stiffen up now."

"Kilcurry, there somebody lyin' out there on top of a berm. Who is it?"

"It's Dougherty. He's been up there a long time. I saw him and Sergeant Mortensen both get hit when the VC opened up. I think they're both dead."

Whew! I thought. *I knew it wasn't Tremaine!* "Where's everybody else?" I said impatiently, not really digesting the data I had just received. "Where's Tremaine?"

"He's okay. He was shot in the back of his leg near his ass but he'll be okay. He's already been dusted-off."

I was relieved to hear that Tremaine was okay. I started to question Kilcurry about the others who were truant when Reynolds jumped into the trench. Reynolds instructed Foos, Wortman and Kilcurry to hustle to the paddy where the dust-offs were landing. Another chopper would descend in less than one minute.

Doc Addison assisted the wounded to the PZ, then he sprinted back to the canal. Concluding that Doc would probably know the status of the others, I scuttled to him. He advised me that Padbury, Yerby, Jackel, Tremaine and Scherbarth had all been hit and evacuated. Jackel, shot twice in the back, was in the worst condition.

"Doc," I said, "Kilcurry told me that Dougherty and Mortensen are both dead. Is that true?"

Doc faltered and wiped away a tear. "Yeah. They're both dead."

"And Norton, where's he? Still out there with the Third?"

Doc looked at me with his moist blank eyes. "Didn't you hear?"

"Hear? Hear what? *What?*"

"Norton's dead too!"

"Dead?"

Norton dead? The sheer concept of it seemed impossible. To me Norton was indestructible, bigger than life. How could this be? This isn't so! There's a mistake!

"Are you sure? Are you sure? Did you *see* him?"

"Affirmative!" Doc sobbed as tears of truth streaked down his cheeks. He paused a moment, wiped the droplets, and sucked in air. "Norton's dead! He got shot in the neck a few times. Jackel and Norton were pinned down for a long time. I was way behind them. Norton finally had enough, and he screamed at Jackel that he was goin' to "Shag ass." I heard him say it. He stood up and started runnin'. He didn't get three meters. A gook was waitin' for him and he cut him down. All he had to do was to stay low and crawl out of there but he stood up! What a dumb ass! And now he's dead!"

Doc's exposition left him gasping. I was numb with astonishment. I felt light-headed. My stupor was fractured when Taylor knifed into the canal. "The tanks are here! The tanks are here! We've all got to get out of here right now!"

Collecting our weapons, we vacated the ravine and retreated into the open paddy. There we joined Tex and Splash and the others who hadn't been wounded. We took cover behind a sizable berm.

Next I did something that I had always considered taboo: I asked another soldier for water. I chose Calhoun as my victim. His canteen was nearly empty but he tossed his supply to me without hesitation. I gulped down all but a swallow. I flipped the container back to him. He lobbed it back to me. "Finish it," he said.

I downed the last of his water. My thirst was insatiable. Next I torpedoed Ramirez, another Tay Ninh recruit. He reluctantly cast his canteen to me. When he did so, he dropped his ammo bundle. The bag was nearly full. I hurled his canteen back at him.

"You lousy son-of-a-bitch!" I screeched.

"What?"

"What the fuck you doin' with a full ammo pack, you fuckin' bastard? We got three guys dead and a whole dust-off full of wounded and you got a full ammo pack! What the fuck you doin' with it? Don't you know some of 'em magazines might have saved the dead guys?"

Ramirez went to sling his canteen back at me. Seething, I started for him when Taylor leaped between us. He told me to shut up. He ordered Ramirez to take "his sorry Mexican ass" down to the end of our line. Taylor, perceiving that I was losing control, admitted that I was right but to take it easy. Relax. Cool it. Bitching at each other wouldn't bring back the dead.

My outburst had obvious foundations. The whole ordeal: heat, terror, injuries, explosions, screams, rockets, death, thirst, fire, gunships, and fatigue. I had difficulty focusing my eyes, controlling my balance. I saw everything through a swirling, satanic, blurred, infrared film—a bloodswirl. Down, down I went, like a runaway elevator. I felt close to going under, to letting my rage, frustration, and sorrow spew forth unchecked. Then Reynolds announced that the tanks were ready for action.

"Be ready for any VC tryin' to run off!" my squad leader alerted.

Jamming on my emotional brakes, I shifted my attention to the tanks. Like gargantuan beetles, two tanks propelled across the canal and fired into the VC positions. The tanks withdrew. The Third moved in. It was over. Two VC bodies were recovered, battered beyond recognition. Two valiant but doomed subterranean warriors had ambushed twenty-two Americans, killing or wounding exactly half. Despite our superior arsenal it took us nearly three hours to subdue our foe. Ho Chi Minh could be proud of his two guerrilla heavyweights.

The tanks rumbled away. The battlefield lapsed into a bizarre hush, the soft wind moaning in pain as it did at Brandywine, Shiloh, Chateau-Thierry, Tarawa, and every field of hell in history. A dismal haze of smoke hovered over the paddy. The stench of cordite, sweat and burnt earth permeated everything.

The Third placed our three deceased comrades on stretchers and hauled them to a clearing beyond the canal. A dust-off arrived to evacuate the KIA's. Reynolds, who was now commanding the First, requested assistance in loading our dead onto the chopper. Taylor, Rojas, myself and some others responded.

I drifted to the bodies. Although ponchos were spread over the upper half of each man, I recognized Norton. He still had a gas mask attached to his hip; he was among the few men in the First who always carried one. We seized the litters and toted the blood-saturated soldiers to the dust-off. I helped carry Dougherty. It was a long trek. The gale from the chopper's rotary flipped over the ponchos covering the faces of the dead. Dougherty's blue eyes were locked open. His face was frozen in the same terror he had showed on the flight to battle.

Enfeebled from our long ordeal, we struggled to elevate the stretchers onto the airship. A corpsman bounded off the chopper and helped us to hoist the dead aboard.

We backstepped from the aircraft. Stunned beyond words, we stood like statues while the dust-off rose and flew off to Graves Registration in Cu Chi. Cloaking our eyes and squinting into a sinking red disk, we followed the chopper until it eclipsed the horizon. Reynolds was first to crack the trance. "There's nothin' more to do," he choked. "Let's get back to the berm."

Separately we turned and tramped back to our positions. As I trudged along I pondered how the fate of my mates would be described in the casualty figures for the operation. Light? Medium? Heavy? Light to medium? Medium to heavy? And did it really matter? No. Because to me fatalities were no longer inanimate statistics. They were real people whom I had known in life and death. In my grieving heart they were as vivid and potent as their blood and dead weight.

Back at the berm we were ordered to gather the equipment strewn about during the battle. This accomplished, we were shepherded into the boundless terrain where we had landed earlier. We thought we'd be splintering into groups to await the choppers. Instead we were commanded to assume a defensive stance.

As we waited for the next earthquake of danger to rattle us, I noticed how much my body was trembling. My knees were shaking the most. The last occasion I could recall them vibrating as much as they were now was back in high school when I had to deliver a speech before forty classmates. *Oh God,* I thought, *only to be back in school or anywhere but on this dreadful paddy waiting for who knows what.* Kneeling behind the berm, out of water, exhausted, expecting the VC at any moment to burst out like bats fleeing a cave, rumor circulated that we were going to spend the night in the paddy.

Rumors. In Vietnam you educated yourself not to believe any rumors. Unfortunately, this rumor had a factual basis. Battalion ordered DeFreeze and his two platoons to entrench themselves for the night. Enemy activity was accelerating all over III Corps. With hordes of VC evidently in our area, our warlords had decided to entice the VC into a raid against a hastily-constructed, undermanned perimeter. Once the gullible VC attacked they would be exposed on the open paddy. Gunships and artillery from Jackson would massacre them.

As daylight settled into dusk, a flurry of choppers arrived with sandbags, ammo, shovels, C-rations, water, wire—everything except the one thing we most desired: another company to replace us. The tools were distributed and the First was appointed to construct three bunkers. Like glum chain-gang prisoners, we chopped into the hardened soil. No one spoke. The eerie, hypnotic reports of our implements were the only sounds echoing through the idyllic evening.

Fatigued and depressed over our paltry progress in establishing a perimeter, I took a break to reload my empty magazines. I was resting on an ammo box when Reynolds approached, looking grim. "Kitch, I got some bad news for you."

I shook my head no. I knew it. LP time. My quivering, which had subsided somewhat, resumed its prior intensity. "You want me to go out on an LP."

"Roger, Kitch. Sorry. But not only do I want you to go out, I want you to take it out."

"What?"

"There's nobody else to do it. I know you can handle it. You'll be takin' Splash and Rooks with you and you only have to go about a hundred meters."

"Why the fuck does the First have to pull an LP?"

"I guess because the Third is pullin' the other two. Don't ask me. I don't say what platoon pulls what!"

"Why do *I* have to go then?"

"Because it's our squad's turn, that's why!" He mopped his brow with a slimy rag I had used to wipe my rifle. "Don't worry about any GI's firin' on you. You'll be right out in front of this bunker. Report to the CP now. The arty officer wants to talk to you." He flipped the rag to me and strolled off.

Disbelief. Self-pity. Splash and Rooks? Fuck! I felt squeamish about chaperoning those two no matter what type of operation I was effecting. Splash's reputation as a triple A flake was still intact. I knew what to expect from him. Rooks, a quiet man from Illinois, was suspected by some to be unreliable. They were third stringers on any team but I'd have to depend on them.

As I started for the CP I heard someone yell, "Gooks! Gooks!"

Everyone traded spades for weapons. Sergeant Houston, the person who had detected the VC parading through a distant hedgerow, pounced on a sixty and blitzed the treeline. Under a barrage of bullets the VC scattered. The presence of VC in that particular hedgerow had a striking import to me. It was in the exact direction I was taking the LP!

Cursing and dejected, I roamed to the CP. There the young artillery officer was poring over a map. The lieutenant looked up tentatively when he heard me approach. "Are you the guy from the First who's taking out the LP?"

"Roger."

"Did the platoon leader show you where you're going?"

"No."

"Okay, look here." He turned the map so I could see it. "We are here. You're supposed to go here. It's about a hundred meters out. The nearest hedgerow will be almost another hundred meters away."

"You mean the hedgerow where Houston just saw the gooks?"

"Roger that." He kept his eyes on the plastic-covered map. "We'll be firing recon rounds from Jackson into it all night."

I scratched my head and carefully said, "Sir, I know I'm supposed to go a hundred meters. But I don't know about that shit. My knees are still shakin' over what happened today. Man, I'm scared shitless over what might happen here tonight."

The officer peered at the darkening sky. It was his manner of remitting attention by looking away. He shoveled back his thick black hair with his hands. "Okay, you're supposed to go a hundred meters. How far *are* you going to go?"

Hey, I thought, *this officer is hip!* "Sir, I'm goin' out fifty meters and then I'm gonna set up behind the first berm I can find!"

"Okay, okay, that's all I need to know. I just want to be sure where you're going to be in case we get in the shit and we have to drop some arty around you."

I shivered with horror over his remark. "Thanks, lieutenant." The officer nodded and burrowed his eyes into his map. I trooped back to the platoon thinking, *What a time and place to be commanding my first night patrol!* LPs at Reed now seemed like Boy Scout outings.

Our fear surged as the inescapable darkness, like a fiendish shroud of death, slowly engulfed us. How erroneous were my earlier predictions to Reynolds that we'd be rewarded for our hardships by relaxing on the bunkerline at Jackson. Not only were we marooned in this hazardous locality, but I had to go on an LP! *Would this nightmare ever end?* I wondered. *And what would the LP be like tonight? Live VC stalking in a hedgerow only a hundred meters from my LP! And only three of us on the LP! Rooks and Splash? Fuck!* Ultra was hustling on all cylinders.

Under the glow of flares we slaved on the bunkers. The luminosity from the aerial torches would breed flitting shadows, shifting light. Was that silhouette over there a lurking VC? And that profile out there, was that the enemy or a friendly working on the perimeter? Dread buried our souls. With one eye on our shovels and the other eye on the darkness, we slogged away, not knowing if some intrepid VC was preparing to pop us on the head with a Chicom grenade. If you were a night person, an individual who liked dark, scary places, then nighttime in suburban Vietnam was for you.

Finally the last flare fizzled out. Total darkness came. Work stopped. It was time for the LPs to leave. As I donned the radio I advised Reynolds that I was going only fifty meters or so. He winked and told me not to take any chances and not to fret about another Aires debacle because he'd make certain we'd be recalled if anything nasty developed.

Splash and Rooks came over. I made sure they had claymores, hand flares, grenades, and full ammo packs. I radioed to the CP that we were leaving. Clicking my sixteen off safety, I pioneered the trail through the two rings of concertina. We marched fifty meters through absolute darkness. We didn't even have starlight to help us; a blanket of clouds had rolled in. I foraged for a satisfactory place to pass the night. Much to my horror there wasn't one instantly visible. I strained through the inky blackness to see a berm, a mound, a hole, anything to give us shelter without advancing closer to the hedgerow. We tiptoed on. Each fleeting step took us farther from the potential deliverance of the wire, paces perhaps we'd have to retrace while under fire.

Furious that I already had gone farther than I desired, I halted. I knelt and forced my eyes to see in the dark. Splash, the Bedouin who liked to cruise back into the perimeter by himself, squirmed up next to me.

"Kitch," he whispered, "we've gone too far already. Let's get back some!"

"Shusss," I murmured harshly, putting my finger over my lips. "Shut up and wait here!"

I crept a few meters onward. I thought I saw a berm just ahead. I snooped three meters more. Yes! A berm—a tiny one but still a berm! There was even a slight depression adjacent to it! Sighing relief, I jumped into the cavity and looked around. It was a puny dike but it would have to suffice. Tramping farther from the wire was simply inconceivable.

I jaunted back to Splash and Rooks. We rushed into the hollow and quickly dispersed five claymores. My partners grumbled something about what a marginal post I had selected. When I asked if one of them would volunteer to scout ahead for a superior location, their complaining ceased.

I assumed first guard while my two compatriots lapsed into a restless sleep. Settled down and under sixty-five meters from the perimeter, I relaxed somewhat. My mind drifted to what had transpired that horrible day. I tried not to think about it. *Forget it. Concentrate on the problem at hand,* I goaded myself. But that was impossible. As I peered into the Far Eastern sootiness, I saw the face of Dougherty when he had looked at me on the chopper. I realized now that his face had emitted more than simply raw terror. His look was that of a man who was also ill-fated, lost, already dead. *I had been staring at a dead man! No! Ridiculous! Over-reaction, Kitch. Man, you're letting this shit get to you! It's over! Forget how he looked at me!* Routed and confused, I gazed into the night, trying to forget, hoping it would all go away, wishing I was anywhere but trapped in a war, praying I'd never glimpse another mosaic of death.

A breeze rustled some reeds. Since my clothes were sweat-drenched, the draft chilled me. I reached for my poncho liner. It was back at Jackson. Then I recalled that there were worse things than being chilled. At that very moment other men in green uniforms weren't only cold, but rigid. I turned up my shirt collar and fended off the chill.

My shift expired. I aroused Splash. Mumbling incoherently, he exchanged places with me. I gave him the wristwatch and radio microphone. I stretched out, using my steel pot as a pillow. But my eyes wouldn't close. I was still too overwhelmed from the events of the day. Also I didn't trust my two associates not to fall asleep. So throughout my confederates' sentinel duty I remained awake, hypnotized by the glittering nuggets now peeking over dispersing clouds and pondering topics like, Where was Norton now? It seemed like a dream when I saw a dull purple line forming above the eastern horizon. Singly the stars winked off. Soon a pink mantle swelled across the sky, gradually evaporating into a pearly sheen. I woke my two mates, one of whom was supposed to be on guard. We collected our gear and left for the wire. Just as the tip of a fiery wafer singed the horizon, we hit the perimeter.

After a listless breakfast of C-rations, DeFreeze announced that we had ten minutes to saddle up. First and Third Platoons were going to sweep a region south of yesterday's firefight. In order to dissolve our perimeter, two men from each platoon were needed to stay behind. Since I had pulled the LP, Reynolds asked me if I'd like to abstain. Learning from my blunders, I accepted. So Rooks, two men from the Third and I drudged through the morning emptying sandbags, rolling up wire, and gathering equipment.

About midmorning small arms fire erupted in the hedgerow complex where our comrades were working. There was a plethora of shooting and shouting. We could see our troops moving along the treeline. Alarmed, Rooks and I scampered to the CP where they had a radio. Our pointmen had surprised two VC perched on a log, laughing and munching rice. Under a volley of slugs the VC dived into their warren. An interpreter tried to lure them out. When they failed to respond, grenades were heaved into their asylum.

This time there were no injuries for the First. It was a distinct victory for the visiting team. But there was no jubilation as the men of the First wobbled into the dismantled base later that morning. Only the consciousness of surviving yet another contest embellished their faces. In victory and in defeat combat veterans all wear the same stunned look of survival, the universal mask of war.

Satisfied with the results of the brief operation, battalion ordered DeFreeze's platoons back to Jackson. We saddled up, gathering the weapons of our dead and wounded. By coincidence I drew Norton's rifle. I recognized it by the unusual sling he used; it was a seven clip bandoleer which he had fashioned into a comfortable strap. Inside one of the clip chambers was an oily shaving brush, a device which we used to whisk our weapons. Holding Norton's sixteen saddened me. Desiring to keep a remembrance of him, I pocketed the shaving brush. In the peculiar way that mementos mollify us, the brush helped to soothe my grief.

We lined up for our air chariots. As we waited on berms a passenger jet flew over. En route to Penang or Bangkok or wherever, these airliners would often soar over our field positions and ignite pangs of jealousy, hope, sorrow, glee, and self-pity. It seemed cruel to taunt us like that. Overhead, only a few thousand feet distant, was an air-conditioned tube complete with English-speaking women transporting soldiers away from the war.

While the First watched the jet disappear into a wisp of clouds near the sun, we heard the hum of our flotilla. Choppers had never sounded so good to us. Soon they landed and with immeasurable relief we boarded our airships and departed that terrible place.

As the remnants of the First wearily tottered through the Jackson wire, each of us encumbered with extra weapons, our clothes and bodies reeking, our ears ringing from the firefight, our minds dulled by shock, the first thing we heard as we approached the bunkerline was the familiar American Forces Vietnam Network. With the stereophonic effect from all the Jackson radios playing on the same channel, welcoming us home was the song of the year from the Broadway musical *Hair*, "Aquarius/Let the Sunshine In," sung by the 5th Dimension. The bunkerline rocked with lyrics announcing the new generation of "Aquarius," a new era of love for all mankind, a new age of lasting peace.

15

A Booby Trap

Some days after the March 28 ambush, First and Third platoons were again airlifted to the Boi Loi Woods, the place of the attack. Our daylight sweep was routine, which was salient to the First because we were the point platoon all day. We had two scout dogs working with us, one to a platoon. Two men from the First marched behind the handler in a sort of triangular formation, hoping the dog would find the VC or their traps before any humans did. The territory we searched was purportedly booby-trapped. But neither man nor beast discovered any traps.

The next day all of Bravo returned to the area to pull a night ambush. The afternoon patrol concluded once we traversed a lengthy swamp. The trek was strenuous, especially for dogs. The mud was knee high. The heat was insufferable; it took nearly three hours for the company to cross the swamp. One of the dogs, upon successfully fording the bog, collapsed and died of heart seizure. The dead mutt—and distraught handler—were dusted-off.

The remaining handler, a conceited individual from Rhode Island, assured us that no VC could creep up on our ambush site without his dog giving an alert. Weren't German shepherds excellent watchdogs? And *his* dog was the best scout dog in the Army. Convinced that the handler knew the capabilities of his canine, that night after my guard shift I slept well.

As the morning sun charred the horizon we deactivated our ambush. *Whew,* I thought, *another night without incident!* After a C-ration meal, DeFreeze radioed to Reynolds that the First would take point for the day patrol. Our mission was to sweep a village three clicks distant. We were to have lunch under the palms in the village, then be extracted and returned to Jackson. It was a brief, standard assignment. The only complication was that the area was booby-trapped. I felt queasy when I gazed out at the countless rows of berms we had to cross before entering the hamlet.

When the order came to form up, Reynolds, Nash, myself and others grumbled about our predicament. We were fuming over again having to assume point. Still reeling from the ambush, our morale and efficiency— not to mention our numbers—were plummeting. There were only sixteen of us left in the platoon.

Reynolds petitioned the captain for permission for us to take the rear, at least for this hazardous operation. Permission was denied. Swearing and growling, we assembled. Reynolds selected Tex and Mabry to accompany the handler on point. The balance of Bravo was dispersed, as usual, in two parallel rows. I was pointman for the left column. Nash headed the right.

We advanced across the paddies, carefully negotiating each berm. My sixth sense again skipped before my eyes. Waves of fear thundered in my head. DeFreeze kept ordering us to accelerate because we were falling behind schedule; we'd be tardy for the rendezvous with the choppers.

Reynolds dutifully relayed this data to Nash. "Tell the fuckin' CO," Nash hollered, "I've got one hundred and ninety-six days and I'm not in any hurry! And Reynolds, if he doesn't like the fuckin' way I'm walkin' point he can get somebody else to do it!"

Reynolds laughed. He knew we were snaking toward the village slower than necessary. We did this to vent our displeasure over being assigned point. We felt the selection was a penalty for having stumbled into the recent ambush. But was the ambush the First's fault? Some in Bravo thought the CO was responsible because we should've been on-line instead of in our usual columns. That would've increased firepower and probably reduced casualties. Tactics made a difference.

Our present tactics were simple: take it slow, keep alert, and keep apart. I'd occasionally peer back at DeFreeze. He'd be pacing back and forth with one hand on his .45, glaring at us.

The closer we came to the village, the more suspicious the berms looked. Finally the point team signaled a halt. Ahead was a mean-looking dike, abnormally high, with bushes and tall reeds riveting the place where we had to cross. The dog handler requested recon fire. Weaver popped some rounds. There were no secondary explosions. DeFreeze waved us on. The point crew approached the berm. The silver and black dog sniffed a few moments, then leaped over the berm. The handler placed one foot on the dike and when he lifted his other foot a detonation torpedoed the morning stillness. The air screamed with shrapnel. I reeled around, simultaneously stooping and covering my face. I turned back to the berm. The pointmen were scattered across the paddy, wailing, grasping their legs. I dropped my helmet, rifle and ammo pack and raced to them. Mabry appeared to be hurt the worst. I knelt next to him and stripped his gear. His bleatings deafened me. Doc Addison rushed forward and tended to Tex's thigh and knee. Seconds later the CP medic bounded to the scene. He ripped off Mabry's shredded pants and applied a bandage to a nasty gash on one calf.

"You jackass!" the sergeant snarled at me while he worked.

"What? Whatta you mean?"

"Jerk, you're not supposed to run up to the wounded when somebody hits a trap! That's my job! What if there were more traps here, you shit-bird? You should just call for a medic and wait!"

"Fuck you, sergeant! I'm sorry if I broke the rules! But I just couldn't watch 'em scream and bleed while I waited for you to get up here!"

The sergeant gave me a fierce stare. "I know that, man. Just don't get in the habit of taking chances you don't have to take." He wiped sweat from his brow. "Help me with this other leg."

Mabry was groaning, writhing. He asked for something to clench his teeth on. I yanked out a putrid handkerchief. He rammed it into his mouth.

"Hold this leg up while I wrap some bandages around it," the medic said.

Mabry's entire leg was saturated with blood. I winced, hesitated.

"Lift his leg, goddamnit! It's only blood!"

I grabbed it. Mabry's warm crimson fluid quickly covered my hands and streaked down my forearms. Blood everywhere. So much blood it was impossible to tell the number of wounds. I looked away while the Doc did his job.

"Okay, man," the sergeant said, "I got it. Thanks."

I squirmed over to Tex. Doc Addison had just finished bandaging Tex's knee. It didn't look too bad. Not much blood compared to Mabry. Tex mumbled that his ankles were stinging. Doc removed his boots and socks. Thick droplets of scarlet blood bubbled from holes in both ankles. Neat little drops, like those released from an eye dropper. Doc went to work.

I drifted out of the way. The dog handler was sitting on the deadly berm, smoking, holding a compress to his knee. Rin Tin Tin cuddled at his feet, licking his paws. I wondered if in the future the handler would still be bragging about his dog.

"Is it bad?" I asked.

He forced a smile. "No. It doesn't hurt much."

"Did the dog get hit?"

"No, not a scratch."

"Who hit the trap?"

"I did."

"How come the dog didn't pick it up?"

The handler shrugged and looked away.

Once the dust-off arrived several of us helped the medics load our wounded onto the chopper. Mabry was in tremendous pain. As we settled him onto the floor of the aircraft he laid back, eyes closed, still biting the rag. The chopper rose and Tex flashed the peace sign and a slight grin. His war was over. We waved back. I wished Tex and Mabry luck, friendship, and a long and happy life.

Disheveled and trembling, I staggered back to my position at the head of the column. I wiped my hands and arms on my shirt and pants. Mabry's blood had begun to dry under my fingernails. As I gathered my gear a simmering fury ruptured inside me. *How much more of this insanity were we supposed to endure?* I wondered. It was mind-clogging, unbelievable. Neither Tex nor Mabry had been involved in the March ambush. They were spared that tragedy only to hit a trap days later. *Why, why, why? How much longer will I escape injury? Christ, how many days left?* I sat in the brain-frying heat counting the months, then the days. *Too many days. Far too many.*

While all this was happening Reynolds had conferred with the balance of the platoon. He had decided that the First wouldn't take point for the remainder of the operation. It was time to draw the line. He lumbered to me. "Kitch, once DeFreeze tells us to move out, I want you to stand fast."

Now there was an order I could handle. "Okay."

Time to go came. DeFreeze ordered us to step out. Reynolds cooly requested that the First assume the rear. The CO refused. An argument erupted. Reynolds insisted our unit needed a reprieve. He emphasized that the other platoons had double our numbers. He said he couldn't stand to see the First lose more men. The CO trooped about, cursing and snorting, red-faced, pounding on the holster of his .45. He called forward the other platoon leaders. He asked if one of them would volunteer their unit to walk point. They refused. Since DeFreeze didn't want to lose face with Reynolds, he hesitated from ordering one of the other platoons to relieve the First.

At this strategic juncture the artillery officer proposed that DeFreeze call battalion and recommend that we terminate the operation. The lieutenant said the CO could inform battalion that in the captain's knowledgeable opinion the area wasn't worth investigating. Besides, the officer discreetly injected, *all* of us would have to journey through the booby-trapped terrain, and *none* of us were enthusiastic about it. DeFreeze, perhaps sensing a physical as well as a professional catastrophe, relented. He radioed his commander. To everyone's unmitigated shock, permission to terminate the operation was extended. Within thirty minutes we were airborne for Jackson. The traps would have to wait for another day and another unit.

DeFreeze seemed jovial about the turn of events, apparently satisfied that he had eluded a showdown with the First. We were grateful to Reynolds for his grit and determination. Since I would've been the pointman had we continued, I was especially appreciative.

Even the loss of Tex and Mabry couldn't deflate our exuberance with our victory in the battle of nerves with the Army. Within minutes we had gone from the agony of despair over the injuries to our friends to the ecstasy of threatening mutiny and getting away with it. We had stood up to them! We had won! First Platoon returned to Jackson that day brimming with confidence and ebullience – all fourteen of us.

16

Diamonds

For the ensuing two weeks we continued operations out of Jackson. Except for an occasional mortar deluge, which to us four or five month veterans was now blasé, we had no enemy contact.

Some of our wounded returned to the field. Tremaine, who had been shot in the fleshy portion of his thigh, reported healed and threatening to re-up. Scherbarth had only a minor wound but he couldn't eat or sleep. He came to Jackson for a day which he spent heaving, trembling. He was quietly dispatched to Cu Chi and a supply room job. Padbury, who had taken shrapnel in his leg, returned bragging about sleeping twelve hours a day in Cu Chi. Foos and Wortman came to the field only to be allotted to the Third. Jackel, severely injured, was exported to a hospital in Japan, then rotated home. Yerby, who stuttered for a month after the ambush, was apportioned to a rear occupation. Weaver was also finished with infantry. He volunteered for duty as a chopper doorgunner, concluding that life in that capacity posed fewer risks than service with Bravo.

The principal strife in the Wolfhounds' theater of operations now shifted to the territory along the Cambodian frontier known as the "Angel's Wing." The Angel's Wing was a segment of Cambodia which jutted into Vietnam in the contour of an angel's wing. Alpha and Delta companies were airlifted to within a mile of the border. They established three bases in the middle of enemy infiltration routes. Since American progress in the war was being calibrated by body counts, Diamonds I, II, and III, as these perimeters were known, were built to tempt the VC into major battles. Of course, the price of the strategy—American lives—was computed to be worth the harvest in VC corpses.

The anticipated onslaughts materialized with hefty VC body counts. Through the grapevine evolved horror tales of what the guinea pigs in Alpha and Delta experienced at the Diamonds. At Diamond I the attackers were dispersed by hand-to-hand combat, a circumstance which dazed even the most swaggering soldier.

Even more tormenting were the Diamond listening posts. One night three LPs were diffused from Diamond III. A VC mortar foray drove two of the LPs back to the perimeter. The third LP was surprised and annihilated by a VC sapper unit advancing for its thrust on the base. Eight men from one platoon were killed.

All of this intelligence was sufficient to alarm even the most languid among us. Even Padbury wasn't sleeping well. Our Jackson operations were trivial compared to the activities at the Diamonds. Then our worst fears were realized. It was our turn. We'd relieve Delta Company at Diamond III.

The appointment terrified us. I was frightened to the extent that I again broke my sacred vow. I volunteered to carry the radio permanently. It was a tradition in Bravo that regular RTOs didn't participate on LPs. I calculated that by assuming this task I'd eliminate at least one hazardous type of mission once we got to Diamond III.

Also Kilcurry, who had recovered from his shrapnel wound and was awaiting assignment to a rear job, had returned to the platoon as the senior RTO. Thus I'd be the junior RTO. I'd toil with the platoon sergeant at the end of the formation. That was another plus.

Not having to participate on LPs or walk point on regular patrols seemed to compensate for the extra weight and responsibilities of the radio. I tried to ignore the fact that our RTOs had a high turnover in recent months.

On a cloudless, brilliant April morning we flew to Diamond III. Of the Diamonds, III was the nearest to the border, roughly a half mile from the vertex of the Angel's Wing. The terrain was arid, devoid of human habitation. Few hedgerows. Good visibility. It was scary to peer across the border into the notorious Communist sanctuary of Cambodia. The Diamond III bunkers were well-constructed. No doubt Alpha and Delta comprehended their roles as sacrificial lambs.

It was the height of the dry season. Diamond III lacked any natural source of shade. We improvised tents out of ponchos and poncho liners. But it seemed we were always in the sunshine. The blast furnace heat was so intense that by midmorning we could cook an egg on any metal object left in the sun. The water in our canteens would cool overnight. But by the first mouthful on a sweep the next morning the water would be warm; by lunchtime it would be hot.

Chinooks brought our supplies. As the choppers lowered they swirled the brownish-red dust of the torrid paddies into an aerial maelstrom. Wrapping towels over our heads, we dived into bunkers to escape the dust storm. We tried to protect our valuables—such as cameras—by storing them in plastic bags which the radio batteries came in. But it was impossible. The red powder infiltrated everywhere.

Diamond III was an incredible salad of dust, vastness, sun, and danger. And it was all ours.

Our initial patrol out of Diamond III was enlightening. Dangling from the concertina were hands, feet, pieces of flesh, and clothing. During the cleanup after the fight, the VC who had perished on the wire were ripped from it. Whatever portions that had clung to the concertina were left in place. Birds picked at the larger chunks. Strewn outside the perimeter were VC corpses putrefying under the sizzling sun. Scorched black and saturated with tiny white maggots, the bodies were bloated so much that it seemed they'd explode. Their faces were unbelievably distorted. As we meandered downwind from the cadavers the odor that slapped us was overwhelming.

A hundred meters from the wire we stumbled onto the location where Delta's eight-man LP had been killed. In the depression where the men had deployed were portions of clothing, metal fragments, and red-stained patches of earth. In our cleverest Monday morning quarterbacking, we evaluated how the tragedy must have occurred. It wasn't difficult to figure how a crafty enemy in the Vietnam blackness could sneak up on the GI's, lob explosives into the cavity, and dispatch one American squad.

A few hundred meters from our outpost we encountered recently-dug, shallow graves. DeFreeze, sensing a body count without firing a shot, ordered us to exhume some corpses to confirm that VC were in fact interred there. Holding handkerchiefs over our noses, like grave robbers we went to work on three tombs. A few inches down our spades hacked into decaying flesh, heads, arms, legs. We could tell what we had hit by the sound. A sharp crack meant bone; a dull thump meant flesh. Colonies of feasting maggots burst from the decaying meat and spilled over our jungle boots. We had to jump up and down and kick our feet to rid ourselves of the worms. The smell was so horrible and pungent that you knew the unmistakable stink of death would be with you forever.

No surprises, they were VC. We counted the remaining graves and reported nineteen kills to battalion. Our jubilant colonel recalled us. For our good work we were permitted to lounge in our Oriental paradise for the balance of the day.

Our first nights at our sweltering border camp were uneventful. Then intelligence revealed that the enemy was massing for another assault on Diamond III. We posted double sentries on each bunker rather than the usual one. Our alertness intensified.

One moonless night at about two-thirty everyone was awakened with harsh news. A ground attack was imminent. Radar had detected movement all around us. Thousands of VC and North Vietnamese troops ostensibly were in the area. By three o'clock our perimeter glowed from illumination. Cobras swirled above, firing into coordinates provided by our radar. Artillery cracked their payloads into the distant darkness. Three of Bravo's LPs, including one from the First, ratified movement through starlight scopes. One LP from the Second radioed that the enemy was on all sides except their rear. The sergeant commanding the patrol requested that they retire before it was too late. DeFreeze, after the usual grumbling, withdrew all of the LPs.

Those of us on the bunkerline were exultant to see our comrades sprint for the wire. It meant more safety for them and more weapons for us. We felt we'd need every rifle. After all, what were all those VC doing out there if they weren't going to attack?

There were five of us on my bunker. While the others hovered inside, Tremaine and I squatted behind the sandbag wall outside. We thought we'd have a better vantage point. We checked our claymore firing devices and made them handy. We stuffed our pockets with grenades. We loaded and reloaded our weapons. Everything was placed within arm's reach. Tremaine lined extra duper rounds on the ground in neat little rows.

For the ensuing hour we shivered in anticipation, horror. Of course, we had a distinct edge in firepower. But if our emplacements were breached, that advantage would be neutralized. On some bunkers there were only two or three men. A hand-to-hand situation could be ugly. The spirit of the bayonet. In training we thought it was all a big joke. The joke now was that we didn't even have bayonets.

Mosquitoes buzzed up my nose and into my ears. I couldn't find my bug juice. Rather than sneak to the other side of the bunker to get my canteen, I tried to appease my thirst by sucking the salty perspiration from around my mouth. My imagination stirred. I vividly pictured pajama-clad Orientals, armed with RPGs and AK-47s, huddled up to berms, ready, determined to slay American imperialists.

My fear was tumbling, landsliding. But it's amazing how coherent and alert you become when you're functioning as an energetic machine propelled by adrenalin. Tremaine and I strained to see into the darkness beyond the flares. We rehearsed what we'd do if we saw them coming. Once within claymore range, we'd ignite our mines. Then we'd click our weapons on rock 'n' roll and fire, fire, fire. We decided to husband our grenades until last.

A shaking lieutenant came by with orders not to open fire unless we had targets. If we saw a green star cluster we were to take cover inside the bunker. The cluster would be the signal that the VC had pierced the wire. Then our artillerymen would dip their muzzles and fire into the invading hordes with beehive rounds — projectiles that contained 8500 tiny metal arrows.

As our destiny hovered between a night of death and merely a false alarm, I scanned the perimeter. Hissing flares, spitting sparks and expelling a thin, dark tail of smoke, hung in the sky like miniature suns. Officers clutching pistols darted about giving orders, inspecting defenses. Some men cowered with their arms over their helmets. Trying to muffle the constant blasting of our ordnance, others plugged their ears but kept their eyes on the wire. And others—the totally fearless—walked around bunkers as if they were on a Sunday morning stroll.

But most of us scrunched behind our ramparts honed and poised, hoping something would happen, anything, just so the waiting would cease. "If they're comin', then why don't they just come!" I screeched loud enough so the men on adjacent bunkers turned and stared a moment.

As the hour bars of our watches crept to four it became apparent that we'd be spared from invasion. At four-fifteen it was relayed to all bunkers to resume normal guard duty. No further movement was being ferreted by radar.

With relief we discarded our firearms and collapsed to await dawn: the crowning benediction of another night concluded at war in Vietnam. The survival of that terrifying night only made each of us, in our shivering bodies and souls, more determined to live another day.

17

The Fifty Day Hard Spot

After that unsettling night in Diamond III, we dismantled the base. Like a customer dissatisfied with his purchase, the High Lamas of war decided to cash in Diamond III and construct Diamond IV. Diamond IV also proved to be disappointment for the tacticians because our duty there was without incident. By June 1 we were relocated to a site which we later christened the Fifty Day Hard Spot.

The Fifty Day Hard Spot was a company-sized perimeter we built in a hedgerow twenty-five meters square in an area of sparse population. It was a tight, secure outpost. We had only our mortar section as close fire support. Again we were in the pivot of an infiltration artery to the Saigon theater.

By this time the rainy season had commenced. As the monsoon opened late afternoon thunderstorms appeared and imperial warships traced eastward, dimming the greenery, jolting the earth with potent explosions, exhorting man and beast to scurry for shelter. The weather gradually deteriorated and more showers punctuated the day, the first storm usually sweeping over about midmorning. Then it rained every day, sometimes all day. The pattern was as timeless as strife in Vietnam. As one cloudburst tumbled away, another was fomenting on the horizon.

A swarm of new faces reported to the platoon. Much to our astonishment, Sergeant Houston and Lieutenant Duncan were transferred to the First. Duncan, a burly, competent, tight-lipped West Virginian was, unlike many officers, respected for his leadership. He was intelligent enough not to take needless chances.

Houston, no stranger to us, was a popular, capable E-6 with steel-blue eyes. Also esteemed as a leader, when he arched his eyebrows and focused his penetrating x-ray irises at you, only the most stalwart person could challenge him. He was tough but fair with everyone. He disliked the platoon's shammers—every unit had some—and he had little patience with them. Anyone who feigned illness or injury to avoid operations while in the field would draw Houston's ire. Malingerers only made things more difficult for everyone.

Meanwhile, three of my friends were leaving the First. Kilcurry, with his second Purple Heart in tow, was finally relieved of field duty and transferred to Long Binh to complete his tour. I was glad to see him get a safe rear job. His departure meant that I'd be the senior RTO. I'd work with Duncan.

Another emigrant was Reynolds. He was assigned to the Second as their platoon sergeant. After our Reynolds-led confrontation with DeFreeze over walking point, the CO had decided that Reynolds was too chummy with the men of the First—hence the customary military strategy of deporting organizers and potential troublemakers.

Taylor left the First for the best reason of all—DEROS. Although he had been wounded his first month in-country, Taylor went home healthy. Once he left, the First missed his humor and his expertise with the machine gun.

One evening the First was lounging behind a hedgerow waiting for dark so we could proceed to our ambush site. We had just finished eating C's. Everyone was relaxing. We had marched through a violent rainstorm to get to our holding location. Some men had their boots and clothes off, letting them dry. Others were clowning or sleeping, their weapons halfway down the treeline.

In the field we often let down our guard. We slept in the shade or showered at a well or a water-filled bomb crater without concern for the enemy. Despite our training and the obvious danger, sometimes we acted like we just didn't give a damn, which we didn't. Sometimes it was just too much trouble to remain alert.

Duncan and I were resting against a berm when I glanced over my shoulder. I saw a half-dozen individuals, crowned with saucer-like tan helmets, carrying weapons, bobbing across a paddy fifty meters distant.

"H-H-Hey look," I stuttered. "There's some people walkin' out there!"

"Christ, Kitch, they're gooks!" Duncan croaked. "And they're NVA! Everybody get down! Everybody get down!" I couldn't believe my eyes. The Phantoms of the Orient making a guest appearance directly before us. It would be a bloodbath, a St. Valentine's Day massacre!

Our hysterical shouts and our scrambling for weapons and gear alerted the North Vietnamese. Duncan crowed at us to get saddled up. Meanwhile the NVA sprinted for a treeline.

I donned my radio. Circling behind Duncan while he frantically organized the platoon, I notified DeFreeze back at the Hard Spot of our sightings. When we were all on-line, we coursed across the empty paddy. Tripping over berms and buttoning our fatigues, some of us without boots or ammo packs, we raced after the already-vanished NVA.

"Which way'd they go? Which way'd they go?" Duncan brayed, jerking his neck back and forth. Nobody knew. Not a round was fired. We lumbered back to our hedgerow, openly elated that our inefficiency had frightened off the enemy. DeFreeze radioed, "Way to go, First!"

The rain and mud at our Fifty Day encampment were our most persistent, exasperating foes. Each day our principal goal would be to try to remain dry for as long as possible. Worries about the VC became secondary. Sloshing along in a torrent on a sweep, we became soaked to the bone. Would our weapons function in the rain? It was irrelevant. Once we pivoted for the return hike home, we darted like lunatics trying to get out of the rain. We were saturated, tired, miserable, chilly, and no one cared about anything, even VC. We couldn't see much through the pelting rainstorms anyhow. Once we arrived at the perimeter we used the sun and wind to dry ourselves. If it rained again we tried to maintain our dryness by huddling in bunkers or under makeshift poncho tents. If we were lucky we stayed dry until the next operation.

If sweeps were horrendous in the muck and precipitation, night patrols were worse. On night missions first we had to slop through water-filled paddies to our ambush site, becoming drenched at least from the knees down. Then the ambush leader would try to find a dry location to set up. Dryness was the touchstone; cover and visibility were subordinate. But invariably we had to deploy in a wet paddy.

After you mounted your claymore on top of a berm, like a swimmer testing the water, you gently slid off your cover berm into the brown water. If you half-reclined on the dike, then you could remain dry from your chest up, provided of course it didn't rain. Ponchos were banned on night patrols because they emitted a glare when wet.

It's difficult to envision being cold in tropical Vietnam. But as you wallowed in the moisture, a numbing chill would envelop you. Before long you were shivering. All the same dictums applied as when you were on a dry season night mission: no ponchos because of the glare; no sitting on dikes because your silhouette would present a superb target; no standing because a friendly might mistake you for a VC; no sleeping on guard unless you welcomed the wrath of your buddies or, worse yet, a VC tiptoeing up to your position. But the regulations were often ignored. How could there be a greater punishment than infantry duty in Vietnam?

So you lay there in the darkness in your outdoor bathtub, fully clothed. I could never sleep when resting in cold water at night. But some men could. They draped poncho liners over their heads, arms and shoulders and somehow dozed off. Mind over matter. Padbury was an expert in this technique.

Sleep was a cherished treasure in Vietnam. If you got three or four continuous hours of sleep you were elated. That was considered a full night's sleep. In the field you were always tired. You slept whenever you could, both to rest and to kill time. Like using drugs, sleep was another way to escape the war and to bring you closer to DEROS. So naturally you were angry when you were cheated out of sleep on a rainy season patrol.

Sometimes I wished that a few VC would trip into our ambush just so I could arouse the men who somehow could sleep in the water and cold. But it never happened. I postulated, probably incorrectly, that the VC were too brilliant to be out in inclement weather.

During our spell at the Hard Spot Sergeant Houston granted me a three day pass to an R & R center in Vung Tau. Houston said that I deserved it but I didn't warrant it more than anyone else. Not one to scorn a splendid opportunity, I was able to engineer the pass into seven days out of the field, killing four days in Cu Chi with in-and-out processing.

Vung Tau was a coastal resort city from French colonial days. Like all Allied enclaves in Vietnam, it was as posh and secure as Cam Ranh Bay or Long Binh. In Vung Tau you could procure anything you desired. There was no harassment or hostility; it was mind-boggling to know that the military was administering the retreat. To accommodate the enormous demand, drugs, liquor, and females were in ample supply. You could wander around the Gomorrah in civilian clothes. You could sleep all day on a golden strand or in a sheet-coated bed.

After dark you hit the club. It's dusky, crowded, sumptuous, air-conditioned and heavy with smoke. With a rum and coke in each hand and a slender, willing, black-haired Oriental at your shoulder, you sing with the band. Another round, another round please. Who's counting? Soak it up, deeper, deeper, going under now, dive, dive. You savor the sensations of her closeness. You slide your hand under the table and touch her thigh, squeezing gently. You kiss her full lips. You watch her soft, shapely breasts breathing in and out, life, life. So much to live for, so much to see and do and learn. Fuckin' war! Why? Why? The band, playing The Beatles' "Hey Jude," goes down with you.

You laugh and sweat and cry and sing and hate and dance and love and drink, drink, drink, trying to wash away the war with swallow after swallow of sweet blindness. Soon Vung Tau has slipped off into the South China Sea, you're drifting in Nirvana, you're as one with Lennon and McCartney. You're gliding to her place. And it's all happening in the same country in which you're dodging bullets, straining to locate booby traps, and sleeping in water.

But in three days it's over. Your flight back to Cu Chi is waiting. You think of deserting but there is nowhere to go. So equipped with photos, souvenirs, and tales of prostitutes, you go back to the war.

When I returned to Bravo nothing had changed. The patrols, monsoon, and drudgery had proceeded unabated.

Sometimes when the weather cleared in the afternoons, we stripped to a towel, sandals and a weapon and strolled like beachcombers to a nearby cluster of hootches for well showers. For C-rations or a bar of soap, the children drew water and helped us wash. Chuckling over our nudity, the kids then executed matchless back rubs. The gigolos among us slithered off behind bushes with young girls, bare American rumps stroking delight on obliging females.

Unconcerned and unafraid, we lolled away some afternoons fraternizing with the rural folk of Vietnam, helping ourselves to anything we coveted. After all, weren't we protecting them from the evil Communists?

During July I became ill. One misty afternoon we returned from an uneventful sweep. I was unusually tired, weak. I discarded my radio and gear and crumbled outside a bunker. I had a high fever. Unable to eat or move, I slept until dark. The First was scheduled to go on ambush that night. When I heard the platoon saddling up I just rolled over. Someone took the radio and my place on the patrol. I crawled into a bunker and slept undisturbed until morning.

When I awoke the fever had dwindled. I dueled with diarrhea for two weeks. But I wasn't sick enough to refrain from operations. I had swallowed my orange and white malaria pills since I had arrived in-country, so I assumed the affliction wasn't a full-blown case of that dreadful disease. I didn't know for sure; I never got a diagnosis. But I finally recovered, disappointed that I wasn't able to parlay my illness into a respite in a Cu Chi hospital, clean sheets and all.

One morning, pregnant with the threat of rain, the First slushed in from an ambush patrol, the chilly paddy water oozing inside our boots. As usual we expected to eat breakfast, sleep and dry off. Waiting for us were liaison officers from division who had just flown to our installation. They had other ideas how to spend the morning: clean weapons and gear, shave, straighten up the bunkerline, conduct police call around the entire perimeter. Like trainees at Bragg we glossed ourselves and our fortress to a proper military sparkle. The nonsense was ordained because a quartet of Congressmen were visiting our post to see how the troops in the field were coping.

After an hour of scrubbing and retrieving cigarette butts, First and Second platoons were ordered to saddle up. Our mission was to set up observation posts to provide security for the VIPs. As we marched out we set a new record for the most curses on one patrol. Once we established our cordon, nearly all of us fell asleep. We were too tired to care about statesmen or security.

Third Platoon's assignment was to remain in the perimeter and to recite the proper answers for the politicians. With coaching from the liaison majors and captains, the Third memorized the lines. Getting enough food, soldier? Yes, Sir. Enough soap, ammo and Coke? Yes, Sir. How about mail, getting through regular? Yes, Sir. Any problems? No, Sir, no problems, Sir. Everything just peachy, Sir. Our morale is terrific, Sir. The Army is treating us fine, Sir. We're licking the Cong in this AO, Sir. Charlie better not mess with us, Sir, because we're the Wolfhounds, the meanest counterinsurgents alive, Sir. And so it went. Once the civilians departed we trudged back to the perimeter cursing the phoniness of the whole episode. We probably set another record for profanity.

That night we went on an ambush patrol in the rain.

At the Fifty Day Hard Spot we had a mess sergeant. One dreary day he rolled out of a resupply chopper like a massive cheese ball amid food lockers and water jugs. He was a middle-aged E-6 who had been a mess sergeant for fifteen years. He was supposed to rescue us from the starvation level of C-rations.

Stout, untidy and unskilled as a cook, he was an aggravating individual who made few friends with remarks glorifying the war and American participation in it. He was really gung-ho. Every dusk he reposed outside his bunker like a fat, contented squirrel perched outside his hole. He laid back, fleshy arms crossed over his stomach, thick glasses magnifying his eyes while he relaxed his way into nightfall.

One occasion we returned from a sweep soaked from a deluge, exhausted and thirsty. Our sergeant was reclining by his bunker fumbling with a ragged American flag. Tremaine, Nash and I tramped to him. Nash asked him for some Kool-Aid.

"Can't do it," he said, picking at a stitch on the flag with his grease-caked fingernail.

"What?" Tremaine said.

The sergeant looked at Tremaine over the top of his glasses. "No can do, troop!"

"Why?" asked Tremaine.

"Why? I'll tell you why. Number one, I got to finish sewin' this here flag. And number two, I'm not supposed to give out Kool-Aid until supper time. There's some water over there if y'all are thirsty."

"We don't want water," Nash said. "We want Kool-Aid, and we want it now!"

We always felt audacious when we reappeared from a no-contact operation. At times like this we weren't intimidated by anything, especially obnoxious mess sergeants. Besides, we were a demanding, haughty outfit. We expected our Kool-Aid and milk and one hot meal a day without interruption or delay. Everyone knew that the infantry moved on its stomach. How could there be a twentieth century war without the amenities? Wasn't this the Modern Army?

The sergeant stood up. "Now look here, you grunts. I got to finish sewin' this here flag for the CO. Beat it!"

"Oh hell, let's go!" I said. "This asshole won't do nothin' for us."

"Who you callin' an asshole, troop? Don't you know this flag is important business? We're gonna have this flag hangin' over our Hard Spot here!"

"I'll tell you what, Sarge," I said. "Why don't you take that flag and shove it?"

The sergeant tucked the flag under his arm and stepped closer to us. "How dare you be disrespectful to the flag!"

"What of it?" Tremaine snapped.

"That's the trouble with you new troopers today! No respect! No respect for anything! No wonder we haven't won this war yet!" The sergeant's face and neck were flushed. He was panting and swaying from side to side. His fists were clenched.

"Fuck you!" said Tremaine.

We laughed in his face and sauntered to the water bag, leaving the seething non-com grasping his tattered flag.

Among the rookies who came to the First was a Virginian named Mundorff. He was a handsome guy, with a model's smile and body. He reported to the field with a low, nagging cough — one of those coughs that you could make worse by coercing yourself to hack. Unhappy over his assignment to infantry, Mundorff couldn't believe that LPs and APs were sometimes effected with only a squad.

Houston took a squad, including Mundorff, on an ambush patrol. Mundorff coughed most of the night, which was dangerous and against the rules. We warned him several times to muffle his noises. He did a sloppy chore of it. A genuine shammer, on his next night patrol he again coughed, although he didn't cough in the base prior to the mission.

The following morning Nash, Houston and I confronted Mundorff. Any further noise-making while on night patrol, we advised him, could result in Mundorff encountering an "accident." "Keep messin' around and you'll be lyin' around!" Nash warned as he poked his finger into Mundorff's hairy, bronzed chest. "I've only got ninety-eight days to go, and I don't want you or anybody else interruptin' my countdown!"

That afternoon Mundorff left the field. He had an urgent appointment with a Cu Chi reenlistment officer. He had elected to extend his Army career in exchange for a rear job.

One sprinkling morning an accident occurred involving the Third. Sheridan, one of the fellows who had reported to Bravo with me, was cleaning his sixteen. Somehow he pulled the trigger on his loaded rifle. There were screams, panic, and confusion. Sheridan hit three men in his platoon, including a short-timer. One was struck in the cheek. He staggered around a moment blowing red spray. Then he collapsed, his face cloaked in blood. One was wounded in the calf, which quickly became a mass of carmine jelly. Another was shot in the testicles. Blood gushed from the wound like water spewing over a ruptured dam. His fluid spilled over the ground creating marbleized patterns in mud puddles. The medics took control and did their best.

After a dust-off evacuated the wounded, Sheridan began crying. His eyes rolled. He screamed and writhed in agony around a bunker. The medics pounced on him and called a dust-off. A week later he was driving a jeep in Cu Chi.

Sometimes the enemy stumbled into us at inopportune times. Once we were in a holding site waiting for the Southern Cross to brighten. I wandered off by myself to answer nature's call. Automatic rifle fire rattled through the humid air. In a second I purged my bowels. I pulled up my pants and hopped back to the platoon. I grabbed my radio and followed Duncan to where the shooting had erupted. Rojas reported that two NVA had walked up to him as if they were going to ask the time of day. They fled when they realized that Rojas was from the wrong army. Rojas and others fired without hitting the NVA. Since it was dark enough, we dropped the matter and went on our ambush patrol.

Another occasion we were bivouacked inside a hedgerow containing a farmer's hut. The sun had dropped into the paddies and the heat of the day had subsided. Stars were beginning to mirror on the paddy waters. I was slouched in the hedgerow. A violent storm had doused the area before we arrived. The hedgerow's ferns and branches trembled from a breeze. A residue of raindrops spilled on me. In the distant north lightning sparked up behind screens of mist. Feeling a chill, I seized my equipment and went into the hootch.

It was cozy inside. I sat on the dirt floor. On a wooden table a solitary candle glowed, casting giant shadows against the hut's thatched walls. The farmer squatted in a corner smiling and nodding whenever anyone peered at him. Minus front teeth, lean and beardless, like most Vietnamese men he was probably older than he looked. Nash lounged in another corner scribbling a daily letter to his wife. Duncan and Houston conversed in muted tones about what route to use for the ambush. The choice involved either a brief jaunt through some water-filled paddies, or a longer, probably drier approach. Tremaine swayed in the old man's hammock, humming and smoking, nervously flicking ashes onto the floor. Serene and detached, my mind drifted to home and freedom and all the things I was going to do once I left the war.

Suddenly small arms fire shattered the peacefulness. We jumped up. Realizing that the hootch would probably be the primary target for an attack on our holding position, I gave the candle a chop, plunging the hut into absolute blackness. Not a brilliant move. Like the Keystone Kops we stumbled over each other trying to gather our gear and flee.

Tremaine located his duper and ran outside. Thinking he was diving for cover, he took a belly-flop into the farmer's yard-high pile of cow dung. Nash fled the hovel and promptly tripped over someone's ammo pack, banging his head on his own rifle stock. Duncan, unable to find his weapon, screamed "Fuck it!" and dashed outside. He slipped on a mud puddle and skidded into the manure mound. I discovered my sixteen and negotiated my way to cover. But like a crack RTO, I had left my radio in the hut.

Four VC had strolled into a machine gun team in one corner of the hedgerow. Rickenbrode and two new men fired, sending the VC scampering. No one was injured. We quickly assembled and went on our patrol.

At daybreak we returned to the hooch. Our host had our canteens, poncho liners and other gear which we had left behind ready for us, all neatly piled and cleaned. Smiling and bowing, he waved to us as we filed off. A few of us left wondering why the VC had been coming into the farmer's hedgerow the night before.

In the middle of July the First pulled an ambush in a terrain of expansive paddies and berms. It was a bad night. I was cold, wet. I had spent my sleeping time watching thunderstorms stalk each other across the sky. A half-hour before dawn the rain had stopped but the dark-bellied heavens were still flashing with jagged light. Nash and I were sharing the last guard shift in our group. A man on guard in another unit reclined with his head bobbing, his eyes flickering at a juncture of berms before him. His partner was sprawled next to him, snoring and panting. Like a sunbather on a beach, another sentinel in a third team laid back on his elbows while he studied the canopied sky with half-mast eyes. Nash and I stared to our front, struggling to stay awake, gaping at the nothingness before us like two caged apes.

It's easy to become complacent on night patrols. After a while you become acclimated to the environment, the danger. You're apprehensive but you're not trembling. Guard becomes a hypnotic mechanical process, a deadly exercise in stupidity. Will you see Charlie tonight? Of course not! Nothing happened last night or the night before or the week before that. In fact you've gone months without any problems on an ambush. And even if the VC do come, there is no doubt they'll make enough noise that we'll hear them first. It's impossible for *us* to be surprised by *them*. We're the ambushers. They're the ambushees. We're the heavily-armed, competent professionals. They're the ill-trained, ill-equipped kids in pajamas and sandals. So it's okay if you're not wide awake. Besides, *someone* in our patrol is always awake and ready. An officer, a sergeant, someone. You bet your life on it.

At five or six in the morning you assume the VC have concluded their prowling for the night. But in the nippy, pre-dawn blackness of this night suddenly Nash exclaimed, "Listen!" He nodded to our right. We heard a thrashing noise in the distance. We couldn't see anything but already my heart was punching my breastbone.

"Better get Houston," I whimpered.

Nash sneaked to Houston and aroused him. Wiping sleep from his eyes, the sergeant squirmed to us. The noise became louder, closer. "I don't know what it is," Houston murmured, "but we're not gonna wait to find out!"

Houston crawled around and made sure everyone was awake, ready. He returned to us and placed two claymore firing devices in his palms. When the disturbance seemed to be directly before us Houston whispered, "Put your heads down!"

We ducked. Houston blew the mines. Then we opened up with automatic weapons, grenades and more claymores. For some reason it felt good to fire our weapons after going so long without using them. The noise was deafening, horrible, and deadly. It was enough to make even King Kong scamper off. Nothing could survive that incredible display of wrath.

While reloading we paraded on-line towards our target. The eastern sky began to lighten up. We trekked until we hit a cart trail. We fanned out and searched the area. Houston discovered two skinny old men cowering in a ditch. Although unhurt, they were terribly frightened. A small herd of water buffaloes grazed nearby. We towed the papa-sans from the hole and checked their ID's. Their documents were in order. We let them go.

First Platoon's initial night attack in seven months was over. We had ambushed two grandfathers who were piloting their livestock to pasture for the day.

We learned of Neil Armstrong's moonwalk. We weren't that impressed because, while the dauntless astronaut was stepping around the Sea of

Tranquility, Bravo was stepping on booby traps. In the track of Apollo Eleven the reflection soared through Bravo with the thrust of a Cape Kennedy launch: they can land a man on the moon, but they can't stop the killing in Vietnam.

The traps were our cardinal adversary at the Hard Spot. Most of the areas we worked were booby-trapped. Each operation was a morbid tournament between you and the traps. In open terrain, where traps were unlikely, you grazed the paddies, ditches and hedgerows. You reconnoitered for potential VC ambush sites, for movement where there shouldn't be any. But in a booby-trapped locale you bored into the two or three meters around you. You probed for evidence of human presence, unusual depressions or elevations, trip wires or anything out of place.

Like walking barefoot on hot sand or pavement, you hopscotch, tiptoe, sidestep. You set your own pace, you speed up and slow down. You don't know where to step next because everything under you is lethal. But you move, you roll the dice. You must. How else will you get out of there?

It's a private little war: Berm junction ahead. Ultra rings between the ears. *Danger, danger. Be ready. Easy, Kitch, easy, slow. Still five months to go. Gotta go home in one piece. No hurry. Concentrate. One mistake and it's on your back.* Your adrenalin boils. Closer, closer. Bent over, looking, searching, praying. Sweat rolls off your forehead in big drops. *LOOK!* Close now. Last chance. *Nothing. Did I miss it?* There. *Okay, Kitch, this is it.* Resist the temptation to rush. *Easy, easy, take a long high step over the berm. Stretch, Kitch, stretch, don't touch it, get over, over, hurdle it, high jump it.* Over. Alive. All clear. No explosions, no bloody, mangled, gushy leg in your hands. *You made it, Kitch, good job. Now get ready for the next berm.*

Some fellows hike in the paddy water beside the dry berm. But most tempt fate and take their chances on the dike. Better to avoid all the mud and leeches and murky Asian water. So the VC bet with the odds. They know that Americans often are lazy and stupid, hence they sabotage the berms, especially those outside villages.

If you're on point you must be Daniel Boone, Charles Lindbergh, and Christopher Columbus all packaged into one. But not only pointmen hit traps. Sometimes a column will tread over, around, and beside a trap, then the last man will ignite it. Usually you're marching too far apart to see exactly where the trooper before you goes, so in a sense everyone is a pointman. Each man must choose his footsteps and meet his destiny.

Rest time comes and you're tired; you want to get off your feet. But where do you sit? Do you sink to the dike and pray that you aren't lounging on a VC mine or a rigged .105? Or do you squat in the water? What, sit in water? That's crazy. That's for hippopotamuses and beavers and gooks and all those sub-humans. Not for clever American foot soldiers. So you put ten meters between you and your partners and you select a dry place to sit, your very own personalized chunk of Vietnam. Is it booby-trapped or not? Sometimes you're so exhausted and hot you say "Fuck it!" and drop. After you cool down you wonder if the next berm you pick will be benign. You wonder what it's like to have your foot or leg blown off. Do the Cu Chi doctors make a sincere attempt to save your mutilated extremity? Or do they just shrug and hack it off? At the call to move out, if you're not feeling brave, you linger for others to go first and begin the duel again. You follow their trajectory, hoping you'll be lucky like them.

Sometimes you have luck popping out your ears. One afternoon I was following Duncan down a berm, much too closely, daydreaming. It was near the end of the operation. I was weary. We heard a tiny click. We froze.

"Kitch," Duncan said, "I just hit a trap. Step backwards real careful like."

"Roger that," I chanted, already moving.

Duncan scanned the area and found a booby-trapped American grenade. The explosive was a dud. Shaking our heads, we quit the berm and trudged through the knee-high mud.

An hour later one of our new men sliced the trip wire on another trap. He had been ambulating parallel to me, only a few meters distant. That trap also was a dud. Of course it was a dud. What other possibility was there? It couldn't happen to *me*. I was immortal, the Lucky One. I entered the perimeter that day drowning in bravado. When you challenged the traps daily, operation after operation, you became filled with a crazy cockiness, a crazy sense of invincibility. The whole thing was crazy. It was zany, preposterous, irrational. It was war.

If I had been drawing aces for the day, there were others who weren't. That evening after a tasteless spaghetti dinner, I was idling on a bunker, pondering my marvelous luck. I noticed a man from the Second gaping at me. It was a very intense stare. The eight-month veteran was prone on top of a bunker about ten meters away. I nearly vomited my sauce and noodles. Dougherty again! From my vantage point the guy looked like Dougherty. The whole wave of emotion about an incident which I had tried to excise from my mind inundated me. Knowing that the Second was going on an ambush patrol that night, I had a cryptic premonition of death.

Wyatt, the gawking rifleman, finally rolled over and looked elsewhere. I was shaken. I thought I was losing my mind. *I've got to stop making such a big deal over how other soldiers look at me! Forget it!* I thought.

But I couldn't forget it. That night on my radio I monitored the progress of the Second as they marched to their ambush site. About ten o'clock a distant explosion in the direction of the patrol turned every head on the bunkerline. Soon a frantic voice yelled over the radio requesting an urgent dust-off. A man had hit a trap. The Second had paused on berms while the patrol leader scouted ahead for a place to set up. When the victim stood, he detonated a manipulated artillery shell.

A chill thundered through me. *I knew it!* I stared up at a lonely moon. The name Wyatt passed my lips. Taut and perspiring, I glanced around to see if anyone had heard me.

"What?" Rickenbrode said. "What did you say? Kitch, what's wrong? You look like you just saw a ghost."

"No, nothin', it's nothin'. I'm just talkin' to myself." I was relieved that Rickenbrode hadn't heard me.

After the dust-off extracted the soldier, the chopper pilot radioed to DeFreeze that his man—Wyatt—was a KIA.

Coincidence? Exaggeration? Insanity? Clairvoyance? Hallucination? Some of these? None of these? One thing about Vietnam. It always gave you more questions than answers.

18

"Just Heathens Here"

"Any Catholics in here?" sniffed a raucous voice into the bunker.

No one stirred. We had just returned from an ambush. It had rained all night. There wasn't a day sweep scheduled, so five of us were trying to recover the lost night's sleep while our clothes dried.

"How about just some Christians?" the man pleaded with a weak chuckle.

"Yeah, whatcha want?" snarled Tremaine.

"I'm Major McDonough, the battalion chaplain."

"Protestant or Catholic?"

"Catholic." The officer crouched inside the low, damp bunker. "Well, any Catholics in here?"

Tremaine, Rojas and I raised our hands.

"Good. Mass in ten minutes at the mortar platoon bunker. Expect to see you there."

"Hey," said Tremaine as the chaplain began to leave, "we just—"

"You mean, Sir, don't you soldier?" He grinned. "I might be a priest, but I'm still a major in the U.S. Army. You may address me as Sir, Major, Father, or Chaplain. Please continue."

"Yeah, well, Sir, I was just wonderin' if maybe we couldn't have mass in, say, a few hours? We're from the First Platoon and we just got in from an AP. We need a little sleep. It was wet out there last night—Sir."

The major shook his head no. "Sorry soldier, but I have three more masses to say today in three different locations here in the field. Wish I could help, you know, but sorry, orders are orders."

"Yeah, but you're a major. Don't you give orders, Sir?"

"We all have superiors, Specialist. See you at mass shortly." The portly father scrambled out of the bunker with a huff.

Rojas rolled over, religious medals and rosaries jingling. "Good night, fellows."

"You goin', Kitch?" quizzed Tremaine.

"Yeah, I guess so. Haven't gone to mass since I got in-country. Are you goin'?"

"Yeah, let's go. But I don't know why."

We were piqued over the major's pompous attitude. The clergy was one domain from which we expected understanding, cooperation. But old habits die hard. As we crawled over our friends while leaving the bunker, someone mumbled something about there being nothing worse than a stupid Catholic.

At the mortar bunker the cleric nodded and smiled at everyone as he distributed mass pamphlets. He donned colorful vestments and erected an altar on top of the bunker. He raced through a Latin service in which he gave a pep rally sermon about the complexities of war and the sometimes unpleasant task of defending one's country. God loves us. *Then why did he send us here?* God is looking after us. *But why didn't he look after Norton and Doc Hernstein and all the others?* We must love our buddies and commanders. *Love our commanders?* We're here to prevent the Communists from overrunning a freedom-loving nation. *Oh. Lately I've been wondering about that.* Did we desire to battle the Reds here or on the California beaches? *But there's ten thousand miles in between!* Avoid the evil temptations around us such as dope, whiskey, and Vietnamese women. If possible avoid Vietnamese men, too! *Very funny.* Do our best to be Christians. *While we're killing people?* Try not to count days. *Should we count bodies instead?* It won't be long before we'll all be home with our loved ones and attending mass in pews and not on sandbags. *Yeah, in a hundred and fifty-four days.* Amen. *Amen is right!*

After mass he collected his booklets, counting to make sure he had them all. He packed his mass gear. Any questions or problems? One pimply-faced lad from the Third inquired if maybe the major wouldn't mind coming out more often? We hadn't seen a clergyman in the field for seven months. Either that or stay longer when he did come? Or how about spending the night with us? Maybe we wouldn't get mortared that night!

"Well Private," he said after he recovered from giggling, "it is Private, isn't it?"

"No, Sir, it's Sergeant."

"Well, Sergeant," the priest continued, not a trifle embarrassed, "it's like this. I have my duties in the rear. You know, my mass schedule there, hospital duty, counseling, so it's impossible for me to stay here overnight. Besides, chaplains have orders to be back in Cu Chi before nightfall."

The squad leader looked away. "Yes, Sir."

Someone from the CP disrupted the uncomfortable hush by announcing that the major's chopper would arrive in three minutes. The parson waved to the messenger, turned to us and said, "Now men, please kneel."

We stooped. He gave us his blessing.

"Men," he said, looking as somber as a mortician, "good luck to you, and thanks for coming."

The flock dispersed. Tremaine and I remained at the bunker looking at each other, speechless, aggravated. The priest's Loach arrived. The round-faced man jogged over to the chopper and hopped aboard. He gave our camp a wide smile, a V salute (peace or victory?), and a sweeping wave as his aircraft slowly rose, canted forward, and flew off to another congregation.

One morning two months later, another Catholic reverend hustled customers along the bunkerline. When he put his head into our bunker and jovially queried if there were any Catholics catching up on our "beauty sleep," someone blurted, "No, Sir, just heathens in here."

The padre lurched out. We all laughed and went back to sleep.

19

Kolchek

We disbanded our Hard Spot and returned to Jackson for a few days. We were scheduled for a three day stand-down in Cu Chi. But events along the Angel's Wing necessitated a postponement.

After enduring a heavy mortar attack on our last night at Jackson—two men from Alpha Company were killed—we were ferried to the border. Our assignment was to establish another perimeter on the threshold of Cambodia. The site chosen for Kolchek was close to a hedgerow network, thus not very attractive in terms of security. We fabricated our bunkers in the rain, toiling listlessly and not terribly concerned when we'd finish building the fortress, if ever. It was our mode of communicating our displeasure over having our stand-down canceled.

Our pace was so deliberate that even Houston was agitated. He tried to motivate us but we weren't in a cooperative mood. Filled with frustration, within earshot of Houston I made a disparaging comment about platoon sergeants, comparing them to overseers on a Southern plantation. Not one to ignore insubordination, Houston confronted me. We hollered and glared at each other. He ordered me to get back to work. Yielding under Houston's blue lasers, I picked up my shovel and went back to work.

The next day I apologized. But Houston wasn't a fellow easily upstaged. Some hours after we had our altercation, along with Nash, Rojas and Tremaine, Houston nominated me for promotion to sergeant.

A different kind of promotion came for Lieutenant Duncan. He was rotated to a Cu Chi job. Wolfhound officers, like medics, generally served only five or six months in the field before referral to a cushy rear position. We were distraught to lose him, especially when we met his replacement.

Lieutenant Prigmore was a finicky, pugnacious man who swaggered and impersonated the hardcore infantry officer. But lurking behind his synthetic face was a compound of marshmallow and rhinestone. He was a disaster. It was late in the war and no doubt the Army had reached the bottom of the pool. His flaws were multiple: no command ability, no common sense, no coolness, no ears, all mouth. Prigmore couldn't read a map, thus he was often lost on patrols. Houston would have to advise him that he was guiding us astray. Prigmore would argue with Houston that we should turn left at this hedgerow. No, said Houston, not this hedgerow, the next one. No, insisted Prigmore, this hedgerow. On it went. Thanks to Houston, we always made it back okay.

Prigmore's tactics were equally deficient. He liked to use the same locations for ambushes. That was taboo. On night missions he rampaged about shouting orders, names. Whenever he became lost at night he called in illumination rounds so he could see where he was. The VC must have loved him.

One night they were after him. On our way to one of Prigmore's favorite ambush sites, the First stumbled into the VC, who weren't quite ready for us either. There was a brief skirmish and some wild shooting. The only casualty was Velasquez, a new rifleman. He was hit in the forearm. Doc Addison ordered Velasquez to be dusted-off. After some complaining Prigmore called a medevac.

The next morning Prigmore said that a "candy ass pussy like Velasquez shouldn't be in the Wolfhounds." He said that after he was hit, Velasquez was "out there rolling around over nothing because he had only a small hole in his arm." Besides, Prigmore grumbled, calling the dust-off had allowed the VC to escape.

We were infuriated. Velasquez was in fact severely injured. We later learned that he almost lost his arm. Someone predicted that our omniscient platoon leader would also be leaving soon. Whether his departure would be due to regular rotation or fragging was unclear.

I disliked Prigmore from the moment I commenced carrying the radio for him. He was constantly badgering me about little things: keep closer, walk faster, talk louder, did I bring an extra radio battery? I could never get the microphone into his hand quick enough.

One day I yelled back at him. During the ensuing argument I called him an incompetent fool. He threatened me with disciplinary action. Casting the radio at his feet, I told him to get another sucker to carry his commo. Since there were no volunteers, Houston picked someone to substitute for me. Relieved and feeling wonderful about myself, I went back to being an ordinary rifleman.

At Kolchek we had a company of ARVN troops stationed with us. Their function was obscure. They occasionally went on a sweep or ambush. Mostly they just swayed in hammocks. Their fighting proficiency was suspect. We frowned upon going on patrols with them, especially night missions, because they always made more noise than we did.

Bravo returned from a sweep one rainy afternoon. As usual we were tired, thirsty, and wet. Some men in the Second reported thefts of marijuana, cigarettes, and cookies from metal ammo containers in which we cached personal items. With the exception of the pot, the pilfered merchandise was recovered from two ARVNs cowering in a bunker.

Bravo was disturbed over pulling an operation while the ARVNs lounged at Kolchek. After all, whose war was this? Then to be robbed by light-fingered ARVNs was too much to bear. Soon a fracas ensued between the thieves and the Second. One thing you don't do in the field is help yourself to another man's dope.

Hawkins, a muscular black machine gunner, concluded that fisticuffs wouldn't teach the ARVNs anything. Incensed over his missing marijuana, he took his sixty, leaped onto a bunker and fired into the slate-colored sky. He got everyone's attention. He snarled that he was going to kill every Oriental in sight. Brandishing his weapon, his biceps bulging like cantaloupes, he warned everyone to stay clear of him.

The CO approached. Hawkins cursed him and the Army, making drill sergeants' language sound like nursery rhymes. Then he fired another burst into the rain. DeFreeze, who always seemed to know when to recoil, paced backwards. Two of Hawkins' friends finally persuaded him to relent. Later in the day he took the supply chopper to Cu Chi, contrite and laughing.

Bravo Company received new troopers at Kolchek. One of them was a sergeant E-5, not the instant NCO draftee variety, but a career soldier. Sergeant Krueger was assigned to the Third. He was twenty-five, short, solidly-built and littered with tattoos. His chest muscles undulated like sand dunes. A Southerner, he was the embodiment of the sabre-rattling hawk, the paladin of the Bible, the flag, chauvinism, and conservatism. Mister Army had already served two tours as an infantryman. Now he was voluntarily back for a third.

Of course, we couldn't believe it. Here was a guy who had volunteered for combat in Vietnam. He didn't have to be here! Like the circus freak or the rarest animal at the zoo, we marveled over him.

The battle lines were drawn. Fervid soldiers usually scared us. But on operations Krueger wasn't a hazard. He was an efficient, knowledgeable combat veteran. Perhaps, we rationalized, his expertise would enable others to rotate home right side up. So we weren't dismayed to have him.

One dawn the First and Third saddled up to return to Kolchek from ambush patrols. We had set up in different locations. Thunder from heavy clouds mumbled overhead. It began raining. As we slogged back from our AP site, huge raindrops splattering on our helmets, a tremendous explosion occurred. At first we thought it was thunder. But an imperial genie curling into the downpour revealed the horrible truth.

We halted and clustered around the radio. Sergeant Krueger was dead.

He had struck a sabotaged .155 shell, absorbing the full impact of the trap. Sergeant Blehm, the Third's platoon sergeant, was injured. A clump of falling sod had smacked him on the bridge of his nose, resulting in a bloody facial wound. There were no other casualties.

DeFreeze radioed to the bewildered novice lieutenant commanding the patrol to get the body ready for a dust-off. The lieutenant called back saying that they couldn't find the remains.

"What?" screamed DeFreeze. "Whatta you mean? Then how the fuck do you know Krueger hit a trap? Over!"

"Because he's the only man I got missing, Sir. Over."

"Now goddamnit, the man has to be there someplace! You find him and you find his weapon! Over!"

"Roger. But it might take a while. Over."

"I don't give a fuck how long it takes! You keep lookin' until you find something! Don't come back in until you do! Out, goddamnit!"

"Wilco. Out."

The CO called Prigmore and instructed him to wait in place until the Third recovered Krueger and his weapon. There was no reason for us to delay because of what had happened to the Third. But DeFreeze was so flustered that we thought it best not to complain. We counted our blessings; at least he didn't order us to help the Third search for Krueger, thus possibly igniting more traps.

At last the lieutenant relayed to DeFreeze that they had collected Krueger: a mangled arm, half a foot, chunks of flesh, part of his head, metal and gear minced together, and bloody sections of clothing. Everything was heaped into a plastic body bag. It was left outside Kolchek in the rain. Later that morning a dust-off extracted the grisly booby-trapped mess.

Sergeant Krueger's third tour lasted fifteen days.

Kolchek was a miserable span of duty for Bravo. We had no hot meals or showers. Our larger perimeters, like Reed, had wooden stall showers with fifty-five gallon drums storing the water. But at the smaller bases we had to rely on local wells. At Kolchek we had access to neither. We tried to wash in the rain but it never rained hard enough at the right time. So we literally washed ourselves in our own sweat. We were as filthy as any outfit in Vietnam.

Nor did we have the security implicit in a well-selected perimeter. Hedgerows capable of concealing VC were simply too close. One night the Second and Third platoons were on ambush. Only the First was stretched thinly around our twelve bunker complex. We had a duplication of that tense false alarm at Diamond III: the ghostly flares, the pounding artillery, the frantic dashes from bunker to bunker, the fire raging in our stomachs, the coarse, hysterical commands blaring over the radios, the stench of gunpowder, the dreadful uncertainty over what was going to happen. We were fortunate the VC didn't attack that skittish night because it wouldn't have taken much for them to overrun us. We were physically and mentally depleted, undermanned, poorly situated, and ripe for a defeat.

At Kolchek our squalid living conditions were more exasperating than our black-haired rivals. The mud was usually ankle deep. After a storm our camp quickly became a shin-high swamp. We tried using wooden artillery shell boxes as boardwalks. But before long they sank and disappeared like they were in quicksand. There was little we could do about the muck; it rained too often. Kolchek was just one great caldron of mud.

Another mark of the rainy season was leeches. The blood-sucking worms clung to us like, well . . . leeches. There was just nothing like them. They were right up there on the Vietnam hate list with snakes, traps, and incompetent officers. They loved us because we were damp. After waking up or returning from an operation, the first maintenance we performed was to examine each other for leeches. We normally couldn't feel the parasites. They absorbed their fill of blood, turning black. Then they dropped from our skin and burst inside our clothes, leaving us with a slimy bloody mess. If we found them in time we could flick them off with a finger. Usually we had to use a cigarette to burn out the worm's mouth, often charring skin in the process. We had contests to determine who carried the most leeches. It wasn't a game anyone relished winning.

One afternoon Tremaine received two bottles of grog in the mail. That night we had no duty other than bunker guard. Six of us spent the evening demolishing fifths of Jim Beam and Johnnie Walker Red. In the field, liquor was nearly always consumed the day it arrived.

By nine o'clock I was inebriated. In the midst of a Tremaine joke, a messenger poked his head into our bunker and told me to report to the CO. Worried over what DeFreeze could want with me—I never spoke to the man except on the radio—I staggered to the CP. Jamming a chunk of gum into my mouth, I ducked into the murky bunker. Two RTOs were playing chess by candlelight, drinking sodas. The CO was resting in a corner, oiling his .45. He looked up. He swept his arm across the dirt floor. "Kitchin, Kitchin, have a seat." Hoping that distance would conceal my breath, I plopped down as far from him as I could. I kept my lips together and waited for him to speak. Peering at his weapon he said, "Kitchin, I like your work with the radio. You're a strack trooper. You do okay when we get in the shit. I liked the way you talked to me that night on the ambush. I want you to be one of my RTOs here in the CP."

One of the chess players glanced at me and smiled. When his opponent muttered "Check!" the man scowled and said, "Fuck!" The CO kept toying with his pistol, waiting for my reaction. I was thunderstruck. I recalled the ambush. One night we had marched to our coordinates, set up, then DeFreeze, back at the Fifty Day Hard Spot, screamed at us over the radio asking why we didn't see any VC. He said that radar had detected movement all around us. I calmly advised him that we didn't see anything, that we had our claymores out, that our guard shifts were established and our ambush was active, and that if we did see VC he'd be the first to know. My report seemed to assuage him. "Okay, out," he replied meekly.

Perspiration burst on my forehead. *Terrific,* I thought, *I get my first taste of spirits in weeks, then I have to be put into a situation like this!* Stalling for time to think, I asked him what my duties would be. There's nothing like foraging for appropriate words with your brain swirling in alcohol.

"Well, you know," he said with irritation. "Just follow me around and give me the damn horn when I need it. You know what your fuckin' duties will be!"

I reddened. "Well, Sir," I began, avoiding his eyes and speaking slowly as I reached for the words, "I don't know. I'm scheduled to go to LCLC on August 20."

Lightning Combat Leadership Course was a training program for potential squad leaders. Houston had designated me for it. It was mainly a vacation, a farce. The basic advantage was that you got a minimum of ten days in Cu Chi.

He scratched his considerable bald spot. "Well, the hell with LCLC. I want you up here. Shit, if you do a good job for me, you might even get an RTO job back in Cu Chi in a few months."

There it was—the magical, elusive dream. The Job in the Rear. But I was feeling high, brave. And stupid.

"Yes, Sir, but LCLC is ten days in Cu Chi, plus I got my R & R, my seven-day leave, and if I quit humpin' like everybody else at thirty days before DEROS, well, Sir, there just won't be much more field duty for me anyway."

He stuffed his pistol into its holster. He glared daggers at me. "Fuck, Kitchin, you're crazy. I'll get somebody else. You're dismissed."

The captain knew I was spewing nonsense. Even with my anticipated respites I still had plenty of time left for field duty. The advantages of his offer were tantalizing. Although I'd still have to participate on sweeps with the CO, I wouldn't have to go on ambush patrols. Like the chess players, the job would mean every night inside a bunkerline and later perhaps a battalion RTO slot in Cu Chi. I knew he wasn't exaggerating because I had witnessed others follow the same scenario.

But I couldn't accept the offer. I was drunk but I knew what I was doing; my drunkenness only made it easier to tell him no. My reasons were both personal and political. On a personal level DeFreeze was a bit too gruff for me. I was worried about having another spat like the one with Prigmore. Captain DeFreeze wasn't an officer whom you could yell at without consequences. The other thing was that my negative feelings towards the war were multiplying daily. If I went to work for DeFreeze, then I'd be slaving with a person who represented the forces who were, I was beginning to believe, responsible for prolonging the conflict.

Even though the hazards were greater staying where I was, I couldn't bring myself to compromise and to take the initial step that might propel me to Cu Chi for my final month or two in Vietnam. After seven months of war, the old craving for a rear job had sprouted criteria. I wanted to go directly to a clerk's desk or a paint brush, no strings, no compromises. And no working two or three months with a captain who symbolized America's imperialism.

Besides all that, I didn't want to leave my friends in the First. The friendships, the sense of belonging, the fraternity of fighting men, had a headlock on me. I knew that I'd feel squeamish about marching behind the CO on a sweep while the men I had come to know and love were cruising ahead of me. Not being with them would make me uncomfortable, despondent. And what would *they* think of me carrying the captain's radio?

And so I skidded back through the mud puddles to the bunkerline, hoping that DeFreeze wouldn't obstruct my appointment with LCLC.

I told Nash and Tremaine what happened.

"Jesus," said Tremaine, "it was tempting, wasn't it?"

"Yeah. In a way."

"I don't blame you for not wantin' to work with DeFreeze," said Nash. He took a long drink. "How many days you got left?"

"One hundred twenty-eight." My two pals laughed. "Okay, okay, you guys." I pointed at Nash. "I know you got about seventy."

"Sixty-eight."

"And Tremaine, you got—?"

"Fifty-eight."

"Hey," said Nash, "don't worry about it. You're gettin' short too. I'm glad you're stayin' with us."

"Roger," said Tremaine. "I'll drink to that!" He toasted me and took a mouthful. "I'm sure you'd rather be down here gettin' goofy with us."

I gave Tremaine my cup. "Pour me another bourbon and Coke. Lots of Beam."

On top of the physical dangers and difficulties at Kolchek, the gnawing mental strain of fighting in Vietnam was beginning to take its toll on the veteran members of the First. We were angry over not getting our three day retreat in Cu Chi. We were perturbed over losing Duncan and, worse yet, receiving Prigmore. Constantly fatigued, wet, hungry for a decent meal, sick of booby traps, mud, fear, mortars and patrols, our Kolchek assignment seemed to be the last straw in an interminable list of straws. We were disintegrating as a fighting unit.

We discussed the war. There were some Galahads like Krueger, but most of us concurred on one basic premise: the war was wrong. For my part, answers to the doubts and questions I had about Vietnam were coming into focus. The cumulative effect of my experiences had set me to thinking and thinking. While you pulled guard in the abyss of the Vietnam night, there was ample time for thought. By the time we left Kolchek I was certain that our presence in Asia was unjustified. I regretted that, like the biblical Thomas, I had to see to believe.

The war seemed to defy simplification. But I tried. I reckoned that the war was a civil war, Asians versus Asians. Thus our intervention on behalf of one of the combatants only made the war more intense, lengthy. For me it came down to one question: were America's vital interests and national security threatened by a Communist takeover of South Vietnam? No. But if I was wrong, if I had missed something, then what about Cuba? Why was it okay for Communists to control Cuba, only ninety miles off shore? It didn't add up. I felt Ho Chi Minh was right. Americans were the true imperialists in Vietnam. This time, at least, our intervention in a distant conflict was wrong.

The politicians at home proclaimed that the war wasn't a battle for territory but a war fought for the hearts and minds of the Vietnamese. But how do you win a man's heart by burning his hearth, napalming his children, abusing his wife, damaging his crops, slaughtering his livestock, and then using his head as a punching bag? And all this was often done before we knew for certain if the person or village was VC. In a civil war how do you determine who the enemy is?

But the supreme testimony for the wrongness of America's involvement was inscribed on the faces of the Vietnamese peasants entangled in the holocaust. Radiating from their soulful, war-weary eyes was a solitary message: leave us alone—please.

20

The Sugar Mill

The Vam Co Dong river was an expansive, deep, turquoise tributary. The current was swift and the riverbanks were coated with foliage, which afforded the VC superb ambush sites. Like a baleful serpent, the river threaded a sinuous route through our AO. Our next duty post was at an abandoned sugar mill along the river. From the sugar mill we pulled ambushes and amphibious operations.

Like a brooding Stonehenge, the principal building of the sugar mill towered several stories above the lush countryside and the other edifices in the complex. The interior of the statuesque structure had been gutted by previous battles. But the steel and concrete portions of the skyscraper had endured. First Platoon was quartered on a upper floor of the steeple. It wasn't a very safe place. A few timely RPG rounds fired through the windows would've been disastrous.

The sugar mill reminded me of a ferocious duel fought for monopoly of a grain elevator in Stalingrad in 1942. Forty valiant Russians defended the elevator for several days against the Germans. Finally the attackers eliminated the last of the determined partisans who were barricaded on the top deck. If things ever became tacky at the sugar mill, like the Russians' Alamo, there was no exit for us either.

On our sweeps from the plant we were transported down the river on converted World War II landing vessels piloted by Vietnamese sailors. Usually two boats holding a platoon each would convey us to our debarkation point, then return at another location to pick us up. Our assaults weren't as gallant as the Hollywood Marines storming the beaches. We simply drifted to shore and filed off the boats, usually into knee-high muck.

Endeavoring to diminish the possibility of ambush or snipers, the ships would ply the river with wide-open throttles. The lead craft would maneuver unencumbered. But the second vessel would be violently chopping through the wake of the point boat. Like on some scary amusement park ride, the potent whitecaps would lift us from the wooden benches that lined the sides of the ships. There wasn't anything to grasp onto but each other. Any equipment not moored would tumble overboard. We became drenched from the spray. In the trailing boat our paramount concern was drowning, not ambushes. More than once I was certain that the next breaker would capsize our craft, spilling one American platoon without life preservers into the murky depths.

The terrain around the river was replete with brown canals, marshes, snakes, leeches, impenetrable hedgerows and thickets, but fortunately, no VC. Most of our efforts were spent retrieving each other from the mud. Each operation was identical. The pointman ambled into a swamp and was promptly stranded. The next man waded in and attempted to liberate the pointman, becoming stuck himself. Then DeFreeze conceded that the mire was impassable. We spent the next two hours dragging out the marooned men.

At the sugar mill we lost Sergeant Houston to DEROS. We hated to see him go. Replacing him was Sergeant Blehm from the Third. Blehm was lanky, somber. We wondered how he—or anyone—could fill Houston's big boots. Blehm had an occasional problem on ambushes. One drizzling night we took a ship down the river. We left the boat and wandered for a half-hour behind Blehm while he tried to locate a suitable ambush site. He finally discovered a huge patch of elephant grass on some high ground near the river, not twenty meters from where we had docked. Damp, exhausted, frustrated by the terrain and no longer giving a damn, we hid in the high foliage and let the Vam Co Dong sing us to sleep. We didn't even bother with claymores.

Our delayed stand-down materialized. We were trucked from the sugar mill to Cu Chi. The journey was meaningful for DeFreeze because it was his final day in the field.

Bravo's arrival in Cu Chi was always a clamorous affair. Like children whooping down a staircase on Christmas morning, we leaped from our transports anxious to embrace the rewards of the rear. We were hosted at the Cu Chi Hilton, another cleverly-named stand-down area. There was formation, weapons check-in, assignment to barracks, a lecture on the do's and don'ts and dismissal. Then our first company break since March began.

First we bribed the Oriental bartenders at the Wolfhound enlisted men's club to sell us liquor. It was ten dollars a bottle. But so what? Grunts in Vietnam don't care about money. We stashed the bottles for later, once the EM club closed. Then we went back to the pub for hours of drinking, bitching, joking, and remembering. We built beer can pyramids on bar tables. We sang with the jukebox. Arguments erupted over what kind of music to play. The black men wanted soul. The Southerners and Westerners wanted country. The rest wanted rock. Sometimes arguments turned into wild West saloon fights: wooden chairs smashing, bottles, glasses and cans flying, bodies crashing through doors. The MPs would enter and haul off a few drunks. After a perfunctory clean-up we went back to drinking. We learned always to select a table near an exit in case of brawls. After surviving traps and ambushes, a bar scuffle was no way to die.

We wallowed in the corpulent life of the rear. We were issued new fatigues, boots, and equipment. We took three showers a day. We slept away mornings in bunks. We caught up on our letter writing. We stuffed ourselves in the immaculate mess hall, where it seemed weird to eat hot food while sitting at a table. With CIB's festooned on our chests we strutted about Cu Chi, drunk, rowdy, and cocky.

As the moon climbed the sky on our final evening as guests of the Hilton, Bravo assembled for the climax of our stand-down: a floor show. Before the presentation began, a thirty-six year-old black captain stepped onto the stage. Smiling, he called the company to attention. A hush descended over the cramped bleachers. "As you were. As you were. Good evening, men," he said. "My name is Simpson. Fred Simpson. I'm the new CO of Bravo Company."

A subdued mixture of cheers and hisses sounded. From most of Bravo there was no reaction. What did it matter who was commanding us? We hadn't had a CO who could inspire us since Captain Hoy. With people constantly going and coming, the faces, like the patrols, were beginning to run together.

Our new CO moved about the scaffold with an easy gait as he surveyed Bravo. He was stubby, slightly paunchy. While he was a clean individual, in his dress he wasn't a spit-and-polish officer. He had an effortless grin; it was difficult to imagine the man becoming angry or raising his voice. A receding hairline revealed a tantrum of wrinkles on his forehead. He was perspiring heavily; his shirt was as soaked as our shirts always were when we returned from a sweep.

"Let me tell you about myself," he continued. "I'm from Indiana." He paused while he wiped his brow with an olive-green handkerchief. "I've been in the Army seventeen years and this is my second round over here in the Nam. The last time I was here I was a platoon leader. I got wounded twice and I lost some men, but I learned a lot my last trip here. I learned a lot about leading men in combat, a lot about the Nam, a lot about Charles, and a lot about getting you men home safe."

Breathing in hard, he mopped his forehead again. "I didn't go to OCS right off. I was an EM like yourselves for about ten years. So you see, I know what you men think, how you think, and why you think it. Because of this I think we'll get along just fine. I'm going to run a real relaxed company. Relaxed—that's a word I like. That's the atmosphere I want. I want everybody to be relaxed. I have an open-door policy for everybody. I'm an extrovert. I like exchanging ideas. If you have a problem, any problem, just go through your normal chain of command, and if your problem still can't be solved, then come to me. I believe a problem doesn't exist that can't be solved at the company level. If we have a problem, we're going to talk it out.

"Just remember that my job is to accomplish our mission from battalion. I intend to do that, and also see that all of you men meet your DEROS. I've been told that I'm taking command of the best company in the Wolfhounds. My goal is to keep Bravo the best and, with your cooperation, I'm sure we'll succeed.

"That's all I have now. Enjoy the rest of your stand-down—let's stay in the Hilton area and keep out of trouble—and tomorrow we'll go back to the field refitted, refreshed, and ready to get some body counts. Enjoy the show!"

With a wave and a smile Simpson bounded off the platform, his improperly positioned captain's bars glistening under the flood lights. He nodded to our new first sergeant, a slender, six-foot-eight reservist with the largest Adam's apple in the world. The E-8, who was still sulking over the misfortune of having his unit activated, signaled to a beefy Oriental man dressed in civilian garments. After a puff on his lengthy cigar the man clicked his fingers.

Under a landslide of cheers, an all-female Filipino band took their places on the stage. Arrayed in scarlet mini-skirts and knee-high white boots, the women took their instruments and began their rendition of popular music. Swaying and lurching sensuously, the women kept their lips flush with the microphones as they chanted. Clapping, snapping pictures, and pounding on the stands with our new boots, we joined the show. They were the four most exotic women in the universe. They were the best ensemble we ever heard.

We smoked dope, guzzled liquor. We gyrated and sang the sweet, sweet music from home. We sang louder than any Tigerland training outfit. We sweated more than we did in any firefight. And like a great white eye, the full moon peered down at the rocking Cu Chi Hilton. When I looked at the moon I thought, *It's a good night for an ambush. We could see them coming.*

The lead singer discarded her guitar. She was the stripper. Keeping time with the music, she began her act. As each piece of clothing was peeled, the men roared and jockeyed for the most advantageous angle to photograph her. She had a Playmate-of-the-Year body. Once she was down to a thread bikini, Bravo's eyeballs strained harder than they ever did for booby traps. The band played on. Someone brought a chair to the girl. She took a microphone and sang The Rolling Stones' "(I Can't Get No) Satisfaction" while she exercised with the piece of furniture. With every gesture of the Filipino's sparkling, miraculous, fragile, silken, exquisite, tawny figure, Bravy Company cheered, groaned, sweated, and drooled. And remembered. She donned a transparent robe. Together with Bravo she emptied her lungs into the grand finale: The Animals' "We Gotta Get Out of This Place."

Off to the side of the bleachers Captain Simpson chuckled and looked at his watch.

The next morning, drained, hung over and still panting, Bravo returned to the sugar mill. I hiked to the Wolfhound battalion area and stashed my gear. I killed the day rotating between the library, the snack bar, the PX, and the USO club.

I reported to LCLC the following morning. LCLC was similar to stateside training, minus the harassment and work details. We slept in barracks, ate in a mess hall, and attended class after boring class. We were confined to the LCLC grounds to prevent us from gallivanting at night and reappearing at dawn with a hangover.

The training was ludicrous because we were instructed how to do the things we had already been doing for seven or eight months, but no one complained. The main thing was that it was time out of the field. It was more X's for our pocket calendars—one of our most cherished items. We were the winners, the fortunate ones, the men who had survived long enough in the field to be nominated or promoted to sergeant. And so that qualified us for a ten day break at LCLC.

The climax to our program was an ambush patrol a hundred and fifty meters outside the Cu Chi wire. The greatest hazard to this operation was having the bunkerline guards fire upon us. To mitigate this peril we launched a flare when we were ready to depart. Joking and waving to the sentinels, thirty of us lumbered through the eight rows of wire protecting the Cu Chi noncombatants. Loaded with firepower and commo, bloated from dinner in the mess hall, we thrashed through the Vietnam bush daring one or two VC—no more—to challenge us, but nothing happened. As anticipated it was a snap patrol. However, like all nighttime missions in our AO, the mosquitoes were brutal.

For LCLC graduation ceremonies a staid general from division presented crescent-shaped shoulder patches to us while he shook our hands. Now that we had received additional training, he exhorted, supplemental results in the form of body counts were expected of us. After the sermon we all laughed, discarded our patches, and obliterated another day on our calendars.

I trekked back to the Wolfhound area. Rooks had just returned from the sugar mill to go home. There was some bad news. The First had been involved in a river accident. The platoon was returning from an operation. The Vietnamese skippers were stampeding down the river towards the sugar mill. The First was in the rear boat. As usual the trailing craft was reeling and trying to keep pace with the other ship. A tremendous wave crashed into the boat, catapulting several men overboard. The helmsmen made a turn and arrowed back to where the victims were bobbing and pleading for rescue. The swift action of the balance of the platoon saved the lives of five men, including Tremaine.

Back at the sugar mill, Rickenbrode noticed that one of his ammo bearers, a new soldier from Pennsylvania, was absent. Where was he? Maybe he's taking a shower. Maybe he's goofing off at the dock. Maybe he's at the makeshift mess hall in another building. A quick search. No Chi Chi. And then it occurred to them: maybe he's still in the river! One of the boats was dispatched up the river with a scouting party. There wasn't a trace of him.

Later Chi Chi's partially devoured corpse was recovered by divers. He still had four hundred rounds of sixty ammo coiled around him. He had gone directly to the bottom; he never had a chance. Battalion subsequently ordered that all river operations be effected at speeds that would not create wakes. We'd take our chances with snipers.

21

Putsch!

I was able to sham another few days in Cu Chi before the Bravo NCOIC of the rear realized that I had graduated from LCLC. He berated me for not advising him of my availability for field duty. When I told him that it had slipped my mind, his eyes nearly fell out of his head. "You *will* report to the sugar mill tomorrow!" he bellowed.

My last afternoon in Cu Chi, Padbury returned to the base for DEROS. He was cursing Captain Simpson and griping about going on operations with his DEROS less than a week distant. I asked him what was going on. He mumbled something about trouble in the field. He hinted that the First was considering refusing to go on an operation in order to do something about Simpson. I pressed him for more information but he was in a hurry to get to the EM club. He said that I'd discover what was happening once I got out there.

I arrived at the sugar mill via the daily truck convoy late on the afternoon of September 2. The First had just returned from a river patrol. Tension and grumbling engulfed the sultry riverfront air. Alarmed over Padbury's report, I confronted Nash and Tremaine. They bombarded me with some astonishing revelations about what had transpired since Bravo had returned to the sugar mill. Captain Simpson was a phony. He wasn't a leader. He disliked participating on operations. He often remained at the sugar mill and coordinated patrols from his cot. When he did go on river forays, he lingered onboard the boat until the landing area was searched. Sometimes he tarried on the ship for the entire operation. When he did venture off the boat he always hovered in the rear of the formation. If he was needed up front he found an excuse not to go. From his cordoned position he ordered the platoon to take unnecessary risks such as going through a suspected booby-trapped hedgerow rather than circumventing it.

Equally disturbing were his new personnel dogmas. He had declared that a minimum of thirty men would participate on every platoon-sized operation. This meant that even short-timers would have to go out because no platoon had over thirty field-ready men. In effect, everyone would go on operations until six days before DEROS, the division's SOP. Besides short-timers, Simpson was also coercing men with medical profiles— exemptions from specific duties—to go on patrols to meet his thirty man criterion.

These announcements astounded everyone. For at least several months before I reported to Bravo it had been a tradition that once a fellow achieved the thirty day milestone, he could refrain from operations. The short-timer would stay in the field, of course, but he expedited menial chores in the perimeter. Then about a week before DEROS, he went to Cu Chi. The custom was a sort of reward for doing a good job and serving eleven months in the field without shamming. Your final month was usually the most anxious one. It seemed logical to detain a man from operations, if at all possible.

Moreover, Simpson decreed a cessation to seven-day leaves. He couldn't prohibit regular R & R's, but, as we later discovered, in the 25th Division seven-day sabbaticals weren't automatic. They were authorized only at the discretion of commanding officers. It was the first time since I had joined Bravo that these furloughs were suspended.

Also, Doc Addison had been rotated to Cu Chi. No one replaced him. The platoon was irate over effecting combat missions without a medic. Two men had volunteered to attend an abbreviated medic school in Cu Chi. But neither of them had finished the training and returned to the field.

Simpson's basis for his novel doctrines was succinct: Bravo had a dearth of bodies. The truth was that Bravo had as many men as it ever had. Each platoon had twenty-five to thirty men, which, at least in the past, was considered ample for conducting effective operations. Working with these numbers, previous COs had seen fit to leave back men under thirty days. The real reason, the First surmised, was that Simpson desired to have as many troops as possible encircling him. The more men on the patrol, the more insulation for him.

On top of these grievances, Simpson had proven to be remote, incompetent. The squad leaders, Tremaine, and others had approached him through the chain of command to discuss the problems enraging the First. But like a slick political candidate, he dodged the issues. His Hilton orientation speech was rhetoric.

Simpson was occasionally lost on operations. Then the platoon would be late for objectives and the men would have to march faster to redeem squandered time. It didn't annoy the First not to achieve objectives or to be militarily ineffective. What alienated the men was that they didn't have confidence in their leader.

I was familiar with the feeling. What if we made contact with the VC? Who would be the more lethal enemy? We knew what we had to do to escape the wrath of the VC. But what about the hazards of sloppy command? It sets you to thinking. Mostly you think about how to eliminate the commander.

The disenchantment in the First had swelled until it climaxed on the evening I returned to the field. The men had decided to refuse to go on a patrol scheduled for the following morning. The goal of the rebellion was to coerce Simpson to alter his policies, or at the very least to attract attention from battalion. The latter, it was hoped, would result in Simpson's removal.

Nash and Tremaine inquired if I was with them. I had just reported to the field. The Captain Simpson I remembered was the champion of relaxation and the open door policy, but I trusted my comrades. There was no debate; I was behind them.

The entire platoon wasn't involved. Some men rallied behind the captain. There were twelve or fourteen hard-boiled revolutionaries, most of us with less than four months left in Vietnam. That tension-crammed evening Nash, Tremaine and I did our utmost to persuade the borderline men to join us. Like lobbying politicians the night before an election, we scurried about our cauldron of defiance wooing, cajoling.

As we suspected, Sergeant Blehm flatly rejected our overtures. He told us that we'd all be court-martialed. Our three rookie squad leaders — instant NCO's who had joined us at the Fifty Day Hard Spot — also declined to endorse the plot. They still had nine months before DEROS. With so much time left, they were afraid of the repercussions. However, they were with us in principle. We respected their decision. Our relationship remained cordial.

I felt that we had flimsy justifications for our refusal. I wasn't certain but I doubted there existed any military regulation protecting thirty day short-timers from going on operations. I didn't feel that Simpson could be proven legally deficient on any item in our bill of particulars, but maybe through our provocation, battalion would recognize that Simpson was impotent as a leader and replace him.

What could they do to us? Court-martial a whole platoon? Fine us? Bust us? It didn't matter. We were living in a world where money, power and status didn't mean anything, while friendship, trust and human kindness meant everything.

Beyond this was the backdrop of emotion generated by eight months of spinning in the whirlpool of war. In the crimson blood of your friends — and those who aren't your friends — the image crystallizes. You decipher that greed, arrogance, power and stupidity in high places are responsible for inflicting war on those beneath them. You know that the war is truly a civil war propagated by American aggression. You perceive that your presence imposes only more anguish on an ancient culture.

You wonder about courage. You ponder whether it takes more guts to say no to a war you believe to be wrong than it does to participate. You are there. You have seen the killing, the destruction. You know it's absurd. But where do you desert to? How do you get out of the country? You're not a correspondent, photographer, or civilian volunteer. You can't leave on a whim. You're stuck there for a year. So you play it cool, safe. You tuck your head in the sand. Even though you know the war is unethical, you go on mission after mission. You keep a pace ahead of being *in flagrante delicto*. You're not concerned with doing a meritorious job. Your only obsession is with your own safety and that of your immediate pocket of friends. You feel like a criminal. But self-preservation subjugates principles. You feel nothing but contempt for the intangible System that has deceived you and employed you as their pawn to fight an unjust war. You feel remorse about not extending the time and effort to scrutinize what you were getting yourself into before it was too late. But eons ago, before you departed for Vietnam, way back when you were young, your head was heaped with silliness, heroics, illusions, adventure.

So what do you do? You keep alert for opportunities to resist in your own unique manner. Then one day a big chance materializes. You elect to engage the Army rather than the Viet Cong. You tell Captain Bligh, and the ideology he represents, to go to hell.

Dawn emerged warm, listless. While Blehm was lacing his boots in preparation for the morning operation, someone placed a handwritten note on his bunk. It was the First's ultimatum. The correspondence demanded that men under thirty days and men with medical profiles not go on patrols; that a medic go on all operations; and that a plausible explanation be given as to why leaves were canceled. From previous conversations with Blehm it was understood that unless the grievances were satisfied, the First would refuse to go on the morning patrol.

Blehm raced downstairs to Simpson. The First was commanded to saddle up. No one stirred. Lounging, smoking, and conversing in confident, determined tones, we waited for Simpson's move.

It wasn't a long wait. Simpson summoned us to formation on the ground floor of the sugar mill. Without gear we meandered downstairs and assembled. Simpson strode before us, set his boots, and in a supplicating tongue he commanded us to saddle up. He said that we were already late for the operation. But if we immediately relented he wouldn't castigate us. Wavering under the pressure, PFCs Bruckner and Butler—new men— dropped out of the formation.

This encouraged Simpson. He responded to our note item by item, stressing manpower needs, offering excuses, and reminding us of our roles as subordinates. He said that what we were doing was grave and stupid. He told us to think it over a moment. Sweating copiously and licking his parched lips, he wobbled away with his first sergeant and platoon leaders.

When he stood before us again he gave us a final chance to saddle up. Stealing glances at each other for confidence, we held fast. We were committed now. After more deliberation with his lieutenants, Simpson announced that he was required to individually order us to go on the patrol. The divide and conquer trick.

The initial man mustered before Simpson was a small, baby-faced fellow from Chicago. It was a crucial moment. If the rifleman vacillated perhaps the mutiny would collapse. The captain said, "I hereby order you to get your gear and go out on this morning's operation!" In a sturdy, defiant voice, Wishard, who had been in-country only four months, quickly retorted, "I refuse, Sir!"

We were inspired by Wishard's grit and the risk he took by being the first to refuse. Thereafter Simpson heard eighteen consecutive refusals. He had given us plenty of outs but no one recanted.

The CO asked for a spokesman to discuss the grievances. Afraid of being singled out, everyone hesitated. Nash, Tremaine, and I looked at each other nervously, feeling guilty about our personal silence and hoping someone would speak up. When Simpson queried again, Flores, a short-timer who had been transferred to the First while I was at LCLC, stepped forward. Flores trotted off with the first sergeant. Simpson dismissed us. Giggling and swarming over each other like a hockey club celebrating a big win, we climbed to our lair of rebellion. We lolled away the morning recounting our experience, discussing tactics. Our ebullience soared when we learned that battalion had been advised of the insurrection.

The CO ordered the Second on the operation in our place. The Simpson loyalists in our platoon accompanied the Second. Hours later we heard that the Second was in contact and in need of ground support. Simpson sent his trembling first sergeant up to our floor. With his Adam's apple jerking wildly, he requested—not ordered—that the First saddle up and help the Second. He explained that the Third was on another operation. We were closer to the Second. We unanimously voted to go. The issue was simple: our friends needed us. Now that news of the revolt had reached Cu Chi, anything could happen. We had no ambition to reject further orders. We had made our point. For once, just once, we had said no to their sordid war. Whatever punishment they bestowed upon us couldn't spoil the luster of our triumph. We were euphoric, confident. And why not? Hadn't we been victorious in our April confrontation with DeFreeze over walking point?

But by the time we prepared ourselves, the operation was abruptly canceled. Relieved over not having to go out, we braced for Simpson's inevitable counterattack.

That evening Simpson ordered the First on an ambush patrol, excusing Tremaine, Nash, Gibson, and Flores. He wanted to talk to them about the grievances. Without debate, the rest of us fulfilled the ambush. A few days later we were singly beckoned to the CP. The initial men to return from their caucus with Simpson were armed with company Article 15s.

My turn came. I sat on a rickety wooden crate before Simpson. He appeared sedate, poised, open-faced. Relaxed. Not a trickle of sweat was on him. It was his kind of atmosphere. He flashed a broad, complacent grin. "Morning, Kitchin."

"Morning, Sir."

He gave me a hard look. "Well, Kitchin, I've decided to give you a battalion Article 15. That's a bust to Spec Four and a fine of ninety dollars."

"Yes, Sir."

The CO smacked his lips and frowned. He arched his brow and with an authoritarian glare he growled, "Kitchin, I don't understand you. Why did you go along with this stupid thing? Why did you let these other fools talk you into this?" He cast his arms apart in a gesture of chagrin. "You were in Cu Chi while all this trouble was brewing. How could you be sure about what was going on out here?"

"Sir, they didn't talk me into anything. I chose to go along with the refusal because I knew what my friends said was happenin' out here was true. I don't have to be out here to find out what's been goin' on. They wouldn't lie to me about somethin' as important as this, no more than I'd lie to them. And besides, once I get to thirty days I want to quit humpin' like everybody else has ever since I got here. I think it's only fair to reward a man like that for doin' eleven months out here without fuckin' off.

"Also, I feel we shouldn't have to go on patrols without a trained medic. There's just no way we should have to go out for several weeks without one. About the leaves bein' canceled, Sir, my morale is pretty low over hearin' about this new policy because frankly I was lookin' forward to my leave. How can you do this to us? I'm under the impression that leaves are mandatory because I've never heard of 'em bein' canceled before."

"No, no, they're not mandatory. They're earned and given out only at the approval of the commanding officer."

"Oh."

I was going to grapple only with the obvious. I had decided that a dialogue on the more subtle reasons for our refusal would've been futile; there was no point in provoking Simpson any further. I also squelched the potent urge to inquire what the colonels and generals in Cu Chi had to say about all this.

"Kitchin, you should know that no subordinate has the right to dictate manpower decisions to a commanding officer, so you will just have to go along with the program."

"Yes, Sir," I purred, like a good subordinate.

"Okay, Kitchin, I still don't understand why you're involved in this, but it's too late to do anything about it." He thrust some documents before me. "Sign here." I signed. He stuffed the Army's disciplinary papers into a manila envelope. I was about to ask him if I was dismissed when he cleared his throat and looked at me beseechingly. "Kitchin, you know, I still have some hope for you."

I was perplexed, wide-eyed. "What?"

"I mean, I think that despite this nonsense that you got yourself involved in, you still can become a strack trooper and do a good job your last few months over here."

"Well, Sir, I don't know. I-I . . ."

"Okay, okay, Kitchin, you're dismissed. And Kitchin," he added as I strolled towards the stairs, "you should be more particular about who you pick for friends!"

I turned, nodded. I also murmured, "Fuck you!" Under my breath, of course.

Throughout the day Simpson dispensed his retribution. Six of us were conferred reduction in grade and fines. Nine men received only reduction in grade. The most disconcerting reprisals were special courts-martial distributed to Gibson, Nash, Tremaine, and Rojas.

The courts-martial jolted the First. Simpson had selected the men whom he suspected were the ringleaders. He was determined to teach all of us a lesson that none of us would forget. The trial was scheduled for October 7. It would be held in the field; the long arm of military law would reach into the wilds of Vietnam.

Meanwhile, there was still another war raging.

22

Phuoc Luu

Shortly after our rebellion Bravo departed the sugar mill. We were trucked to a village situated less than two miles from the Cambodian border. For the ensuing six weeks we lived in the hamlet and went on patrols, often accompanied by the local militia.

Phuoc Luu was one of those rural Vietnamese villages whose loyalty shifted towards whatever element was currently dominating it. The inhabitants were rice farmers and craftsmen. The place seemed to be prosperous, no doubt due to the lucrative trading effected across the frontier before our arrival. And happy days continued with us. The black market was incredible. Once we instructed a ten-year-old that we required three bottles of red-eye. He scampered off. Within an hour we had our spirits, whatever we ordered, right down to the label.

Phuoc Luu was a photographer's utopia, a kaleidoscope of activity, spectacle, and color. Snapshots: stick-legged, white egrets camped on the backs of mud-caked water buffaloes, picking ticks. Children riding the smelly buffaloes as they lumbered against an orange sunset. Women carrying choggle sticks across a shimmering checkerboard of green paddies. A schoolteacher dressed in a cao dai, a high-necked, colorful, silky gown split to the waist. A yellow-beaked mynah bird perched on a hedge of red hibiscus. Exotic flowering foliage; orchids and frangipani, jacaranda, and flame trees.

The village huts were mostly thatched edifices with doors front and rear. Some homes had tin roofs. A few buildings, presumably owned by the wealthier folks, were made of brick and mortar, complete with porches and shingled roofs. Brittle, sun-baked branches served as fences around small yards. Palmyra and toddy palm trees dotted the town. A mélange of dogs, chickens, pigs, birds, and children rollicked about. Shallow ditches along the shoulders of the dirt roads functioned as public lavatories and garbage heaps. Makeshift bridges of logs or boards stretched across the gutters. Characteristic of foreign soldiers, we christened three of the more popular thoroughfares Asshole Alley, Defecation Drive, and Dung Street.

Inside the homes were neat, cool, and sparsely furnished. There were no modern amenities. Beaded blinds covered windows. The villagers slept on hammocks or plank beds, maybe four feet by six feet. Woven mats covered the beds and parts of the earthen floors. Usually the back door opened into a diminutive courtyard which contained a well and perhaps an outbuilding or two. In a rear corner of each hootch an aperture dropped into a bunker. Tiny shrines with burning incense, flowers and pictures of deceased loved ones glittered on a table or shelf. This was a sacred place in the home. We kept our hands off it.

The peasants wore their baggy, dingy pajama outfits. The children went barefoot; the adults wore sandals. Everyone donned the traditional broad-brimmed, cone-shaped coolie hats of woven bamboo, which served as umbrellas against the sun and rain.

The women, like civilians in all wars, tried to maintain a semblance of normal life by conducting their affairs without exhibiting much interest in us. While cutting fish for meals or sweeping dirt out of their front door with a bamboo broom, they flashed their betel nut–stained teeth at us. But what were they thinking?

The sparkling brown children were like fledglings anywhere. Inquisitive, friendly, playful, and sometimes awestruck by the giants in green uniforms who packed sundries, C-rations, and lukewarm Coke. The kids were capable entrepreneurs. There was no dalliance in submitting their price for a backrub or to wash our clothes or to clean our muddy boots. They were cognizant of what we toted; they knew precisely what item they wanted in remuneration for their services. And when we paid the youngster it was virtually impossible not to increase our recompense as we looked down, way down, at a smiling, innocent face highlighted by two glistening dark gems.

When we didn't pull ambush patrols there were two outposts we had to populate at night. One post was a squad-sized bunker in a corner of the village. The other fortress was located forty meters outside the hamlet. Protected by tanglefoot and concertina wire and dozens of claymores, the latter was a square base reminiscent of Revolutionary War redoubts. It had dirt mounds for breastworks. Four enormous bunkers were positioned in each corner.

One dusk six of us were assigned to the squad-sized bunker at the edge of the village. While the others observed a fiery sunset, I lounged inside the bunker chatting with Reynolds. Suddenly he told me to freeze. He said that a snake was curling around some bamboo in the wall beside my head. At first I thought he was clowning. When he slowly reached for his rifle I knew he was serious.

I clenched my fists and struggled to control my urge to duck away. Reynolds whispered that when he was ready he'd blink his eye. Then I was to lurch away from the wall. Aiming at the slithering reptile, he put the muzzle of his sixteen a foot from my head. He blinked. With a scream I dived clear. Reynolds fired. The snake, hit in the head, jerked and fell from the wall. It was over a yard long and as thick as a banana.

I thanked Reynolds for his poise and marksmanship. Since we didn't care to meet the snake's relatives, we took it and quit the bunker. Some Vietnamese saw the serpent and indicated they wanted it to eat; to them snakes were a delicacy. We accommodated them. Not all hazards in Vietnam involved the VC.

The days we didn't go on sweeps we mingled with the villagers. Living among the resourceful peasants helped us to understand the culture we were fighting. By our Western standards the people were materially poor. But on another level the Vietnamese seemed rich because they were more ethereal and timeless than our technology-oriented, fast-paced society. They lived in harmony with the environment. Their life cadences were regulated by the elements rather than by the date or clock. Their kindness, reticence and unpretentiousness was arresting. They were an interesting people.

On some ambush patrols we had to journey through the village to reach our ambush site. As we trekked through the streets it was dark, but not quite time to sleep. I peeped into the hootches, which were illuminated by candles and glowing fires. On cool, stormy nights the family hearth was surrounded by a young woman or two, some old people, and the little ones. They were talking, eating or playing, sharing in the miracle called "family."

Jealousy engulfs you. You want to discard your paraphernalia of war and abandon your place in the file. You desire to partake in the warmth flourishing inside a thatched hut. But you aren't the man who belongs there. Where is the person who does? Is he dead? Is he in the ARVN? Is he snooping across a paddy fabricating booby traps? It doesn't matter. You hope, nearly breaching the patrol rules by praying aloud, that he'll return unscathed to his fire and waiting family. And then, with equal fervor, you pray that someday you also will return to your home.

While we had no VC contact at Phuoc Luu, we did have difficulty avoiding injury by friendlies. One night we tramped around the hamlet only to confront the village yeomanry strolling to their ambush site. We heard each other. Neither force knew for certain who the other was. We set up skirmish lines and prepared to duel. Then the Asians thought of igniting a flare to see who was sloshing in the paddy water before them. It was a narrow escape. Incidents like these always made me wonder when my well would run dry.

Another night we were marching west to our ambush coordinates on the border. A few miles to the south a firefight erupted between the VC and another unit. We advanced while intermittently glancing at the fracas, hoping that the VC wouldn't retreat in our direction. Artillery was blasting into the area. Gunships were swarming above the melee, squirting tracers. Suddenly a thunderous, brilliant orange explosion brightened the night. We dropped flat. A huge display of orange fires fanned across the sky like fireworks. An artillery round had hit a chopper, fracturing it into a billion specks of flame. We rose and proceeded to our ambush site. There was nothing we could do. It had happened far away. It was someone else's war.

After months of treading in water many of us contracted skin diseases from our knees down. Caused by fungi, the infected areas were characterized by discolored patches shrouded with vesicles and scales. The itch was unbearable. We scraped and clawed until we were hairless.

The Army wasn't totally oblivious to our miseries. A medical chopper from Cu Chi arrived one afternoon. A doctor and his Asian trainees bounded off the transport. Inside our larger outpost they erected a medical station under a poncho tent. We queued for analysis of our skin ailments. When my turn came I settled my feet onto a stool before the physician.

The major scrutinized my aching red skin. "Un-huh, yep, yep, un-huh," he muttered. "Say, this is quite a specimen here!" He summoned his assistants. The team circled around my feet. "Look at this, this man has contracted two of the principal skin diseases found among our troops here in the Nam." It's just wonderful to be a medical marvel.

"Yes sir, look here, gentlemen," he continued while pointing with a pencil, "these red blotches here are advanced impetigo. Not a doubt about it. And these round patches over here are ringworm. Notice the complete absence of body hair in the infected areas. Hmmm, and these spots here are, hmmm, well, let's see, probably just your basic, ordinary jungle rot. The rainy season sure is rough on American feet. It looks bad, real bad." He looked up at me. "Does it hurt much, soldier?"

"Oh yes, Sir," I cried, twitching my cheek and looking grim. "I can hardly walk. I have trouble keepin' up on patrols. Some nights I can hardly sleep, Sir." I was putting down a thick coat. The doctor's auxiliaries blinked at me pitifully.

"Un-huh, you definitely have an acute case."

"Yes, Sir," I echoed, waiting for his decree that I was unfit for field duty until my feet dried out. *Cu Chi, here I come!* I could already taste the rum and hear "Hey Jude" at the EM club.

"Well, I'll tell you what to do, soldier." He reached into his medicine receptacle. "Go to that well over there and wash your feet with this." He gave me a bar of Ivory.

I was irked. "Hey man, that damn water is filthy! It's the same water that gave me these sore feet! You should know that! You're the doctor!"

The alarmed apprentices leaned back. "Oh no," the doctor said, unfettered and not missing being called Sir, "that water's okay for washing. Go on now, give yourself a good wash. And, oh yes, one more thing, try to keep your feet dry."

When I realized that he was serious I tossed the soap into his lap and limped away.

A particular patrol at Phuoc Luu was unique for me. The First deployed in a cluster of bushes thirty meters from a dirt road trailing from the village. I had first guard in my group. As usual I settled down to think and to consume my two hours. The night was warm and alive with the hiss of mosquitoes. A few hundred meters to the south, lightning forked over the village, brightening chunky thunderclouds and causing dogs to howl in alarm.

Then I saw a figure on the road. Or what appeared to be a figure. Looking twice, three times, it appeared to be moving. I squinted, strained, and gaped. Soon I thought I discerned more silhouettes. Because it was an overcast night the starlight scope was useless. I poked Rickenbrode and Nash. They looked. They didn't see anything except a skinny tree out near the road. I insisted that I saw VC. They were skeptical but they alerted the balance of the platoon. One man proclaimed that my VC was a tree. He rolled over and went back to sleep. After another steady gaze at the figure Nash looked at me compassionately then snuggled into his poncho liner. Rickenbrode tapped me on the back and told me to forget it. He dozed off. I spent the next hour and a half checking my ghost on the road. When my shift expired I conceded to Rickenbrode that the silhouette hadn't moved in an hour and a half. I awoke with the first dim rays of dawn. In the chilly morning placidity, we determined that my VC was a six foot sapling.

It was the initial time that I saw something, panicked, then convinced myself that VC were present. My apparition left me anxious, embarrassed. It wasn't like me to hallucinate, to get the whole patrol aroused over nothing. It could only be due to one thing. I was starting to go. I was under seventy-five days. My nerves were exhausted. From that mission onward I knew that I couldn't contribute much, even if I wanted to.

Captain Simpson remained in command of Bravo. To his credit, he wasn't vindictive towards any of the conspirators. He treated the First no differently than the balance of Bravo. For some weeks he didn't alter any of his company precepts. But when replacements arrived, swelling our ranks, he relented on making short-timers go out. He still, however, vetoed seven-day leave requests. The First received another medic from Cu Chi which alleviated that issue.

More good news was that we were relieved of Lieutenant Prigmore. His term of service was over, thus his Vietnam tour was aborted. He had enrolled in college. Back in the world, back at UCLA, the fall semester was beginning.

Like us, Captain Simpson seemed to be patiently waiting for the trial. Among ourselves we discussed the upcoming proceedings. Our vision of the trial was that, while only four men were indicted, the entire First was on trial. It was still an "us against them" atmosphere. The four knew they could rely on the balance of the First for assistance in their impending quandary.

We were apprehensive that the trial would be a circus, a mockery. Expecting the worst, the defendants went to Cu Chi for a few days to confer with the two young lawyers assigned to the defense. The four returned to Phuoc Luu with some astonishing facts. Captains Rohrig and Bankovich, the barristers, were sympathetic toward what had happened to the First. Remarkably, they also felt the war was absurd. Even the trial counsel had expressed his chagrin over being appointed the prosecution officer. First Lieutenant Engraf was outranked by the captains, thus exiled to accusation chores. We couldn't have had more properly disposed attorneys if we had ordered them custom-made from Harvard. They assured the defendants that the verdict wasn't a foregone conclusion.

We surmised that the reason Simpson selected Rojas and Gibson for courts-martial was so he couldn't be accused of racial prejudice. While Rojas and Gibson were among the hardcore revolutionary element in the First, they weren't ringleaders. There weren't any masterminds in the strictest sense because the idea for the revolt was a grass roots inspiration, a kind of spontaneous combustion.

But if there were catalysts in the broadest sense, then Nash, Tremaine and I were candidates. Once the seed had germinated we helped to nurture it to fruition. Without our persuasion the plot probably would've occurred but it might not have involved as many men as it did.

I was astounded that Simpson had omitted me for court-martial. He seemed to target NCOs and short-timers for that penalty. My E-5 papers had gone through while I was at LCLC, so I met that criterion. However, the four who were picked for courts-martial all had more time in-country. Another reason he skipped me, we theorized, was that he didn't want too many whites indicted. Two whites, a black and a Hispanic seemed to cover the field. We didn't have any Indians or Orientals involved in the refusal, or probably, we joked, they also would've been court-martialed. Furthermore, Simpson knew Nash and Tremaine. He clearly disliked them. Since I had been at LCLC he hadn't had a chance to learn to detest me.

Perhaps he deduced that he'd have a difficult time convicting me because I had reported to the field only the afternoon before the refusal, ergo how could I know what was happening, let alone instigate anything? Another potentiality was that what he had told me during my interview was the truth: maybe he genuinely felt I was misdirected by more corrupt personnel, thus undeserving of a court-martial.

In any event, I eluded being court-martialed. It left me twirling in a nebulous amalgam of guilt and glee. Nobody wants to be court-martialed. I was elated over that. But I felt guilty about two of my best friends being punished more severely than I was, even if it wasn't my doing. I had done as much buttonholing as they had done the night before the refusal.

Should I have asked Simpson to court-martial me to assuage my guilt or to prevent my friends from being jealous of my good fortune? Or would that be an absurd sense of loyalty? I felt that in a way I had already demonstrated my loyalty by declining DeFreeze's offer of an RTO job in the CP. I concluded that volunteering for a court-martial wouldn't be an act of friendship. It would be stupidity. A true friend wouldn't expect me to anyway.

23

The Sleeping Princess

The stretcher carriers lowered their burden in our path in the middle of the dirt road. A multitude of villagers, including members of the local militia, swarmed around the litter yelling and wailing in their native tongue. There was much commotion. Nash, Tremaine and I became unnerved by the behavior of these normally reticent people. We made certain our rifles were loaded just in case. We were bound for a well in the middle of Phuoc Luu to take a shower. We had left behind all our gear except our rifles.

"Looks like someone's been hurt," I said.

"Yeah," said Nash. "Let's check it out. But let's be cool. We're all too short now to get careless."

We maneuvered down the road towards the crowd. A woman in the throng noticed us. She shrieked and pointed to the stretcher. We ambled close to the rack and saw a girl, perhaps eleven or twelve, lying motionless on her stomach. Her slender frame covered little space on the canvas. Her long black hair glistened in the merciless sun.

The horde grew in quantity, frenzy. Medics joined the confusion. Some Wolfhound officers appeared with their Vietnamese interpreters. The village chief and his entourage stormed onto the scene. A cluster of people, probably the girl's relatives, were bawling and embracing each other by the side of the road.

"I wonder what's wrong with her?" said Tremaine. "She looks like she's asleep. She looks just like a sleepin' princess."

We elbowed through the mob and peered over a medic's shoulder for a closer view. No blood or wounds were visible. Her black pajama pants and white blouse were stainless. The soft morning breeze intermittently lifted her radiant hair. Tiny golden earrings pierced her ears. A boy darted to the girl, gently raised one of her fingers, and removed a thin ring. He dashed to the group by the edge of the road.

An important-looking Vietnamese man with a neatly-trimmed goatee squatted next to the girl. He muttered something and nervously rubbed his hands together. After hesitating a moment, he rolled her over. Everyone expounded a gasp. Tremaine, Nash and I reeled back. The girl was without a face. She had no features of any kind. Nothing. From her upper neck to her forehead was gaping chasm. The man placed a blue silk cloth over her head.

An altercation ensued between the Vietnamese officials and the Americans. The Vietnamese were furious and gesturing to the sky and rotating their arms. The interpreters and the somber Americans kept nodding agreement, trying to placate the seething villagers. We realized there was nothing we could do. We left for the well.

Later that morning we heard that the girl had been killed by an American helicopter pilot who thought it was necessary to stampede a herd of water buffaloes grazing in a field. The girl had been standing on a nearby hill when the chopper dived too low and its rotary struck the child. Witnesses proclaimed that it was a small observation chopper, the ones that often scouted around alone, the kind used by high-ranking officers.

24

The Trial

The Phuoc Luu school was situated in the middle of the village. The school consisted of two rectangular, concrete, one-story structures. They flanked a dirt courtyard which functioned as the school recess area. The east section was used by the children for classes. Bravo employed the west side as quarters. Each building had five large rooms. Many of the cubicles had structural damage from previous battles. A few of the rooms were roofless; all were doorless.

When we didn't go on night patrols or pull bunker guard, the First spent the night at the school. I often reflected how simple it would be for a saboteur to toss a few grenades into the rooms as we slept. Half a platoon would've been exterminated with two explosives. The sapper would've had little trouble escaping into the shadows and hiding places in the village. It was difficult to get a good night's rest in Vietnam.

Before the trial began on the morning of October 7, portable metal chairs and tables were erected in one of the schoolrooms. At nine-thirty a military judge, the lawyers, and a court reporter arrived by chopper and hiked to the schoolhouse.

The four defendants, nervous and silent, took their places behind a table on one side of the room. Their attorneys, Captains Rohrig and Bankovich, flanked them. On the other side the judge and trial counsel took seats. A chair for witnesses was placed in the center of the room. No court observers were permitted.

At ten o'clock the judge called the session to order. The accused were arraigned. Charge: violation of the Uniform Code of Military Justice, Article 90. Specification: in that the Four, U.S. Army, Company B, 2nd Battalion, 27th Infantry, 25th Infantry Division, having received a lawful command from Captain Fred Simpson, their superior commissioned officer, to prepare to go on a combat operation, did, at the Sugar Mill, vicinity XT 4307, Republic of Vietnam, on or about 3 September 1969, willfully disobey the same.

The defense motioned that the charges be dismissed on the ground that the four's rights under the Due Process clause of the Fourteenth

Amendment were violated in that the four had been arbitrarily selected for disproportionate punishment. The defense requested that the ruling on the motion be delayed until after the presentation of the cases for the prosecution and defense. The judge agreed.

The accused were asked to enter their pleas. Each pleaded "not guilty" to the charge and specification.

Lieutenant Engraf, the trial counsel, made an opening statement, proclaiming that through the testimony of three witnesses the government would prove that: at zero seven-thirty hours on the morning of September 3, 1969, Captain Simpson gave a legitimate order to nineteen members of First Platoon, including the accused, to go on patrol; that they failed to go on the mission; that the operation was necessary despite the fact that no medic was available to accompany it; and that on the basis of personal conversations, rank, experience, and leadership in the affair, Simpson recommended six individuals for court-martial.

The initial witness was Sergeant Blehm. Under direct examination he related the events of the refusal. Lieutenant Engraf asked him if he thought that refusing to go on a patrol was a violation of UCMJ. The defense objected, stating that the prosecution was trying to extract a legal opinion from the witness which he wasn't competent to offer. The objection was sustained.

Captain Bankovich then questioned Blehm:

"Who gave you the note with the list of demands?"

"I don't know. Someone put it on my bunk and told me to give it to the CO before the operation. I didn't recognize the voice. Up on that floor of the sugar mill there were quite a few people walking around, eating."

"What were the demands?"

"That short-timers under thirty days and people with medical profiles not go on operations; that a medic accompany all patrols; and that seven-day leaves be reinstated."

"Was that the first time you found out the problem with medics was as serious as it was?"

"Well, not really. I had heard a lot of complaints about the lack of medics, and I had talked to the CO about it myself. He said he was trying to get medics. We had been without a medic for three weeks. The First Platoon wasn't really sure whether the CO could send them out without a medic for such a long period without their consent."

"Do you feel a medic should accompany every operation?"

"Yes, Sir, especially a platoon-sized operation or larger. I don't consider it a good practice to go out consistently without a medic. In times past, we've gone a single mission without one, but never for long periods."

"What type of missions did you go on without medics?"

"Daytime sweeps, night APs, LPs."

"How far did you go without medics?"

"We had to go seven to ten clicks on sweeps, sometimes up the river five clicks. We went about seven clicks from the sugar mill without medics."

"Did you eventually get a medic?"

"Yes, Sir, we were able to get a medic from another company about midnight on the day of the refusal."

"What was the company policy for men under thirty days before Captain Simpson assumed command?"

"Captain DeFreeze, our former CO, had a policy in which people under thirty days wouldn't be required to go out unless it was tactically necessary. From what I heard, the policy was in effect before he came, and there was even a sixty and ninety day policy at one time."

"What was Captain Simpson's policy?"

"At first Captain Simpson didn't actually make his policy clear. During our Hilton stand-down he said one thing, but later at the sugar mill he changed. Eventually he stated that men with under thirty days left in-country would have to go out if there weren't thirty men otherwise."

"Were you always able to get thirty men to go on missions?"

"No, Sir, most of the time the platoons didn't have thirty men in the field."

"What about in the past?"

"In the past we never had any problems letting short-timers stay in, but then it wasn't necessary to send out thirty people. It all depended on the AO, the amount of contact we were having, and other information."

"Did you feel that before you were sending out a safe number?"

"Yes, Sir."

"Did Captain Simpson ever sit down with the platoon to discuss your grievances prior to the refusal?"

"No, Sir. Neither did the first sergeant."

"Why do you think these four men were singled out for court-martial?"

"I really don't know. I spoke to the CO and Top, trying to find out. To my knowledge they had done nothing different than anyone else. Someone had told the CO that certain individuals were the instigators of the refusal, although I don't know who it was. Probably the CO chose these people for courts-martial through interviews and discussions with other people. I think the CO determined to his satisfaction that these four were the instigators of the refusal. In addition, these are the higher-ranking people in terms of time in-country, and the other members tend to look up to them. The new people tend to look up to all short-timers."

"Did you ask Captain Simpson not to court-martial these men?"

"Yes, Sir, I did. I told him I realized that their way of handling the thing was wrong, but I was sure the men realized the seriousness of their mistake. I told him that a federal conviction could cost them for the rest of their lives, and I didn't think they should have to suffer for the rest of their lives. He said he already had the paperwork in and he couldn't let them get by with doing something like that or they'd be doing it over and over."

"Do you feel that Captain Simpson's policies were reasonable?"

"There was quite a bit of misunderstanding about the policies. It's unreasonable to think that you can get thirty people to go out on every platoon operation every day. Very few people with thirty days or less will stay back with such a policy. Often twenty to twenty-two men on an AP is quite enough. Canceling leaves is definitely bad for morale. None of these men are professional soldiers, most of them are in for two years. They work just to stay alive and to keep their friends alive, then go home."

"What kind of soldiers are these four?"

"These four men are very good soldiers. In fact, the whole platoon is good. We've never had any problems before and they've always gone out in the past."

"Would you like these men to continue to serve under you?"

"Yes, Sir."

The court recessed for a brief lunch. Blehm, the unpopular platoon sergeant of the First, the prosecution's first witness, the man who wanted no part of a mutiny, had emerged as an excellent attestant for the defense. None of us expected he would say all the good things he did. With his surprising remarks, he proved us to be mistaken about his concern and insight, demonstrating that even headstrong revolutionaries sometimes grossly err.

When the court reconvened, the next witness, Bravo's first sergeant, reiterated the testimony of Sergeant Blehm. He emphasized that the decision as to the type of punishment each mutineer would receive was Simpson's alone. The first sergeant acknowledged that originally six men were recommended for courts-martial, but the battalion commander had authorized Article 15s for the other two "probably because they were PFCs."

Next the prosecution's star witness took his seat before the court. Sweating enough to look like he just stepped from a shower, Simpson wiggled tensely in his chair as he identified the four. Lieutenant Engraf asked Simpson to describe the events of the morning of September 3. Stammering and blinking at the air he began, "I-I-I was sitting down, looking at a map, thinking about that day's operation, when I was brought a list by

Sergeant Blehm with four demands on it from First Platoon. I told him to get First Platoon and bring them downstairs, then I talked to Lieutenant Prigmore and the first sergeant and made an outline of the answers to their grievances. The platoon formed, and then, item by item, I went down the list and explained the points.

"The operation was scheduled to commence at zero seven-forty-five and the formation was held at about zero seven-thirty. I told them that I was aware of the thirty-day policy the previous commander had but I explained that I couldn't guarantee this. The division policy is three days prior; normally, they pull the men out about six days prior. I told them I'd send them in eight days prior. I told them I couldn't make any promises about taking them off-line early. Sometimes I only had twelve or fifteen men on platoon operations across the river. I had two platoons to work with and I needed about thirty men in each. I told them that I could understand their anxiety about the shortage of medics. I only had one medic and I had to have him go out both night and day, I had them keep the medic on the boat and keep the boat as near the platoon as possible. I sent in two individuals from the company for training as medics.

"At commander's call, everyone in the battalion was screaming for medics. As soon as I took the company I told the battalion commander I needed medics. Addison had impetigo and he worked for a few days, but the battalion surgeon finally said he'd have to stay in. We used him as a medic in the CP for a few days, then finally I had to send him to the rear. Right away I called battalion, but still I could get only one medic.

"I told the whole group that we had an operation and that they were to get their gear and get ready to go. The twenty just stood there, so I told the first sergeant to take names. I asked the S-3 over the radio if there was any such thirty-day off-line policy in this battalion, and he said there wasn't. I asked him again about the medic situation, and if there was any policy which prohibited sending out operations without a medic—again, no policy. I told the men I didn't like to do it, but there was no other way. I reminded them that the medic was in a boat and fairly close to the area next to the platoon. I also told them about the OJT program for medics, and that we had sent two people for training.

"I called up each man and counseled him individually. I gave him a direct order, something like: 'As your CO, I give you a direct order to go on this combat operation.' But they all refused this order."

Engraf interrupted Simpson's dissertation by asking him what reasons the men gave for refusing his order. Simpson flitted his eyes and said, "Their excuse generally was that they wanted a guarantee they'd get off-line thirty days prior to DEROS. The people who refused had everywhere from ten months left to thirty-one days, and I told them that in many cases I wouldn't even be their CO when they DEROS'd. Then they said they wanted their friends with thirty days or less to get off-line. Many of them told me that if they'd known the whole story earlier, they'd have gone out. Generally they had nothing against me. As for the leaves, those were a privilege to be earned, not a right. I told them that the whole battalion was short on medics. One man told me he was afraid to go out without a medic. I asked him what he'd do if the medic was the first to get killed. He said he didn't know. The biggest complaint seemed to be the loss of the thirty-day policy.

"A couple of days before I had had a little run-in with Sergeant Tremaine. He seemed to be very nervous and somewhat afraid, so I told him I wanted him to prove himself. He had been staying in the rear, and I asked him why and he said that Top kept him back. One particular night Tremaine didn't want to go out, so another man volunteered to take his place to keep Tremaine from getting in trouble. I had three short-time sergeants and forty-four people in the rear at that time. Tremaine wanted off-line because he was getting nervous and didn't want to be leading people. He was an NCO, however, and I needed to use him as one.

"I sort of took a personal interest in Flores and talked with him a little about personal problems. I asked him during the interview why he was doing this and he said it was because he wanted to stick with his friends. I never got much out of Rojas. The next day they were all together and said they knew they had goofed and they wanted to be treated individually, and I thought they should be punished as individuals. People had different attitudes about the whole thing. Most of them were really concerned over the thirty-day policy. Other people had heard of platoon refusals happening before. I believe Flores said he knew of two platoons that had sat down on an ambush, and nothing was done about it. Others said that if they had to do it again, they wouldn't. I begged Gibson to reconsider during the interview, but he wouldn't."

"Okay, thank you," Engraf said. The Lieutenant turned to Bankovich. "Your witness."

Bankovich leaped up and paced around the room, a faint smile flickering on his face. He halted next to the witness, his agate eyes boring into the black man. Hovering over the perspiring, grim-jawed Simpson like a bee zeroing in on a flower, Bankovich began, "How long were you Bravo's CO when this incident happened?"

"About two weeks."

"Did you ask your predecessor about his policies?"

"Captain DeFreeze and I talked about four hours when I first took over."

"Fine. Did you discuss his thirty-day policy?"

"No."

"Did you talk to the battalion commander about the medic policy?"

"This is my second tour in Vietnam. I had read the battalion SOP and talked to the battalion commander about his policies but I had no reason to ask whether it was against any battalion policy to send a platoon out without a medic, although I did ask the S-3 on the day of the incident, just to be sure."

"What is the difference between a leave and an R & R?"

"An R & R is a right and a leave is a privilege."

"What about those men who already had leaves scheduled when you announced that leaves were being terminated?"

"Those who were definitely scheduled to take a leave did so. What I wanted to do was only postpone or change leaves if necessary, not take them away."

"In Cu Chi did you tell the company there would be fewer Article 15s and courts-martial under you?"

"Yes."

"Did you have any idea whether there had been a lot of these before?"

"No. It's a standard thing to say. I tell them how I treat a company. I said we were going to cut out the courts-martial. If we have problems, I told them, we'll get to the root of them; we'll take care of personal problems, or if there are troublemakers, we'll take care of them. It's a standard speech, a pep talk, that I give anywhere I go. I want to let them know who I am. I tell them we'll take care of any problems: 'Your problems are my problems.' I interviewed the senior NCOs, and told them to alert me to any problems in the company. Also I talked to the platoon leaders. That's why I knew about Sergeant Tremaine's nervousness. They told me when I came in the battalion that B company was the best, then I found out that people were smoking marijuana, and then there was the medic problem. I had to deal with a succession of problems. After the refusal I went to the battalion commander and said, 'Give me a medic!' I took a medic back with me that night."

"Did the tactical situation at the sugar mill demand thirty men on every patrol?"

"The tactical situation varies. Sometimes you'll be able to operate with thirty men, sometimes with fewer. When you're patrolling west of the river, you need a whole battalion; on the east side, you can reinforce easily and get to people, so you need fewer people in the original patrol. You're never supposed to go anyplace you might be required to hold for more than one hour. In the operations we were working, I had to have thirty men. If we couldn't get enough men otherwise, I'd have to send men with less than thirty days."

"Did you in fact have men with fewer than thirty days going on operations?"

"Yes."

"Who decides who will stay back?"

"The platoon leader."

"Did you make any effort to leave back short-timers?"

"If we can afford to, we try to keep those men back, but I can make no guarantees."

"How often does a platoon go out?"

"The platoons at the sugar mill go twenty-four hours on, then twenty-four hours off. First Platoon had stood down the day before, and it was their turn to go out."

"Don't you think there was a communications breakdown here someplace?"

"Yes, there must have been some kind of communications breakdown. Tremaine was nervous and the NCOs didn't say anything about it. Sergeant Blehm should have come to me about Tremaine. Also, I think the leadership fell down in the rear area. I think a man should be able to discuss his personal problems with his superiors. As CO, I don't want to see the man struggle with his problems alone."

"Why do you feel the men refused to go out?"

"I guess, by acting as a group, these men hoped they could change their tour to eleven months. If they could do that, then they'd protest until they'd get a ten-month tour. All of them disobeyed the order for different reasons. Some of them went along with some of the demands, but not all."

"But doesn't an officer serve only five or six months in the field before rotation to the rear?"

"Yes, an officer will normally spend five, six or seven months on-line."

"Why did you interview each man individually?"

"By interviewing each man individually I wanted to find out what type of punishment would be appropriate, on an individual basis. I really wondered why they thought they had a right to do this. After answering their questions, I told them what I could recommend as punishment. I had no idea of the punishment I'd impose at the time. I was trying to see how they thought, and to see who started the whole thing."

"Did anyone tell you who wrote the note?"

"No."

"Did you receive information from a certain person as to who the instigators were?"

"Yes, I got information from someone that Nash, Tremaine and Rojas were the instigators of the refusal, or at least the main participants."

"Who gave you the information?"

"The information given to me by this person was given in confidence. I regard it as confidential."

The judge interrupted to advise the witness that unless he was a physician, lawyer or clergyman he didn't have the right nor the privilege to refuse to give information obtained in confidence from another individual.

"Okay," continued Bankovich, "are you a physician, attorney or priest?"

"No."

"Okay, who gave you the information?"

"PFC Butler was the individual who game me the complete information."

"PFC Butler. Did he go along with the refusal?"

"No. He was one of the men who dropped out of the formation."

"What did he tell you?"

"He told me that Sergeant Tremaine had been doing a lot of talking about the previous policies and how they should be the same now. Butler also implicated Nash and Rojas."

"Is this why you recommended these three for courts-martial?"

"Yes. After the counseling, I felt Tremaine should be recommended for court-martial. I analyzed the entire situation: Sergeant Tremaine is an NCO in the U.S. Army—he could have stood alone on the problem, and the same goes for Sergeant Rojas. Nash just said he was sticking with the rest of the people."

"Did it hurt your pride that your order was disobeyed?"

"No, but it shocked me that an American man would do such a thing, facing the possible consequences of his family knowing about it."

"Where is PFC Butler now?"

"He was medevaced yesterday for hypertension. He was shaky, nervous, and I told him to go take a shower, then I heard a shot fired."

"A shot?"

"Yes. Someone fired a shot. I don't know who. Then I thought it best to rotate Butler to the rear."

"Is PFC Butler the only man who gave you information?"

"This is the only man who told me enough about the situation to really base my judgments on. Another man, PFC Bruckner, didn't say anything right out. He'd not say who wrote the note. I'd say something and he'd tell me whether I was right or wrong. This is the way I got the information."

"Did you get information from anyone else that the original six had more to do with the refusal than the rest of the platoon?"

"No. What I determined was that these people were more vocal in discussing the situation with everyone. Along with what I had determined by counseling, this is how I made my decision."

Under redirect examination, Simpson was asked if he allowed anything to bias his decision in suggesting court-martial. He swallowed hard and said, "I allowed nothing to prejudice my decision. I had had no major run-in with any of the six individuals. In the three weeks that I had been in command I was able to observe the six and to discover with some accuracy who were the weak and who were the stronger, the leaders. I've been in the Army for seventeen years, and this is my second tour of Vietnam and I've learned to analyze people pretty well. I always tell the first sergeant and the NCOs to be sure that they let me know any problems they may spot. I thought about this incident for three days before I made my decision, and the information I obtained from Butler and Bruckner was only part of the basis for my decision."

The judge wanted to know if Simpson consulted his CO concerning the disposition of the case. "No," replied Simpson. "I didn't consult the battalion commander. I received no advice from anyone per se. I got the NCOs together and talked to them about it and allowed them to make recommendations to me, but I never received nor asked for advice from the battalion commander. I recommended courts-martial for the original six. There was another NCO, Sergeant Kitchin, for whom I recommended a field grade Article 15. He told me at the time of the interview that he had heard a rumor that I was going to cancel all leaves. After I explained to him the policy, he said he had made a mistake."

The judge nodded, then Bankovich unloaded a few closing questions at Simpson:

"Did the battalion commander offer to speak to the men?"

"Yes, on the day after the incident."

"What was your reply?"

"I told him to let me keep talking to them and that I could take care of the problem."

"Who did you speak to on the morning of the third when you called battalion?"

"I spoke to the S-3 on the third, but not to the battalion commander. I asked the S-3 if there was any policy I wasn't aware of which said they had the right to do what they were doing."

"Did he give you any suggestions as to the disposition of the problem?"

"No."

"Did you ask for permission to leave the platoon back?"

"No. I used the other platoon."

"Why?"

"There was no reason to delay a prescheduled operation since I had the other platoon."

"What did you tell your CO on the day after the incident?"

"I told him I was looking into the problem and that I had no idea as to the punishments I intended to impose."

"Did any other members of First Platoon ask you to see legal counsel?"

"No one came to me to ask about legal counsel, although some did want to go to the rear to see a 'Captain Bankovich.' I didn't realize at the time that they were referring to you. The first sergeant did say something about some of the men wanting legal counsel, but I don't know whether they got to see counsel or not."

"That's all," sniffed Bankovich, his deep, hypnotic eyes piercing Simpson. Simpson forced a smile at the judge. The judge looked away. The CO shuffled from the room, his half dozen discrepancies—if not outright lies—trailing behind him like droplets of blood from a fleeing, wounded animal.

After an intermission the defense began its interrogation of a lengthy list of witnesses. The first was Captain DeFreeze. He explained his thirty-day policy, stressing that it depended on the man's performance and manpower needs, but that he adhered to the policy he inherited in all but three or four cases. He said he felt it was a good policy. He downplayed the medic situation, but recalled that he never had a shortage of corpsmen. He claimed that he used to threaten to cancel leaves, but that he never did.

Waiving their right to remain silent, the accused took the stand as witnesses in their own behalf. Exchanging glances, the four testified their reasons for refusing the CO's order and their feelings towards his policies.

Tremaine told the court that one of the PFCs who was originally selected for court-martial wrote the note. It was actually Nash who wrote it. In response to a question about racial prejudice entering Simpson's decision to court-martial certain people, Tremaine offered that he felt the only reason Gibson was in court was to eliminate that issue.

Another highlight of Tremaine's discourse was his retelling of his interview with Simpson. During the conference Tremaine asked the CO the reason why things had to be a certain way. Tremaine said Simpson "pushed the bars on his collar towards me, pointed at them, and said, 'That's why!'"

Throughout the rest of the afternoon and the next day a procession of twelve witnesses, including me, recounted our reasons for refusing. We

declared that we felt we had legitimate grievances. We expressed our mys-
tification as to why the four were culled for courts-martial. And, perhaps
most significant in light of Simpson's testimony, we reported that many of
us had requested the CO for legal counsel and hadn't received it.

Among the defense witnesses was Flores. A week prior to the trial he
gave a spirited exposition to Captain Bankovich at the staff judge ad-
vocate's office in Cu Chi. Excerpts from his testimony were read to an at-
tentive courtroom by Bankovich:

"Specialist Flores, how long have you been in Vietnam?"

"Three hundred sixty-four days."

"So you'll be returning home after the taking of this disposition?"

"Yes, Sir."

"What units have you served with during this year in Vietnam?"

"Second of the twenty-seventh Wolfhounds."

"With the Wolfhounds for the whole year?"

"No, Sir. I was with headquarters company, first brigade."

"How long have you been with the Wolfhounds?"

"Almost two and one-half months now."

"While you have been in Vietnam have you been serving in the field?"

"Yes."

"Have you received any awards or decorations while you have been
serving over here?"

"Army Commendation Medal."

"Do you have the CIB?"

"Yes."

"Any other decorations?"

"Bronze Star and Parachutists Badge."

"Now, you mentioned that you know the four accused. How long have
you known them and what was your relationship with them?"

"I've known all four for about a year now and we're just friends."

"Did you go on missions with them?"

"Yes, Sir."

"So, you had the chance to serve with them out in the field and you
saw how they performed in the field?"

"Yes, Sir."

"Did any of them serve in a leadership position over you?"

"Sergeant Tremaine did."

"And what kind of soldier would you say Sergeant Tremaine is?"

"I'd say he's an excellent soldier, as people say, soldier. I mean, there
are only two kinds, that is a bad one and a good one."

"And you feel he was a good one?"

"Yes, Sir."

"Do you feel he was a good leader?"

"Yes, Sir."

"Would you be glad to work under him in the future?"

"Roger that."

"What about the other men? What kind of soldiers would you say they are?"

"Well, I think Sergeant Rojas is a good soldier. And Specialist Gibson, we went out on sweeps together. Specialist Nash and Sergeant Tremaine, like I said, were fine soldiers."

"Would you be glad to serve with any of these men again?"

"Yes, Sir."

"Do you think it was good for the First Platoon to refuse to go out?"

"Yes, Sir."

"Why?"

"Because someone had to do it. I mean, when a man doesn't want to give a man what he deserves when all he's asking for is a medic and with thirty days, or thirty-one days, not to go out, but to go out and see the little man, and maybe not see the little man, and still to go outside the wire and know that you're not protected. That's what it's all about. That's what everybody was really looking for a whole year on-line, anyway, and that's the last thirty days when you get off-line and you can lay back and wonder how you ever got back."

"Then you were in sympathy with these complaints?"

"Yes, Sir."

"Had the soldiers been discussing this for a period of time?"

"As far as I know."

"Did Captain Simpson ask for a spokesman on the morning of the refusal?"

"Yes, Sir."

"What did he say? Can you remember his words?"

"I can't remember his words but he asked us for a spokesman. I stood up and told him that if the people were given what they were asking they'd go out, and they would've gone out that day."

"Then you did act as spokesman on that day?"

"Yes, Sir."

"Did anyone else act as a spokesman or were you the only one?"

"I was the only one."

"If Captain Simpson had stated that he'd take some action upon the grievances and it seemed reasonable to the platoon, then they would've gone out that day?"

"Yes, Sir."

"Now, was there any reason in particular why you volunteered to be the spokesman?"

"No, Sir."

"Well, did you have any feeling that you were correct?"

"Yes, Sir, and I thought I was one of the oldest men in the company at the time in the platoon, and I thought somebody better speak up for the men. I guess I took it upon myself to do it."

"Have you received any punishment for taking part in this incident?"

"Yes, Sir."

"And what is that?"

"I was offered a court-martial. He told me he was going to give me a court-martial."

"Who told you?"

"Captain Simpson. I came into Cu Chi and saw a counsel and then went back to the field and nothing was said of it, and then Simpson called me to the CP bunker and offered me a battalion Article 15."

"And did you accept that battalion Article 15?"

"Yes, Sir. I want to go home tomorrow."

"Do you think that it was fair that you accept that battalion Article 15?"

"No, Sir."

"What type of punishment were you given?"

"I was busted from Four to PFC and charged thirty-four dollars for two months."

"Do you feel this punishment was just?"

"No, Sir."

"Why?"

"Because a man spends twelve months in Vietnam, or eleven months, and they can't take thirty days off, or even just sham for thirty days and work back in the rear like they say they'll do for you? Well, I don't think it's right."

"Did you appeal the Article 15?"

"No, I never got counsel. I asked for counsel but I never did get it."

"Why do you feel you couldn't get counsel?"

"Because my company commander wouldn't let me out of the field."

"Wouldn't he let you come in here for counsel?"

"No, Sir. He kept telling me counsel was going to come up and when counsel did come up he had me out on an LP."

"Do you feel you would've appealed this Article 15 except for the fact that you're going home in a short time?"

"Yes, Sir."

"Do you know what punitive action was taken against the other individuals involved in this incident?"

"Yes. Captain Simpson talked to most of the PFCs and Spec Fours we have in the platoon and he, in my view of things, scared them into taking company Article 15s and battalion-sized Article 15s."

"Do you feel that the four individuals who are being courts-martialed are being singled out for this type of punishment?"

"Yes, because the CO says they're all pushers and he caught them."

"Did he ever call those men pushers?"

"Yes, Sir."

"And when was this?"

"When he called me a pusher."

"On what occasion did this take place?"

"That was that night."

"The night of September third?"

"Yes. There was Nash, Tremaine, Gibson and myself and we talked to the CO and the first sergeant about the whole incident and he kind of made it plain that we were the instigators, or like he said, the pushers of the refusal."

"Did he say why he called you a pusher?"

"He said he had his own information."

"But he wouldn't give you this information?"

"No."

"Do you feel that these individuals may have been selected because they were the shortest individuals in the platoon?"

"Yes, Sir. He told me himself that's why he was putting me up for a court-martial."

"And what did he say to you?"

"He said he'd give me an Article 15 because I was doing so good, but since I refused a direct order and since I was so short that he was going to show me that he wanted me to go back to the world the way he felt I should, with no rank and no money."

"Do you feel that the decision not to go out if something wasn't done about these complaints was a decision made by a certain number of people in the platoon, or was this decision made by the platoon as a whole?"

"This was made, this decision was made, as a platoon. The whole platoon said they weren't going to do this. It wasn't just one or two people, but the whole platoon."

"How many times did you ask to see a counsel?"

"Almost every day."

"Over a period of how many days?"

"I'd say seven."

"And during these seven days you weren't allowed to go in to see a counsel?"

"No."

"Do you know of any regulation that was violated by the CO giving you an order to go to the field without a medic?"

"You mean in one of your books or something? No, I know it's wrong. I don't know the number of it, but I know it's wrong."

"You know there's a regulation?"

"Yeah! I know there is. Anybody in the Army—Sir, excuse me, but I'm not stupid. I might look stupid but I'm not, you know. I come over here to do something I think is right. If I could say no, I don't want that Article 15 right now, I'd take a court-martial and stay. But I can't because I already signed it and I can't do anything about it but take the punishment."

"Okay. Now, you don't know of any specific regulation?"

"No. I can't tell you the reg number, Sir."

"Okay. You said before that it was wrong for him to send you out in the field without a medic?"

"Roger that, Sir, because if you're shot in the belly, Sir, if you're with me and you're shot in the belly all I know to do for you, Sir, is to cover it up and say, 'Wow, I hope you live'!"

"Right. I understand that you feel it's wrong. What I'm asking is that you are aware of the law it violates? The one you say you can't quote?"

"I can't quote your reg. It's a military thing."

At the end of testimony on the second day of the trial, the defense rested.

The next morning, Captain Rohrig made a declaration on the motion that the charges be dismissed:

"The defense has asked that the military judge dismiss the charges against the four accused on the grounds that they had been denied their rights to due process guaranteed them by the Constitution of the United States and the Uniform Code of Military Justice. It is the contention of the defense that these four men were arbitrarily selected as scapegoats to cover up the failures in leadership of their commanding officer. The evidence is clear that there were no ringleaders, no instigators in this refusal. This refusal was the mutual action of all nineteen men in the platoon and stemmed from very real grievances. These four accused are no more guilty and no more innocent than the other fifteen men in the platoon, yet they have been singled out to be court-martialed. Why? The only apparent reason that these men were selected is that they have the shortest remaining time in-country. What more telling example could there be for the company and the battalion than to court-martial four people who have under thirty days left in-country or are in fact past their DEROS? It would be inconvenient indeed to court-martial the entire platoon; it would be a messy trial and undoubtedly create a lot of bad publicity. It is much easier just to court-martial four people, to have the courts-martial in this God-forsaken village far from the news media, but adjacent to the company concerned, and to punish four people, any four, as an example to others not to transgress in this manner.

"The defense recognizes that a commanding officer has considerable discretion in determining punishment, but it is our contention that there was a clear abuse of discretion in this case. The Court of Military Appeals, in the case of the *U.S. vs. Gallagher*, 15 USCMA 391, set out very clearly the criteria that must be followed when making any classification. Captain Simpson in this case clearly classified these four as more culpable and more worthy of punishment than the other fifteen men who committed the same offense. The Court in *Gallagher* stated that such a classification as this cannot be arbitrary and capricious. The classification must rest on some reasonable difference between the parties or things classified. A classification not based on a reasonable difference amounts to a denial of due process for the party so classified. It is clear from the evidence in this case, Captain Simpson's testimony notwithstanding, that there is no rational or reasonable basis for selecting these four men to be court-martialed. Their selection was arbitrary and capricious, based solely on the fact that they had the shortest time remaining in-country."

"In a very real sense these men have been denied the equal protection of the Uniform Code of Military Justice. They have been selected as scapegoats to incompetent leadership and they have been denied the due process guaranteed to them as American soldiers. For these reasons, we ask the court to dismiss the charges against them."

Lieutenant Engraf made his argument on the motion:

"As to the question of the defendants being deprived of due process, the Government argues that there has been no indication of discrimination so unjustifiable as to be violative of Due Process. The Fifth Amendment has never been and cannot reasonably be interpreted to require a commanding officer to justify every move he makes. Confronted with several offenders, the CO must recommend appropriate punishment for each. Much of his decision will inevitably be based on intangible, hard-to-explain considerations. Absent a clear showing of prejudice or complete lack of rationale, a CO's decision to recommend Article 15 punishment for one offender and courts-martial for others cannot be questioned by a court.

"In this case, there has been no assertion of prejudice on Captain Simpson's part. The defense says that he had 'no rational basis' for distinguishing Tremaine, Nash, Gibson, and Rojas from the others. The evidence introduced establishes that Captain Simpson made his decision as to the varied punishments he'd recommend only after long and arduous consideration of each case. He devoted many hours to interviewing each individual. He gained information from PFC Butler and PFC Bruckner that these four were the leaders. He is a company commander who has asked about his people, knows their tendencies and capabilities, and knows the leaders and the followers. This is his job. Much of his decision was based on impressions he derived from his conversations and his knowledge of these men as their commander. He certainly fulfilled the requirements of the *Manual for Court-Martial* by making inquiry sufficient to render an intelligent decision as to each offender. Prejudice, bias, intentional or arbitrary discrimination were no part of his decision, and are not asserted to have been."

The judge, a patient, canny, spare-boned figure, shifted his weight in his chair. After the customary clearing of his throat, he ruled that the motion to dismiss the charges be denied.

Captain Bankovich, noticeably perturbed, rose to make a closing dictum. In an overpowering voice he assailed the court:

"The accused have not admitted to the elements of the offense. The law is for the court to decide. It is one of the responsibilities of the court to determine whether or not the accused are guilty of each element and thereby determine the guilt or innocence regarding the offense. All witnesses say that it is a bad practice to send a platoon-sized element on a combat operation without a trained medic. A medical platoon sergeant of eighteen years experience stated that very thing. But this was not a single occasion. This platoon had gone three weeks without a medic.

"To cite a general principle: express orders should not be given when soldiers are under great emotional stress. The commander must always ask: am I doing enough? Grievances such as those brought to the attention of the company commander are nothing to be treated lightly. These things were very important to the men and they were entitled to an explanation. It is clear that the company commander did not do enough. He went quickly over the complaints and then said, in essence, go on the operation or you will be court-martialed.

"The court must consider the meaning of the testimony of the defendants. They all believed that the order, under the circumstances, was unjust, unfair, and unreasonable. Captain Simpson hurriedly spoke to their grievances. He did not take the time to seriously answer them. The platoon was entirely dissatisfied, and felt they deserved a man-to-man explanation, and when such an explanation was not given, it only served to reinforce their belief that the CO was being unfair and unreasonable.

"Admittedly, they made a mistake as to the lawfulness of the order, but the mistake was based on their past experiences with medics and with reasonable treatment by previous commanders. They felt they had no choice, and their mistake as to the lawfulness of the order was honest and reasonable.

"Consider also the way in which the case was mishandled. This is no simple case of refusal. Upon being confronted by a platoon which had the audacity to present to him a list of grievances with a demand that they be answered, Captain Simpson lost his head."

The prosecution waived a closing argument. The court recessed. When the proceedings reopened, the judge announced his findings. To each accused he stated, "It is my duty as military judge to advise you that this court finds you, of the specification and charge: guilty."

As the verdict was disclosed the defendants sat like four tombstones, stark, lonely, engulfed by the tapestry of disaster. The judge, despite his position of authority, spoke in venerable undertones and seemed somewhat embarrassed while expounding his decision. Captains Bankovich and Rohrig, looking as somber as two presidential bodyguards, gave each other vehement stares. Lieutenant Engraf, the reluctant prosecutor, hung his head.

The judge uttered that he'd consider in the determination of sentence certain personal data concerning the four. Under grilling from the judge the defendants chanted the required information. Once they concluded, the judge expressed that all the accused had gone on military operations since the refusal, including Tremaine, even though he was under thirty days.

With tireless precision Bankovich made an august final statement as to sentencing:

"The court has found these four men guilty of disobeying an order. In determining an appropriate sentence, we ask the court to consider all the facts and circumstances surrounding the incident. The motion to dismiss this case on the ground that the accused have been denied their due process rights were denied by the court; however, we believe the court should take into consideration the fact that these four were arbitrarily and capriciously selected for punishments by courts-martial. Technically, they disobeyed an order, but fifteen other men disobeyed the same order, and those fifteen will not have federal convictions on their records.

"We ask the court to look at the records of these accused. The records of all four are unstained. They have served as combat soldiers in the field for one year, all with distinction. Not one of them has so much as an Article 15 on his record. All continued to serve as infantrymen, even after charges had been conferred. As a result of this incident, several of them have been deprived of their R & R's and leaves. Now, for the rest of their lives, these men will bear the burden of a federal conviction. It is the defense's contention that this conviction, in and of itself, is more than enough punishment for what these men have done. We do not believe that any sentence greater than an oral reprimand is justifiable, nor is it deserved by any of these accused.

"These men have made a mistake, perhaps, but they have been punished for it over and above the other fifteen by their conviction here today. We do not believe that any further punishment is necessary."

In a firm voice Lieutenant Engraf, not a bit inflated by his triumph in the verdict, made a brief closing statement:

"Having listened to all the evidence and having cross-examined many of the defense witnesses heavily, I cannot avoid being impressed. I have prosecuted vigorously and yet each defendant has reacted to me as a complete gentleman and with utter respect. They have shown no animosity. In my experience with military law and people in trouble, I have never been so impressed by the straightforward and truthful nature of the testimony of the accused and the defense witnesses. I cannot in good conscience argue that these four men should receive a more severe punishment than the other fifteen. They each now have a federal conviction for disobedience—a serious blot on their records. Hence, I concur in the recommendation of the defense."

The trial participants took a respite. The First wasn't on a patrol that afternoon. As the trial entered its concluding stages, we milled around our bunker outside the village, waiting for adjournment. When the four related to us during the break that the verdict was "guilty," we were saddened.

Once the court reconvened the judge broadcasted his sentences to the four: reprimand. The tension in the courtroom dissipated. The judge continued, "I would further like to state that this reprimand will not be administered by me, but it will be up to the battalion commander to do so. I hope he does not do so until he has had a chance to read the record of trial of the events which have been related to the court.

"But let me say that the incident of September 3, 1969, at the sugar mill in which each of you willfully disobeyed the order of your commanding officer to prepare to go on a combat operation was and is of an extremely serious nature, and I think you've been duly impressed by the fact that you're here in this courtroom today. This, in addition to the conviction which you've received, I feel is punishment enough. Your disobeying orders was done so at your peril; there can be no discussion of the merits of an order once it's issued. No army in the world can function in any other manner if it's going to be successful. Discussion and question of the orders of superiors once they are issued only results in the festering of chaos and victory for an opposing force. The reasons for this incident are in the record and have been recorded here in these past few days. They speak for themselves, but they are not reason enough to willfully disobey the orders of superior officers.

"Im sure you all realize this now. Let me say in closing that each of you, in my opinion, except for this one incident, have served in the highest traditions expected of members of the United States Army. The fact that you are not career soldiers, but part-time soldiers, the manner in which you have served, as attested to by your contemporaries, both officer and enlisted persons alike, reflects substantial credit upon you."

When the trial was closed the jubilant defendants raced from the schoolhouse to our enclave outside the village. They trumpeted the results to the rest of the First. "They messed with the wrong people this time!" an exultant Tremaine told me.

When Simpson heard the news he was furious. Cursing and snarling, he paced around his HQ like a caged panther. Overcome with anger, he jogged down to the judge and lawyers waiting on the helipad for their shuttle to Cu Chi. He exchanged opinions with them, making them aware of his displeasure with the lenient punishment. The attorneys rebuffed him. Simpson stormed off, flailing his arms and swearing loud enough to be heard in Saigon.

We watched the spectacle and laughed. Of course, the lack of castigation other than reprimand astonished us. It was too good to be true. No stockade! No grade reductions! No fines! Nothing but reprimand! Nothing! Nothing but a subsequent piece of paper from the CO of 2nd Battalion, 27th Infantry, proclaiming that "the sentence is approved and will be duly executed: REPRIMAND. You are hereby reprimanded."

That afternoon the four took the resupply chopper to Cu Chi to prepare for their individual DEROS's. Tremaine's DEROS had already passed. The others were all within two weeks of going home.

Before I left for R & R, I visited with Nash and Tremaine for the last time in Cu Chi. In mid–October they left Vietnam. Reprimanded but unrepentant. And alive.

25

The East Has Come to Call

Two days after the trial I flew to Cu Chi to go on R & R. For three consecutive months I had vied for R & R in Sydney. Each time I was preempted by fellows with more time in-country. Realizing that I was running out of months, I selected Singapore to assure myself of getting an R & R.

In Cu Chi I met Splash, who was there for his DEROS. Late one evening I overheard him grumble an astonishing revelation to a friend. When he had arrived in Vietnam he was supposed to be assigned to the Wolfhounds' headquarters company in Cu Chi rather than a line company. A reception station clerk had misdirected his orders, losing them. Since Splash had no papers, the Wolfhound HQ people shipped him to Bravo. Like an innocent prisoner, he endured one year in the field when he should have been in Cu Chi.

Splash went home bitter. Nobody blamed him.

On R & R you retreat by degrees into another world. From the Wolfhound battalion area you're jeeped to the Cu Chi airport, flown in a C-140 transport to Tan Son Nhut, then bused to an R & R holding base named Camp Alpha. At Alpha you're processed, cleared, briefed, quartered, and fed until your flight departs. The atmosphere is laid-back. There is no harassment, details or nonsense. Compared to C-ration pork slices or ham and eggs, the meals in the mess hall are outstanding. Just having two or three entrees at every meal makes you aware of how opulent life really is in the rear.

At departure time you take one of the Army's olive-green buses with metal grilles over the windows to Tan Son Nhut. Then you're shepherded aboard a cool, antiseptic 727. The thought that you don't have to go on an ambush patrol, confront booby traps, or pull guard staggers you. More stunning is the realization that for the next week your odds of living are infinitely enhanced.

R & R in exotic, balmy Singapore is a six-day dream, a marvelous, sensuous dream from which you hope you'll never awaken.

You select a hotel: the brochure for the Newton Towers was more colorful than the other three hotels' pamphlets, so I picked it.

You get a room: there were no complications or delays. The efficient hotel staff had been alerted to the approaching busload of impatient, horny Americans.

You take a relaxing bath: the thick, bronze tan I thought I had acquired rinsed down the drain in the form of dirt.

You don civilian clothes: it felt weird, wonderful. For the first time in ten months I weighed myself. Eighteen of my pounds were back in Vietnam.

You get a girl: initially the relationship was awkward, strained. I was almost as nervous as when I went on my first night patrol. She helped. She was custom-made to soothe war-weary soldiers.

You get a steam bath and massage: more of the Vietnam grime peeled off. But I still could rub a fingernail on my skin and it would accumulate dirt.

You get high: every evening I celebrated at a different nightspot. I ran out of nights before I ran out of clubs.

You sightsee: I went shopping for clothes. Two street salesmen who lured me into their shop chaperoned me about the island for two days in exchange for my business.

One sight I visited was the memorial to the civilian victims of the Japanese occupation during World War II. A sort of miniature Washington Monument, the memorial was located in a manicured park near the harbor. Simplistic and impressive, the structure's melancholy white starkness propelled my reflections to the realities of that global war.

I thought of the infantrymen who fought in World War II. In that war the European dogface had to deal with bitter winter months and regular attacks from enemy artillery, planes, tanks. Except for a few World War II–type engagements, we Vietnam troopers had a much different, and in some respects, better situation. For us—at least by 1969 in our AO— sometimes weeks passed without enemy contact. Then most of our action was only minutes of electricity. We had better, lighter equipment, more firepower, advanced medical procedures. Due to the swift evacuation of casualties, if you were wounded in Vietnam your chances of living were excellent. Most significantly, the World War II soldier was committed for the duration of the war plus six months. We had a maximum tour of one year; we knew when we'd go home. This realization did cause additional stress for some Vietnam soldiers. But weren't an infantryman's odds better with the one year formula?

America's intervention in World War II was inevitable and correct. The country was proud of its gladiators and grateful for their sacrifices. In some way the war touched nearly everyone. A serviceman who died in World War II died for something. But in Vietnam the dead perished for

. . . what? A man killed in Vietnam was merely a statistic in the weekly casualty figures. Only his buddies and relatives grieved the person behind the number.

Different eras, situations, wars. We build memorials. But do we ever learn from history? Do we ever harken to the dead?

In Singapore I briefly entertained the notion of deserting. The bars were teeming with tales of fellows who had done so. There also were dramas of the authorities zealously tracking down and capturing American AWOLs.

I counted the days. I'd have fifty-six to go once I returned to Vietnam. Would my incredible luck endure? Much would depend on Simpson adhering to the thirty-day tradition.

The thought of jail terrified me. I didn't know what to expect from life as a deserter. But I knew what to anticipate from Simpson, the traps, and the VC. In war, like anywhere else, you learn to adapt to your environment. You become accustomed to it all after a while—even tempting death on a daily basis. The unknown perils of being a deserter, being the pursued, frightened me more than Vietnam. Like America's statesmen and military agitators, I didn't examine what I was getting myself into before I submitted to Vietnam. And once trapped in the mire, I didn't know how to get out. Casting aside my objections to the war, I rendezvoused with my jet for its return flight to Tan Son Nhut. In ethical junctures, sometimes you're courageous, sometimes you're not.

My R & R timing proved to be ideal. The day I was scheduled to return to the field Bravo came into Cu Chi for a stand-down. There was more drinking, bravado, and floor shows. But it wasn't the same without the old gang. Kilcurry, Nash, Tremaine—they were gone. I felt lonely. I was becoming a short-timer.

The last afternoon of our respite Bravo was mustered before Simpson for an awards ceremony. With two Wolfhound battalion officers flanking him, he shuffled between our ranks attaching Army Commendation Medals to fifteen of us. We didn't know who had nominated us for medals but many of the recipients were veterans of the refusal.

When Simpson came before me he pinned the decoration, smiled, and extended a wet-fish handshake. An officer and a gentleman. I wondered if he still had some hope for me.

Once we were dismissed, we stuffed our medals into our ammo boxes. Then we drank into the night.

26

Hard Spot Harris

Next stop for Bravo was Hard Spot Harris, a fifteen-bunker complex built by Charlie Company thirteen miles west of Cu Chi. Like most of our outposts, it was a close, defensible base.

On our maiden patrol out of Harris we filed down a dirt road leading to Fire Base Jackson. Near Harris the thoroughfare was heavily booby-trapped. We were able to negotiate through the hazardous segment without incident. But another unit sweeping towards us wasn't so fortunate. While we were marching we heard an earth-shattering blast in the direction of the mechanized outfit. A feather of black smoke ballooned into the blue.

Assuming the worst, we came upon the site of the explosion. The point vehicle in the mechanized unit had hit a mine. A bandaged survivor, who was on the track when it met the trap, related to us that two men had been killed and several wounded. The smoldering vehicle rested on its side adjacent to the road. Blood, gear and debris littered the zone around the track.

We loitered at the scene until the routed unit regrouped. We left the mechanized Americans licking their wounds and maybe for once, just once, wishing they were strictly ground-pounders.

With my reduction to Spec Four, I was assigned to Sergeant Stofka's squad. Stofka, a jovial, sensitive, sturdy Long Islander was one of the Instants who had declined to join our rebellion. We got along well. We talked in our bunker. Each time we conversed, we opened up a little more. Once you have been in combat for any length of time, you become scrupulous about establishing new relationships. You want to extend yourself, but you're often tentative. You're afraid that someday you'll be seeing the man's blood.

But I liked Stofka. He cared for me. So we got to know each other somewhat. Whenever some of us were in the bunker and Stofka's favorite song—"Lay Lady Lay" by Bob Dylan—would come on AFVN, he turned up the radio and we all sang.

One Army project which met with universal acclaim, at least in Bravo, was AFVN. It played an assortment of tunes but it was heavy on the rock 'n' roll. This was only proper. How could we fight *our* war without *our* music?

Our music. You couldn't separate the music and the war. Impossible. You knew both would be with you forever. To me Vietnam resembled a huge, berserk rock concert. You had a stone sober awareness that you were attending a limited, once-in-a-lifetime engagement. And once the show is over, once you come down from your high, you go home. But the trouble is that only part of you goes home. A part of you remains at the concert. And you know why: because it is such a crazy show, because you are right there sucking in every sight and sound, every beat of the drum, every sensation of life being lived at the edge. You know that you'll never completely come home. You know that part of you will always be back there at the Show of Shows, remembering the good songs, the good feelings, the good friends. Deep in your gut you're glad you went, you're pleased that you had a front row seat. You know that you'll never be as high, you'll never see another drama quite like it, not in a dozen lifetimes. It's ironic, really, because you didn't want to go in the first place.

At Harris, every evening a squad went on a dusk patrol. These operations involved circling the perimeter maybe fifty meters outside the wire. The patrols usually consumed only an hour or so. We never encountered anything but they were nerve-wrenching missions. Unlike our slinking infiltrators, once the purple hue of dusk loomed above, we longed to be behind our earthworks, concertina and claymores. At night it definitely was their country.

One night just before dawn, radar detected enemy movement outside Harris. As was customary, our cannoneers fired into the vicinity. At daybreak we were ordered to forgo breakfast and to immediately investigate the area because the crafty VC usually hauled away their dead. We had to verify that almighty body count before the VC cheated us out of it. It's rough when your opponent doesn't play by the rules.

Of course, we had to traverse the booby-trapped road trailing from Harris. Stofka assigned me to the low-risk district of the formation—the rear. We cautiously maneuvered down the road. We unearthed some traps and exploded them. Soon our pointman ordered a halt. He had stumbled upon a dead VC sprawled near the highway. We sauntered to the corpse. Our new platoon leader, a garrulous, chunky, academic-looking lieutenant named Ressert, commanded some soldiers to scout for more bodies. I dallied around the deceased VC with a half-dozen other men. We were all trying to make ourselves look busy, hoping that we wouldn't be told to ferret for bodies with the others. We didn't want to find traps instead.

The dead VC was diffused in a grotesque octopus position, a classic "response-to-impact" pose—the Army's double talk for describing pulverized cadavers. He appeared to be heftier than most VC we encountered. He was lacerated with shrapnel from end to end. His blood was everywhere. Lots of blood. His bowels had spilled over his legs, a red-yellow stinking mess slowly drying in the morning sunshine. A few trickles of blood ran out of his eyes. He was definitely a KIA. The arty boys had done their job.

I was standing next to the VC's perforated arm when I noticed the handle of a revolver protruding from a mud puddle. I seized the weapon. It was a Chicom pistol, complete with a lanyard and ammo clip. I was agape. A war trophy! I showed the firearm to our ecstatic lieutenant. He notified Simpson at Harris. We scrounged up some local peasants. Through interpreters they identified the man as a VC captain.

The elated Simpson summoned us back to Harris. Someone mentioned burying the VC first. Our ubiquitous lieutenant said that the locals could bury the body. Besides, he added with a frugality of expression and speaking for nearly all of us, it was getting hot and we hadn't had breakfast yet. Without further discussion, we abandoned the body to the pitiless sun and trooped back to camp.

Our battalion commander was so excited over the elimination of a VC officer that he flew to Harris. The colonel wanted to inspect the pistol. I reluctantly submitted it to Simpson. I made it known that I wanted it as a souvenir. Simpson said that it would hinge on the colonel's fancy.

Once the colonel departed, a runner returned my pistol, minus the lanyard. The messenger said that the officer had remarked he "just had to take something." I considered myself fortunate. I thought I'd never see the pistol again.

Later I experienced some embarrassment over wanting to keep the handgun in the first place. I was opposed to the war and the spectacle of dead bodies appalled me. However, I wasn't hesitant about keeping a lethal relic of the war. My inconsistency disturbed me, although not to the extent that I debated relinquishing the weapon. Apparently, for better or worse, I hadn't become a bona fide pacifist.

On October 28 I participated on what proved to be my final operation. Stofka's squad had to pull an LP. We had ten men in the team. Stofka chose three others over me to stay back. Since I was the one closest to DEROS, I was perturbed about having to go. I didn't become hysterical; I still wasn't down to thirty days.

Stofka and I picked a location about seventy meters from Harris. We had marched farther. But I had persuaded Stofka to retreat to a site with additional cover and which was, of course, nearer to the wire. Stofka and I took first guard. I whispered to him my consternation about his selecting me to go. I complained about being short. I emphasized my belief that short-timers should stay back before all others. He agreed, explaining that he wanted me along only because of my seasoning. I understood. I reminded him that on a recent night ambush I had seen something that wasn't there because my nerves were frazzled. Stofka relented. He apologized for taking me, pledging that he'd bypass me for future operations if he could.

Stofka kept his word. Whenever he finished announcing the names of the men required to saddle up for a patrol he winked at me. I was grateful. I displayed it by not whining over any uninviting details or protracted bunkerline guard shifts which were assigned to me because I was refraining from missions.

The concluding night in October First Platoon launched an ambush. It was the first time in my tour that the First attacked the enemy at night. Thanks to Stofka, I was inside Harris that evening.

Two new men were on sentinel duty when a gang of VC strolled into their location. The rookies activated their claymores. The balance of the First awoke and fired their weapons and mines. An exploration revealed three dead VC. The following morning Bravo was convened. The novices were awarded Bronze Stars with V-devices in a ceremony presided over by a brigadier general from division. After the ritual the two men, sobered by their first combat experience, tossed their medals into their personal boxes, lunged into a bunker, and went to sleep.

Days later the First was patrolling down our familiar mined road. A man who had been transferred to the First from an airborne unit only a week earlier struck a trap. He was killed. Three others were wounded. While the platoon was lumbering back to Harris, Stofka hit a trap. Witnesses said that his wounds didn't look serious. A week later we discovered that he had lost a foot and some fingers.

I was at Harris when Stofka was injured. Only minutes after it had happened I heard the bad news over the radio. I was sick, despondent. At the time all I knew was that he was injured severely enough to be dusted-off. I wanted to be alone. I crawled into an empty bunker. Someone had left on a transistor radio. It was barely audible. Hoping to escape the reality of traps and bleeding friends, I adjusted the volume to maximum. After an alluring commercial about R & R in Hong Kong, the AFVN blended the advertisement's closing music of bongo drums into Dylan's gentle "Lay Lady Lay." The song flooded over me. I tried to fight it, to hold it. I tried to sing. I tried to forget but it was hopeless. I covered my head with a poncho liner and cried.

27

Kotrc

By November the East Asian winds began funneling from the northeast. This signaled the arrival of the dry season. The paddies started to dry up. Puffy, majestic cloud formations replaced the brooding thunderheads of the monsoon. The land, replenished from its long drink, braced for a six-month thirst that would be alleviated only when the winds again hailed from the southwest.

With new troopers reporting to the field every day, it was still possible for me to refrain from patrols. The First received a new platoon sergeant, a skinny, genial, tattooed fellow from California. He placed me in charge of the helipad outside Harris. It was my job to load and unload the resupply chopper when it arrived each afternoon. Mornings I assisted a demolitions engineer whose task was to explode hedgerows with bangalore torpedoes. We began with the treelines closest to the wire and systematically destroyed any foliage which could conceal VC.

Another project assigned to me was the vilest detail in Vietnam perimeter life. Our portable wooden latrines were stationed just beyond the bunkerline. Each morning after breakfast I had to take gasoline to each toilet and burn the excrement in the metal receptacles. It was a nasty chore but I never sniveled over it. It beat jousting booby traps.

In mid–November we were rotated to Fire Base Kotrc. Another border fortress, Kotrc was located south of Phuoc Luu in a marshy sea. Unlike Harris, we had superb visibility across the expansive swamp into Cambodia, less than two miles distant. Nightly our radar, ground sensors, and other night-viewing instruments would detect enemy movement across the frontier. Lots of movement. And all of it, fortunately, was going around us. We were mortared several times, however, just to let us know we weren't forgotten. Only once did the VC shells detonate inside the perimeter, injuring no one. The hallmark of Bravo's tour at Kotrc was accidents. Not a day passed, it seemed, without someone becoming injured because of carelessness with weapons or equipment. Some injuries weren't accidental, however. One new arrival to the First participated on an LP his first night in the field. The following afternoon he crawled behind a bunker, put a rifle to his foot, and blew off a toe. Like countless soldiers before him, he opted for a self-inflicted wound over the risk of losing his life. Of course, he claimed that his weapon had accidentally discharged.

On Thanksgiving Day we feasted. Extra cooks and helpers were flown to Kotrc to serve us a turkey dinner with all the adornments. Beer was provided. It was the finest meal we ever had in the field. Irrefutable evidence was that everyone jostled for second and third helpings.

We learned of the Moratorium in the States. I didn't discuss the event with anyone. I was exultant that the anti-war forces at home were making the War Führers in Washington fidget.

Except for exterminating hedgerows, I performed the same bunker-line jobs at Kotrc that I handled at Harris. Since I wasn't going on patrols, I withdrew from the camaraderie of the First. My final weeks in the field were a mesh of elation and tension. I was suspended, distant. My mind was in Pennsylvania. Much of the time I spent alone. I concentrated on reading books, running the chopper pad, burning feces, and marking days off my calendar.

The booby traps were devastating at Kotrc. One afternoon the Second Platoon lost five men. Another morning the First lost two men. Later the same day, two more soldiers in the Third became trap casualties.

The death and injuries made me sullen. It seemed endless. I'd watch the platoons saddling up and leaving, knowing there was a good chance some of them wouldn't return. Then later in the day the hysterical words would wail over the radio: "T-T-Three guys just hit a trap! Their legs are blown all over the paddy! Get us a dust-off! We need a dust-off now!"

And simultaneously over another radio, the mocking AFVN blared to us the lyrics of love and life.

It was all too much. So what to do? You feel like crying. But finally the tears cease coming; you can't cry when you're benumbed. So you turn your back and wander off by yourself to cremate more shit. And in the flames you see and smell a scarred countryside, crying children, burning homes, frightened faces, dead minds, dead hopes, dead dreams, and corpses, corpses, corpses.

In Vietnam mail call was always the highlight of the day. Most fellows received a letter or two a week, occasionally a parcel with sweets or special requests lovingly packed.

One day I received a manila envelope. I thought it contained data pertinent to my recent punishment. But inside were thirty letters from a fifth grade class attending a Catholic grammar school in Sharon Hill, Pennsylvania. The teacher had asked the children if anyone knew a soldier in Vietnam. A relative of mine had submitted my name.

The letters ranged from comical to profound. It was a benevolent, touching deed. I was stirred. It made me wonder what the future history texts would say about America's intervention in the Vietnam War. Would the schoolbooks whitewash the events reminiscent of the warped chronicles that portrayed Native Americans as sadistic, godless savages? Or would the volumes be a candid, unbiased analysis?

Meanwhile, Rickenbrode was receiving mail of another sort. A stateside kinsman of his had spotted a press release entitled "Rebellion Extends Beyond Company A" by Tom Tiede of Newspaper Enterprise Association. Tiede's article was an account of our sugar mill revolt! Remarking that troop mutiny in Vietnam wasn't uncommon, the writer capsulated the events of September 3.

Citing the highly-publicized rebellion of part of a unit—Company A— during a combat action as a example, Tiede asserted that First Platoon's revolt might be the gravest yet because of the degree of the resistance and the number of men involved.

Also included in the piece was the Pentagon's reaction. The Pentagon, stressing the positive side, pointed out that First Platoon, after the initial refusal, actually did go on the patrol. The only complication was that nineteen of its soldiers declined to go. The brass noted that we all participated on an ambush patrol that evening, and that we had all been good soldiers since the refusal. The Pentagon felt that First Platoon was a unit beset with ongoing leadership problems and that we were simply probing a new company commander. The Pentagon emphasized that there was no thirty-day off-line policy and besides, none of the mutineers were under thirty days.

Even Simpson had his say in the papers. He stated the correctness of his position and that he had no choice but to prosecute men who disobeyed orders. He complained that the four court-martialed men weren't punished enough with a reprimand and that they should have, at the very least, been rotated to other units. He whined about some of the other refusal participants still being in his company.

Those of us who were still in Bravo were elated over the publication of our rebellion. We were happy when word of our refusal reached battalion. The fact that tidings of our effort reached the American public, even though the facts were partially distorted, enhanced our joy even more. And by late 1969 any informed, discerning person who read Tiede's report might suspect—reading between the lines—that our action wasn't a test of a new commander, as the Pentagon suggested, but a manifestation of our contempt and frustration with fighting a futile war.

We didn't end the war, or break the System. We didn't get our seven-day leaves renewed. We didn't get rid of Simpson. In fact, we probably burdened ourselves with him longer than necessary solely because of the rebellion. It appeared that Simpson's punishment was that the higher-ups condemned him to field duty for much longer than any other Wolfhound officer. One message I received from a returning Bravo veteran was that as late as March 1970, Simpson was still marooned in the field pleading for a Cu Chi job.

We did get Simpson to revoke his "everybody humps to DEROS" scheme. We did implant an indelible smudge on his career. We did scare him. We made him sweat, curse, squirm, and stammer. Like the resisters in the streets, we did our small bit to challenge the demented, flag-draped philosophy which says that when America goes to war, automatically we are right and the conflict becomes a glorious, moral enterprise. We orchestrated a mutinous shock wave that rippled from an isolated Asian outpost to the Pentagon, to the public. Perhaps we helped to arouse a few minds, perhaps not.

But we tried.

28

Purple Out

"Incoming! Incoming!" shrilled the bunker guard. "Everybody inside! Everybody inside!"

The frantic yelps startled me. I was sleeping in a hammock inside the bunker. I rolled out of the hammock and reached for my rifle. "Not tonight," I protested. "Not tonight of all nights! My last night in the field!" I donned my helmet and cowered in a corner of the bunker.

It was a mortar attack. Like dozens of previous occasions, we huddled in the bunker and prayed that a ground raid wouldn't accompany the mortars. We could hear the familiar sound of the shells whizzing over the perimeter and exploding outside the wire. Our gunnery returned fire. Soon the VC tubes were quieted.

It was mind-boggling. My first night in the field we were mortared. Now again on my final night. A year had elapsed but what had changed? Nothing. We ambushed them. They ambushed us. They fled. We pursued. They mortared us. We returned fire. They absorbed some fatalities. We hit the traps. It was a vicious circle, a stalemate, a mindless concentration camp of futility. Like a swaggering technological Goliath, we tromped about the countryside seeking our clandestine Davids. So we defoliated the jungle, destroyed crops and villages, and resettled civilians to deny the enemy a haven. And it didn't work—none of it. But it was The Policy.

Furthermore, our method of settling Asian wars didn't allow short-timers to get any sleep. Worrying about additional mortars, ground incursions, and national tactics, I endured the balance of my last night in the field blinking at the roof of a bunker while holding my sixteen across my lap.

Relieved, impatient, and praying that nothing would go awry, the following morning I prepared my gear and hid in a bunker so I'd avoid Simpson. I didn't want him to abort my parting.

That afternoon, after a few goodbyes, I boarded the resupply ship. As the chinook lifted off I tossed a purple smoke grenade out the chopper's window. To "purple out" was the traditional gesture when a man left the field for DEROS. While the chopper circled above Kotrc, I watched the smoke sweep across the lonely perimeter in a cold purple cloud.

A few minutes after taking off my helicopter landed. Perplexed, I knew that we couldn't be in Cu Chi yet. I leaped off the bird in a panic. Fire Base Jackson! I quizzed one of the aircraft's officers about what was happening. He said that Jackson was the last stop for everyone. I screamed at him that I was going in for DEROS and I had to get to Cu Chi. He told me they were flying elsewhere. Dreading the potentiality of another night in the field, I cried that I had to achieve Cu Chi this afternoon. Unmoved, he shrugged and mounted his chopper. I told him what he could do with his chinook.

The ship flew off in an easterly direction. The only sizeable perimeter in that trajectory was Cu Chi. I was furious. I raced to the CP bunker. A sergeant told me that the afternoon resupply convoy had already departed for Cu Chi. I spotted two jeeps on the other side of the base. I asked what those vehicles were doing here; they looked like convoy vessels to me. He frowned and strolled away.

I hustled to the jeeps. A PFC was smoking behind the wheel of one. He told me he was part of the Cu Chi convoy. There was a mix-up and the convoy had left without him. I explained my dilemma and asked if he was going to make a dash for Cu Chi or remain at Jackson for the night. He said that he and the other driver were going to Cu Chi and they'd welcome extra rifles.

Convoys between Jackson and Cu Chi were rarely ambushed but the possibility always existed. Road mines were always a worry too. For us the principal hazard would be a mechanical malfunction and the contingency of having to pass the night stranded between the bases. We'd be traveling without commo.

I was desperate. I told the driver I'd risk it with him. A few other voyagers who also had been ejected from the chinook volunteered to go. We absconded with ammo and grenades from the bunkerline and jumped into the jeeps. I told my driver to forget the VC and to set a new Vietnam land speed record. As we pulled out of Jackson the driver floored the accelerator, spinning dust across the camp. He laughed and said, "Fuck it all!"

As far as I was concerned, he set a record.

I spent a week in Cu Chi out-processing, drinking at floor shows and grinning. Despite the moral ramifications, serving a year in the field is an unmatched feeling of achievement. You feel good about yourself. You have nothing to prove to anyone; you have passed the test. You're a genuine combat veteran. You scowl at the droves of Cu Chi noncombatants and silently but angrily ask, What have *you* done for a year? These sensations partially explain why there is such a thing as war. Among cooks and clerks in Cu Chi it's easy to feel triumphant, bloated. They have heard of ambush patrols and Eagle Flights; they sense what you have been through. They respect you. And you love it.

From Cu Chi you're transported to Long Binh, another station on the long road home. There is more processing. Lines for everything. Hair short enough for fighting and dying is too lengthy for the stateside Army. Baggage is checked and rechecked for drugs, unauthorized weapons or souvenirs.

In Long Binh I met acquaintances I had trained with at Bragg and Polk. It was like a reunion. I discovered who was killed, who lost a leg or arm, who re-upped, who was court-martialed, who made E-5, who went home early because of a family crisis, who went AWOL on R & R, and who went crazy. One fellow I knew at Polk sauntered into a USO facility one afternoon and blew a claymore, slaughtering five soldiers. He succeeded in fragging his CO before they netted him.

I was assigned to a noon flight out of Bien Hoa airbase. During my final hours in Vietnam the happiness which I had experienced earlier in Cu Chi gradually drained from me. By the time I wobbled from the waiting area to my jet, the glee about leaving—something which I had harbored for a year—was totally absent. Nothing abominable had happened since I had left Kotrc. But for some mysterious reason, I was anxious, disconsolate, hesitant about departing.

Once aboard the plane I settled into a window seat. With the broadcast "Okay, girls, grab a seat!" the pilot opened the throttle and the aircraft soared across the runway. Once we were airborne everyone expounded a roar. I opened my mouth in a muted grunt. I kept staring ahead, immobile.

Weird reflections popped into my mind. I remembered when I had worked as an usher in a theater during high school. Sometimes the management would play the national anthem before the movie. The Stars and Stripes would be on the screen. I recalled how agitated I used to become when the Saturday night crowd, still burping and picking meat from their teeth, would lounge in their seats conversing during the paean. I recollected how at baseball games people would shuffle and laugh while the hymn was played. I used to be outraged.

How patriotic I was then. But what is patriotism? Are you patriotic if you blindly swallow everything your government says is good for you? Are you patriotic if you blindly follow the leader? Is that patriotism, or mere stupidity? If you're really patriotic, if you really love your country, shouldn't you intelligently evaluate the judgment of your leaders? And when you believe your government is effecting a vital error in national policy, shouldn't you express those reservations? Aren't dissent and debate keystones of democracy?

Patriotism is more than flags, songs and blind allegiance. You love your country if you care enough to think, to question, to educate yourself on issues. True patriots challenge their leaders. But did I care now? No, I admitted, as my airship canted to the northeast towards home, towards America. For now I knew I still wouldn't clown during the national anthem. But I wouldn't sing either.

I felt nauseated. My emotions were logjamming. I had a basketball lodged in my throat. I comprehended that I had just lived a whole lifetime — several lifetimes — in one year. I realized that I had made some lifelong friends and I had lost some friends forever.

My mind was blitzed with rapid-fire slides flashing like neon signs: a rainstorm, Norton, a berm, an explosion, the mountain, Simpson, a chopper landing, the crack of an AK-47, the river, Dougherty, an LP, Reed, the stench of dead bodies, Stofka, a bleeding detainee, a hedgerow, Doc Hernstein, a village, and ebony-eyed, laughing children. *Oh God,* I thought, *the children, the children.*

A tremor struck me around my knees. *You're supposed to be happy! This is what you've waited a year for! It's done. Be happy!* The quiver crept higher. The thumping in my head intensified. The swelling and choking in my throat burgeoned. The tears came individually. I tried to hide them. I bent over and covered my face with my hands.

The man next to me fled to the toilet. By the time he returned I was composed, mute, and straining downward trying to glimpse a fleeting patch of land through the cumulus clouds. But there was nothing below except the sea. And instantly Vietnam became a time frozen, a cold-sweat dream, a throbbing memory: Vietnam, Vietnam, Vietnam . . . Vietnam.

While I was out-processing in Cu Chi, I noticed that many of my records still labeled me as a sergeant. I had already been fined the ninety dollars but my grade reduction papers were muddled. Aside from some fiscal documents, there was nothing in my dossier indicating that I had been demoted. I had been wearing Spec Four insignias in Cu Chi but all the bored transcribers had typed me in as a sergeant because of the bulk of my credentials classified me as an E-5.

So on the jet, inspiration struck. Without a moment of reflection, I sifted through my personnel file. There were only three or four papers that branded me as a Spec Four. I ducked into a toilet with my folder. All the evidence which stamped me as a Spec Four I stuffed into my pocket. In an airplane's latrine, midway between Okinawa and Hawaii, I promoted myself to sergeant.

I didn't mind being a Spec Four in Vietnam. But stateside there was a galaxy of difference. I still had six months of active duty. A sergeant's stripes would mean fewer details and harassment. However, my overriding motivation for my devious act was that I wanted vengeance against the Army. I wanted to retaliate in any way that I could against the System that had put my friends and me through a needless war.

But these were shallow excuses, rationalizations. I had forfeited a sergeant's privileges at the sugar mill. By my fraudulence I was able to slither through the inefficient system of military punishment with only the loss of ninety dollars. Meanwhile, two of my closest friends, who ostensibly meant so much to me, had federal convictions on their military records. But the possibility of hurting others—or myself—had never entered my mind. Revenge and anger had blinded me. I had an opportunity to elude some retribution for my involvement in the refusal, so I took it. In the military, officers and career men don't have a monopoly on cowardice and vice.

In the dreary light rain of a winter's day, I took a limousine from the Philadelphia International Airport to a shopping center near my home. The December chill numbed me. Although the temperature was only in the forties, I was freezing.

More chilling was the atmosphere in the limousine. When we had loaded up, the driver gave me a half-smile and a question, "Vietnam?" I nodded and said, "Yeah." He winced and scurried behind the wheel.

The other five passengers were businessmen. I detected immediately that it was going to be a long trip. With their sleek leather briefcases, drip dry shirts, double-breasted suits, and plastic faces insulating them, they sat rigid, distant. They were tense, uncomfortable, worried, like they had just been notified that profits were down and heads would roll. Gawking at the urban madness of Philadelphia, they pretended not to notice the bleary-eyed soldier in a uniform sprinkled with colorful patches and medals. But I sensed their frigidity and negativism as acutely as I sensed booby traps.

And no wonder they were unnerved. I was perched in the midst of them. Was I one of the wildcats they saw nightly on TV who was vaulting out of choppers and annihilating villages and babies? Was I an alcoholic? A murderer? A drug-crazed sadist? Would I go berserk, commandeer their limousine, and hold them hostage? So, I thought, *this is what it's going to be like: silence, suspicion, embarrassment.* To me the situation was obvious. The home front saw the killing on TV and they knew that the war was a fiasco. Perhaps they realized—finally—that we shouldn't have been involved in the first place and that we should get out. Then returning veterans, untimely symbols of the catastrophe, reminded them of their country's intransigence, stupidity. It *was* a long ride.

From the retail center I hiked to my house. During the jaunt the rain ceased. The sagging sun peeped through the regiments of livid clouds in the west. The slanting rays beamed into my eyes. It felt good. I smiled. For the first time since I had exited Cu Chi I felt joyous, vibrant and alive. I was home!

I thought ahead some months to the summer when the heat would be almost as stifling as it was in Vietnam. I visualized the trees and grass being lush and verdant and the heavy summer air replete with swarming insects. It wouldn't happen soon enough for a warm weather zealot like me. I couldn't wait to see the butterflies.

Military History
of Dennis Kitchin

Dennis Kitchin was drafted into the Army on July 17, 1968. He attended basic training at Fort Bragg, North Carolina, and advanced infantry training at Fork Polk, Louisiana.

On December 15, 1968, Kitchin departed for Vietnam. He served a year in Hau Nghia and Tay Ninh provinces on infantry operations with First Platoon, B Company, 2nd Battalion, 27th Infantry (Wolfhounds), 25th Infantry Division.

After his Vietnam tour, Kitchin was sent to an infantry unit at Fort Carson, Colorado, to complete his active duty. He was discharged on July 16, 1970.

Kitchin was awarded the National Defense Service Medal, the Vietnam Service Medal with two Bronze Service Stars, the Vietnam Campaign Medal with 60 Device, the Army Commendation Medal, the Combat Infantryman Badge, and the Republic of Vietnam Gallantry Cross with Palm Unit Citation Badge.

Index